DATE DUE

MODERN SCULPTURE

modern sculpture

ORIGINS AND EVOLUTION

by Jean Selz

Translated by Annette Michelson

GEORGE BRAZILLER

NEW YORK

PRINTED BY JOH. ENSCHEDÉ EN ZONEN, HAARLEM, HOLLAND

CONTENTS

I. In the Labyrinth of Forms   1

Subject and Technique
What Is Sculpture?

II. The Weight of Tradition   27

Mid-Nineteenth-Century Art
An Epidemic of Monuments
The Last of the Classicists

III. A Breath of Freedom   57

Honoré Daumier
Jean-Baptiste Carpeaux

IV. The Age of the Academicians   77

Mannerism and Solemnity
Some Isolated Experiments

V. Revolutionary Visions   89

    Impressionism and Sculpture
    Auguste Rodin
    Medardo Rosso

VI. Continuity and Change   131

    Rodin's Influence
    An Advanced Classicism
    Painter-Sculptors

VII. The New Aesthetic   203

    The Discoveries of Figurative Sculpture
    and the Road to Abstraction

A Summing-up   244

Biographical Dictionary of Sculptors   251

List of Plates   272

Bibliography   279

Index   289

MODERN SCULPTURE

I. IN THE LABYRINTH OF FORMS

Subject and Technique

The Museum of Fine Arts in Rouen possesses a large picture, *Friday at the French Artist's Salon,* painted in 1911 by Jules Grün, a fashionable artist of the time. The scene is the vast sculpture hall of the Grand Palais, site of the annual Salon; the artist has assembled a hundred or so prominent figures of Parisian society. In the midst of this elegant crowd, among the potted palms and top hats, stand some large marble figures: heads of famous actresses, mythological concoctions, academic nudes, allegories of various kinds, and commemorative monuments. A common style, a common concern with anatomical precision, a common affectation of the gracious or noble gesture, give them an air of kinship; they might all have been carved by the same hand.

This picture revives memories of visits I made as a child, shepherded by my father, to these Parisian Salons. I always emerged exhausted, having learned once and for all (again!) what bad painting was, and convinced that all works of sculpture were monuments of boredom.

These Salons, from which any work deviating from the aesthetic values or technique endorsed by officialdom (the Academy) was systematically weeded out, probably reassured admiring visitors, for they presented an art which involved no problems of any sort. A "real" artist was one who conformed to tradition, and what was then termed "tradition" was simply the diligent representation of scenes from real life, rendered in the most exact, scrupulous, and colorless way.

I have managed to locate a copy of the catalogue for this 1911 Salon. Apart from François Pompon, who was showing a plaster *Turkey,* most of the exhibiting sculptors are now utterly and deservedly forgotten; the names of a few remain familiar as subjects of irony. One can quite easily imagine that the visitors confronted with these 860-odd pieces, *Old Folks, Breaths of Spring, Nymphs, Motherhoods, Italian Bandits, Arab Dancing-Girls,* and portraits of bishops and senators, were able to recognize what the critics of the time hailed as "precision of attitude and genuineness of feeling."

This period is not so remote that it does not awaken a secret nostalgia in

Plates 3-5

1

2

3

4

5

1 Alexander Falguière. Woman with Peacock, 1890. Marble. Museum, Toulouse.

2 Jacques Lipchitz. Seated Bather, 1917. Stone. Otto Gerson Gallery, New York.

3 Jules Franceschi. Fortune, 1886. Plaster. Paris.

4 Raoul Larche. Monument to Corot, 1904. Marble. Paris.

5 Léopold Morice. Diana and Endymion, ca. 1900. Plaster. Paris.

certain elderly art lovers. They used to be able to *understand* sculpture; today they no longer can. They do not realize that they never really did understand it. But even those whose artistic education has not been formed, or deformed, by the official art of the turn of the century, may have some difficulty in acquainting themselves with the multiple forms of contemporary sculpture. The young visitor to an exhibition of modern sculpture may, without in any way sharing his grandfather's tastes, have difficulty in grasping the frequently mysterious intentions of the artist and in submitting to the spell of an art which often refuses to surrender its meaning. The unity of style and technique which formerly characterized the statuary of a given period has, moreover, been replaced by a diversity which cannot fail to appear baffling to many.

Plates 1, 2   Between the new forms of figurative sculpture and the constantly renewed inventions of abstract art, there exists an entire range of works constituting innumerable ambiguous intermediary stages between these two categories. One can see them either as last vestiges of representation or figuration, or as pure abstraction, content, apparently, with a vague resemblance to a familiar form.

    Limiting ourselves to the main tendencies of contemporary sculpture and taking into account the work of more than two hundred artists, we may establish the following types or kinds of sculpture:

Plates 7	1. Representation deriving from a classical tradition.
6	2. Figuration at some distance from reality.
10	3. A tendency toward surrealism.
12	4. Creation of a fantastic zoology.
11	5. Representation of the human body in a degraded form.
8	6. Reduction of the human body to the state of an object.
9	7. Schematization of the human body, verging on abstraction.
14	8. Abstraction, implying a meaning or association.
13	9. Pure abstraction.

4

7

6 Alberto Giacometti. Slim Bust, 1955. Bronze. Galerie Maeght,
Paris.

6

7 Volti. Sleeping Nude, 1960. Bronze. Galerie Chardin, Paris.

8

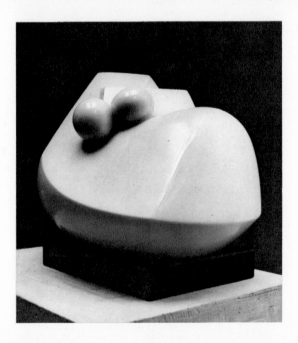

8 Henry Moore. Reclining Figure, 1939. Lead. Collection Sir Kenneth Clark, London.

9 Emile Gilioli. The Sleeper, 1946–61. Marble. Collection Carozzi, Pisa.

10 Apel'les Fenosa. Hair, 1960. Bronze. Private Collection, Paris.

11 Robert Couturier. Hollow Woman, 1954. Bronze. French Institute, Milan.

12 Germaine Richier. The Wasp, 1953. Bronze. Galerie Creuzevault, Paris.

9

10

12

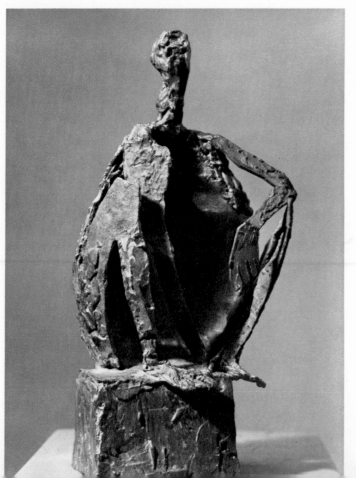

11

7

13 James Rosati. Hermes Trismegistus, 1958. Stone. Owned by the artist.

14 Claude Viseux. Petrified Crowd, 1959. Bronze. Collection D.B.C., Paris.

13

14

This essentially ideological classification, which seems to constitute an outline of the historical development of sculpture in the twentieth century, does not allow for those differences of style and technique which would have to be listed within each category, were we to attempt an all-inclusive formal inventory. One would then be led to see that abstraction—to consider only one category of form—has its purists (Arp), and its baroques (Stahly); those who limit themselves to the exploitation of the monolithic block (Lipsi), and those who assemble (Robert Müller); those who juxtapose and solder metal rods (Pevsner) or work with sheets of metal (Lardera); those who use steel for linear constructions (David Smith); those who co-ordinate bits of carpentry (Nevelson); those who engrave surfaces (Adam) or work with burned material (Consagra); and finally those who have made sculpture a kinetic experience, using movement, either through the natural displacement of forms in space (Calder) or through the action of electrical energy (Tinguely).

Plates 15-26

The seven general aspects defined above suffice to show the divergent and frequently contradictory ways in which sculptors attempt to solve their problems. While, for some artists, sculpture still involves a really manual labor—modeling clay or wax, carving wood, stone or marble—others have adopted methods borrowed from industrial technique—use of the acetylene torch or soldering iron, for example—thereby calling into question the very notion of sculpture.

Given this labyrinth of forms, conceptions, intentions, and materials, it seems impossible to determine the direction of sculpture's development, and it is frequently difficult to define the intellectual, visual, and technical developments that have led to these stages of accomplishment. When we realize that twentieth-century art is largely characterized by precisely that development which led the artist to sculpt not only *different subjects* but also in *different ways,* we may begin to wonder about the reason underlying such a radical development. What were the stages, influences, and upheavals which led to a conception so removed from that which had heretofore characterized sculpture? Who were the artists responsible

16

15 Morice Lipsi. Lava, 1960. Volcanic stone. Galerie Denise René, Paris.

16 François Stahly. Combat of Birds, 1960. Wood. Park in Louveciennes (Seine-et-Oise).

17 Jean Arp. Extreme of an Outer Mythology, 1952. Stone. The Art Institute of Chicago.

18 Robert Müller. The Pyre, 1959. Iron. Collection Myriam Prévot, Paris.

19 Henri-Georges Adam. St. Matthew, 1960. Bronze. Editions La Hune, Paris.

20 Louise Nelson. Royal Tide V, 1958–60. Gilded wood.

18

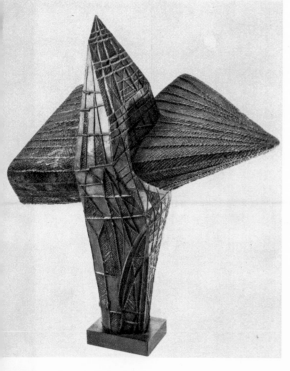

19

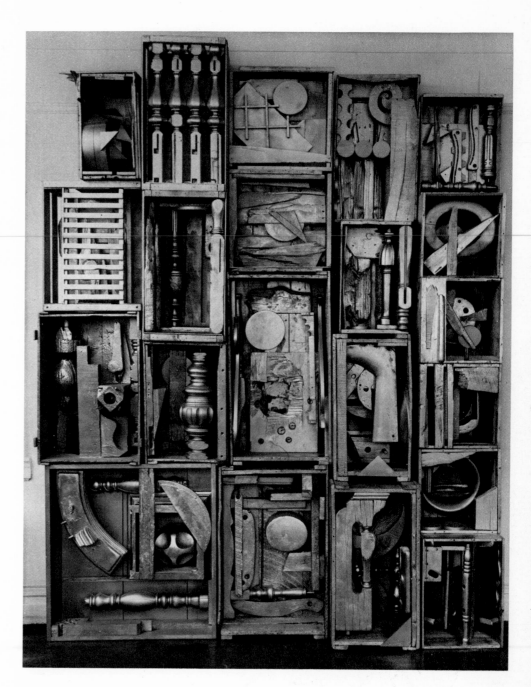

20

11

for this great revolutionary movement? These are the questions I propose to discuss in this study.

If we compare a work of sculpture made a century ago, at a time when artists were ruled by the Academy, with one of the more obviously abstract works of our own day, we may seriously begin to wonder whether the meaning of the word "sculpture" has not changed. However, before we attempt to see whether the act of sculpture has now assumed a meaning which differs from that of the past, it will be necessary to consider the very nature of the act and to attempt to define its basic, determining factors independently of those particularities which originate in individual schools and periods.

What Is Sculpture?

The difference between sculpture and painting is more than the difference between real and suggested volume. The reality of this volume necessitates an object which is part of our world of immediately tangible forms. Pictures, like books, take us out of ourselves, lead us into a novelistic, poetic, or at least different, universe. The statue, on the contrary, approaches us, puts its universe in our hands; man and statue share the same space. This fact alone is enough to establish between sculpture and viewer a physical relationship which is not without psychological consequences.

Any statue commands our attention by the mere force of its presence. Moreover, what is present is not only the material of which the statue is made, but also the object which it represents. A stone horse is not merely a reference to the idea of horse. Even though it refers the imagination to a live horse, the model for this stone one, or to the place where such a horse may be found, it is above all a *real stone horse*. Thus, by its form, volume, and material, it exists as a compromise between reality and fiction. This compromise is of cardinal importance in the history of sculpture. It was particularly apparent and essentially exploited during those periods in which the work of sculpture was invested with a spiritual character, whether of a magical or religious kind. It assumes its most patent forms in prehistoric art, in polytheistic antiquity, and in the art of the so-called primitive societies and of the Middle Ages.

When considering the spiritual domain of sculpture, we must not overlook the correlation between aesthetics and function. The paleolithic statuettes of the Aurignacian period, such as the *Steatopygeous Venus* of Willendorf or that of Lespugne, were not merely "artistic" interpretations of the feminine figure. At a time when secular life was closely bound to the sacred, these statuettes undoubtedly played a magical role in fertility rites. Statues of the Greek gods were worshiped in temples as if they were actually gods themselves. Anthropomorphic figures from the Ivory Coast and from Gabon also played their roles in ritual ceremonies. Finally, it is significant that the prevalent figure of Christ, which came to dominate the Christian church, is not a painted image but a three-dimensional crucifix—a sculpture. Plate 27 Plates 28, 29 Plate 31

The act of making sculpture, for these creators of Christ images, of magical figures, marble deities, and idols, was the act through which a spirit, more or less divine in nature, was embodied in substance and thus brought within the scope of human understanding. Between spirit and matter, a certain confusion was established, sufficient to favor the attribution of power—at least the power of intercession—and to make the statue an object of worship. Through its role in the religious community, sculpture really represents a compromise between the artist's imagination and that spiritual reality which exists for any religious or superstitious sensibility in the idea of a superhuman force.

When we study secular sculpture, it is important to bear in mind, not the meaning which religious sculpture may have acquired in the contexts of so many different civilizations, but rather the fact that this meaning has succeeded in asserting itself through a medium called sculpture. From this, we deduce that sculpture

22

21

23

14

21 Antoine Pevsner. Kinetic Construction, 1953.
   Metal pipes.

22 Berto Lardera. Love of the Stars II, 1959–60.
   Steel and iron. Collection of the artist, Paris.

23 David Smith. Agricola V, 1952. Steel. Otto
   Gerson Gallery, New York.

24 Jean Tinguely. Metamechanical Sculpture, 1953.
   Steel wire. Collection Kramer.

25 Pietro Consagra. Chorus, 1958. Burnt wood.
   Galerie de France, Paris.

26 Alexander Calder. Red Pyramid, 1945. Mobile.
   Galerie Louis Carré, Paris.

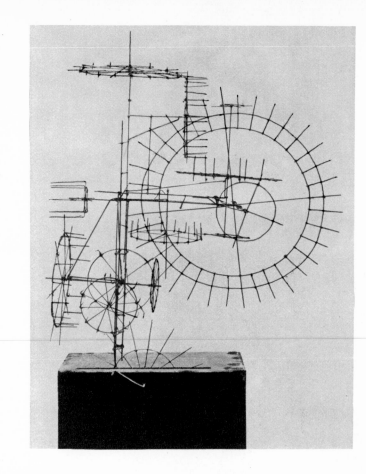

24

25

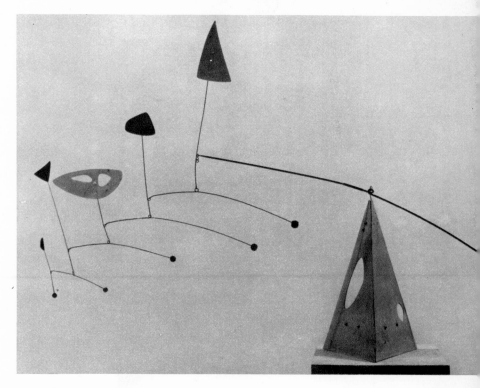

26

15

has always been recognized as a medium particularly well-suited to the expression of what may be defined as a translation of the invisible into the visible. Our present concern is to understand why sculpture, more than any other form, was so particularly qualified for this role.

Two factors, one psychological or moral and the other physical, seem to explain this. Regarding the first, we have already seen that religious sculpture implied a certain ambiguous relationship between the spiritual and the temporal. This ambiguity can also be seen as a link, for it was through the magical statue or idol that a link between man and an intangible spirit—or between man and the divine—could be established. The ambiguity of form was necessary in order that the statue belong both to the supernatural and the human world. The balance between these two worlds, as it appears in its sculptured figures, has shifted in favor of one or the other, according to the nature of the civilization and its beliefs, and the predominance of the human element in sacred statuary can be interpreted as a sign of cultural evolution.

Plates
30, 32-34 Paleolithic art, including the well-known *Venus* of Savignano, provides some examples of a mixture which is half realistic representation of a human figure and half geometric schematization. This geometry is accentuated in Cypriote idols and we meet with it again in areas as diverse as Africa, Colombia, the Philippines, the New Hebrides, and others. The human element is sometimes merely a very slight anthropomorphic accent in an animal form of a fantastic or monstrous kind. In a case of this sort, the plastic realization of a supernatural life adds an aesthetic of terror to the idea of mystery. On the other hand, the art of statuary, for the Greeks particularly, was in keeping with their polytheism and their mythology of the superman and the hero. The gods could assume the form of Man among men. Their strength, and often their beauty, inspired admiration, much as the God of the Christians was later to win the compassion and devotion of the faithful through suffering. Here schematization gave way entirely to a naturalism suited to the emotional atmosphere in which the Christian religion developed. This led the

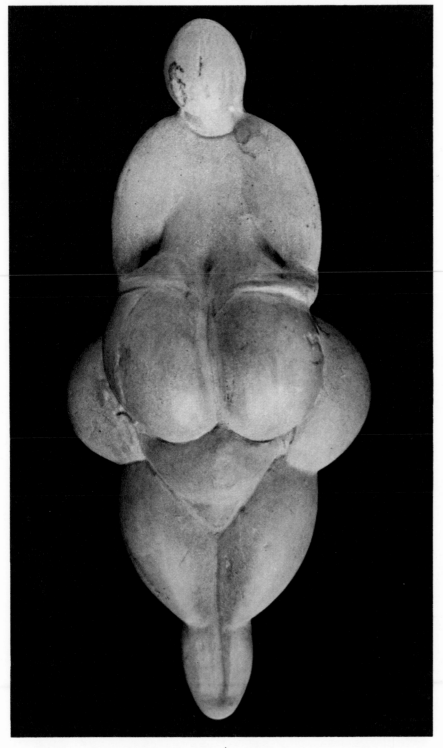

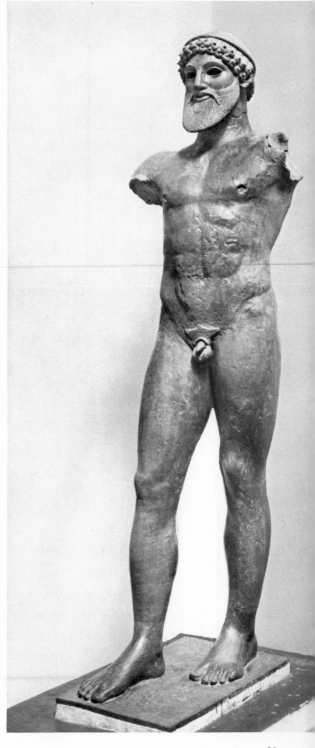

27

28

27 Venus of Lespugne, Paleolithic Age. Ivory. National Museum of
    Antiquities, Saint-Germain-en-Laye.

28 Poseidon, Early 5th Century B.C. Bronze. National Museum, Athens.

29 Anthropomorphic Statuette from Ossyeba (Gabon, Africa).
Copper. Museum of Man, Paris.

30 Head of a Cycladic Idol, ca. 2500–2000 B.C. Marble.
Louvre, Paris.

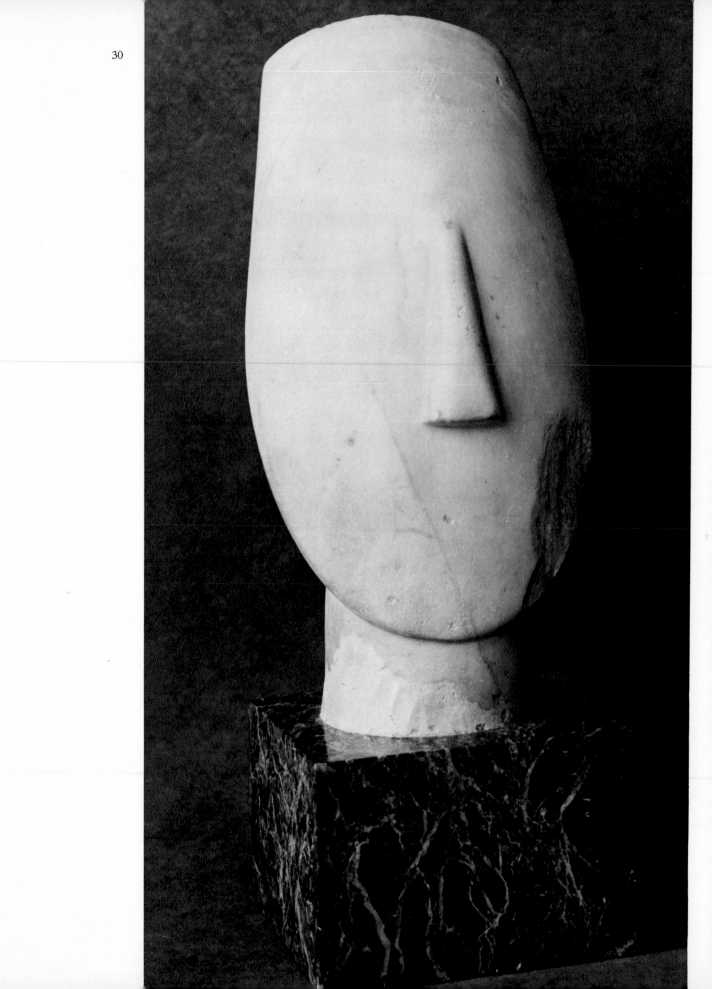

31

32

31 Crucifix, 12th Century. Painted wood. Louvre, Paris.

32 Cretan Idol, ca. 2500–2000 B.C. Marble. Louvre, Paris.

sculpture of certain countries toward a realism so highly developed that Spain, for instance, produced Christ figures of almost super-reality, whose bodies drip blood that has been traced in relief and painted red. Here the psychological conditions of sacred sculpture found their most conclusive demonstration. Plate 35

Always, even when it departed farthest from the human figure, the statue—through its presence alone—satisfied man's need to believe that the gods or spirits, in forms more or less resembling his own, were part of a reality one could touch with one's hands. It is this quality of the *object* which enabled sculpture to fulfill the physical qualification for its psychological role. This explains the importance of sculpture's role in sacred art: through sculpture, ideas enter a ponderable, tangible world. Sculpture assumes this function in secular art as well, and we may note it as one of the most ancient and fundamental motivations of the act of making sculpture. For the beholder, tangibility as such probably does not figure as more than a possibility, not necessarily to be exploited, although the touching of wood or marble frequently adds to the pleasure of contemplation. "The eye," said Father Jousse, professor at the Paris School of Anthropology, "is the instrument of frivolous curiosity." The hand is more precise in its aesthetic investigation; furthermore, it is an instrument of possession as well.

The tangibility of sculpture is, however, less fascinating to the viewer than to the creator. The creation of a form testifies to the artist's power to change himself, as it were, into this form fashioned by his hands. Thus, it is not only the figure or concept which emerges from the material, but also that which constitutes the irreducible duality of the sculptor's strength and sensibility. This need for self-reflection and exaltation, for personal expression, this need of another form for flight or hiding, the need, in short, for metamorphosis, reveals still another motivation for the making of sculpture. (Its importance will be demonstrated by the analysis of contemporary art.) All the great sculptors, however, all those who have left the stamp of a creative personality on their work, have felt this need—more or less urgently, more or less obviously.

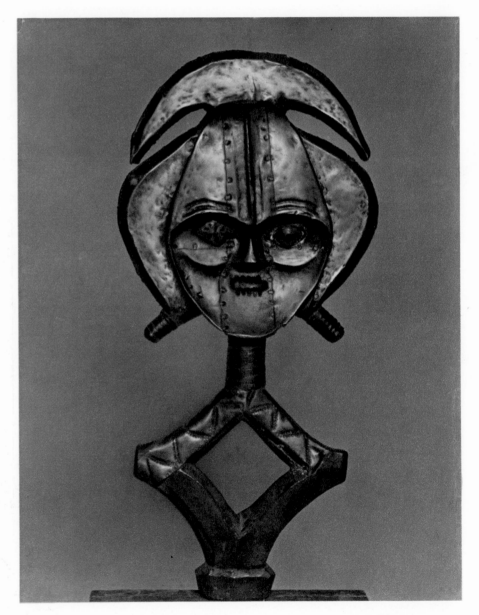

33

34

33 Cypriot Idol, ca. 2000 B.C. Terra cotta. Louvre, Paris.

34 Funerary Figure from Bakota (Gabon, Africa). Wood and copper. Private Collection.

35 Spanish–Peruvian Christ, Late Colonial Period. Agate covered with painted plaster. Museum, Cuzco (Peru).

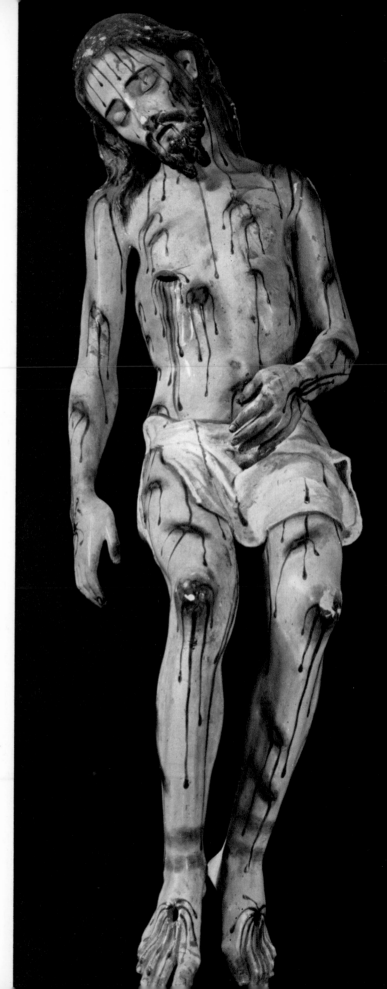

These views, through which I have tried to clarify the why of sculpture, are based solely on the consideration of that which is specifically related to this form, that is, to an art of mass. Nevertheless, we should bear in mind the motivations which are common to all art forms. We are, however, less concerned with emphasizing that which is common to sculpture, painting, music, or poetry than with understanding the ways in which sculpture is fundamentally opposed to, or different from, these other forms. The love of any given form of expression—sculpture, drawing, music, or literature—and the need to establish communication between one's self and the world, the need, as well, to represent this world in one's own way, to explain, modify, and dream it, and sometimes to challenge it, are at the root of all artistic creation.

Although a deep mystery underlies any attempt to explain the genesis of a work of art, we dimly sense that its reason for being lies in a power and necessity through which humanity transcends itself, a power and necessity which are *natural* to us. Like all instincts, that of creation is dictated by an unconscious desire for liberation and tends to realize itself through what the psychoanalysts call playtherapy. For this reason, we are possibly less interested in the *why* of art than in its *how*. And if we have managed to grasp a few of the general, basic reasons which impel an artist to make sculpture, another whole range of problems arises as we begin to observe the way in which he works. These problems grow much more acute when one recalls the upheavals which have marked the history of sculpture during the last sixty years.

Once again, we are faced with the question of how the sculptor arrived at a conception of his art which differed so greatly from that which formerly dominated sculptural style. In order to answer this question, we must turn to the nineteenth century, a period still close in many respects, yet already remote when viewed from the standpoint of aesthetics.

I Honoré Daumier. Bust of Benjamin Delessert, ca. 1830–32. Bronze. The Joseph H. Hirshhorn Collection, New York.

II Jean-Baptiste Carpeaux.
The Violinist, 1870.
Plaster. Petit Palais,
Paris.

II. THE WEIGHT OF TRADITION

Mid-Nineteenth-Century Art

If we observe the unfolding of art history through the centuries, we see that it is subject to two contradictory impulses: desire for the future and nostalgia for the past. In this, it does not differ from social history, which expresses on the collective level the pattern that students of the behavioral sciences observe in individuals: the conflict between attraction toward the unknown or new and nostalgia for childhood.

Although we cannot speak of a literal regression in art, we can say that at certain periods this nostalgia, which is easily identified with the hope of returning to a happier era, has acted to check artistic expression. Viewed as an evolutionary movement, art history assumes an irregular rhythm, rather like the movement of a man who sometimes stops, sometimes rushes ahead, now looking backward, now forward. This tendency is particularly striking in the second half of the nineteenth century. Seen in the general context of artistic evolution, the pattern of movement in painting does not coincide with that of sculpture, tending to confirm the theory that motives underlying sculpture are different from those of painting.

The sculptor's art seemed, for a long time, unlikely to emerge from the paths laid out by the traditionalists. Wilhelm Lübke, the German historian, unhesitatingly stated, in 1880, that "sculpture can never abandon the classical mode." This "classical mode" had, nevertheless, already been abandoned for years by some painters. The appearance of each new tendency, however, caused painting to be considered a somewhat frivolous art, subject to the whims of fashion, inclined to be led astray by eccentrics who stood no chance of posthumous fame. Sculpture, on the other hand, was always an object of reverence. It was considered noble and austere, requiring hard labor and a rigorous discipline dictated by the masters of the past. For a long time, sculptors themselves maintained their belief in the necessity of a formal orthodoxy. In his *History of the Second Empire*, Taxile Delord wrote: "If sculpture played no part in the decadence of painting, this is because the sculptor was protected, by the very nature of his art, from the danger of debasing it. Sculpture is less likely to become an object of commerce

36 Bertel Thorvaldsen Cupid and the Three Graces,
    1817–19. Marble. Thorvaldsen Museum,
    Copenhagen.

37 Antonio Canova. Cupid and Psyche, Late 18th
    Century. Marble. Louvre, Paris.

than painting; it is less subject to change of fashion, more obedient to tradition. Owing to these advantages, sculpture has been able to maintain a more constant respect for greatness than painting."

We realize, therefore, when we try to sum up the situation of the arts in the middle of the nineteenth century, that in a curious manner, painters and sculptors had turned their backs to each other. We might even say that the painters had their eyes fixed on the future, while the sculptors were looking backward. Classicism in painting had certainly not lost all its defenders by 1850. Obviously, a painter such as Ingres, by emphasizing the seductive qualities of composition as taught by his master, David, and by attempting to revive, through these laws of composition, the purity of a Raphael, found more admirers than Delacroix, whose romanticism, though somewhat theatrical, already revealed the first signs of a "disturbing" use of new technique—especially color. But, if Delacroix started a technical revolution in painting, he remained a traditionalist in his choice of subjects.

It was unquestionably Courbet who freed painters from the two great academic obsessions: the mythological theme and the recreation of historical events. It was he who finally opened their eyes to the sights of everyday reality. All of Courbet's teaching is contained in the following lines, addressed to his students on December 25, 1861: "In painting, art can consist only of the representation of objects which are visible and tangible to the artist." We shall later see that a position of this kind was to have a delayed influence on the work of the sculptors. Let us note in passing, however, that these new views concerned the subjects and not the *technique* of painting. Courbet himself did produce a few sculptures of real charm, originating in a realistic sense of observation (among them, the *Bust of Madame Max Buchon,* 1864), but their technique remains entirely classical in its discretion.

Plate 137

It is curious to note that the public did not forgive Courbet for having opened its eyes to everyday reality. The limits of art, for the immense majority of the public, were those of idealization, and ugliness was the quality for which

Courbet was most violently reproached. Because he dismissed the conventional notion of beauty established by classical painting, his influence was slow to take effect.

The dominating fact in the history of painting in the mid-nineteenth century is, consequently, the new interest in scenes from real life. At first, Courbet's importance as leader of the Realist school was, however, less apparent than that of the landscape artists, who were less shocking to the theoreticians of the "ideal of beauty." Corot, Harpignies, Daubigny, Theodore Rousseau and the painters of the Barbizon school helped greatly to accustom the public to the idea of a confrontation of art with nature. The major artistic development of this period, therefore, was the flowering of landscape painting, a development which could hold but little interest for the sculptors.

Although the painters were advancing, slowly but surely, toward what twenty years later was to become Impressionism, the sculptors, for their part, kept their eyes fixed on the "great art" of the past. The notion of "great art" was theoretically linked to the eternal prestige of ancient statuary. The sculptors of 1850 were, however, more directly influenced by the work of those who, fifty years earlier, had in turn been influenced by Greco-Roman sculpture.

The widespread fame of Antonio Canova (1757–1822) and of Bertel Thorvaldsen (1768–1844) had not yet completely dwindled. Both these sculptors had used their great technical skill (coupled with lack of originality) in a neoclassical idiom which corresponded to the taste of a period longing for a return to tradition, both in art and in politics. One sees why Canova, an Italian from Venetia, was welcomed as a "new Phidias" at Napoleon's court. The Empire found in him an artist who conformed to its standards and ideals. Some of Canova's work is, of course, elegant and graceful, but when one considers his predilection for the mythological subject (*Mars and Venus, Paris, Hebe, Terpsichore, Theseus,* etc.), one concludes that his notion of mythology had a certain eighteenth-century frivolity. He was, nevertheless, deeply concerned with the rebirth of classical sculpture. The

Plate 37

31

38

39

38 Giovanni Dupré. Sappho, 1857. Marble. National Gallery of Modern Art, Rome.

39 Vincenzo Vela. Spring, 1857. Marble. Civic Museum, Padua.

40 James Pradier. Atlanta at her Toilet, 1830. Marble. Louvre, Paris.

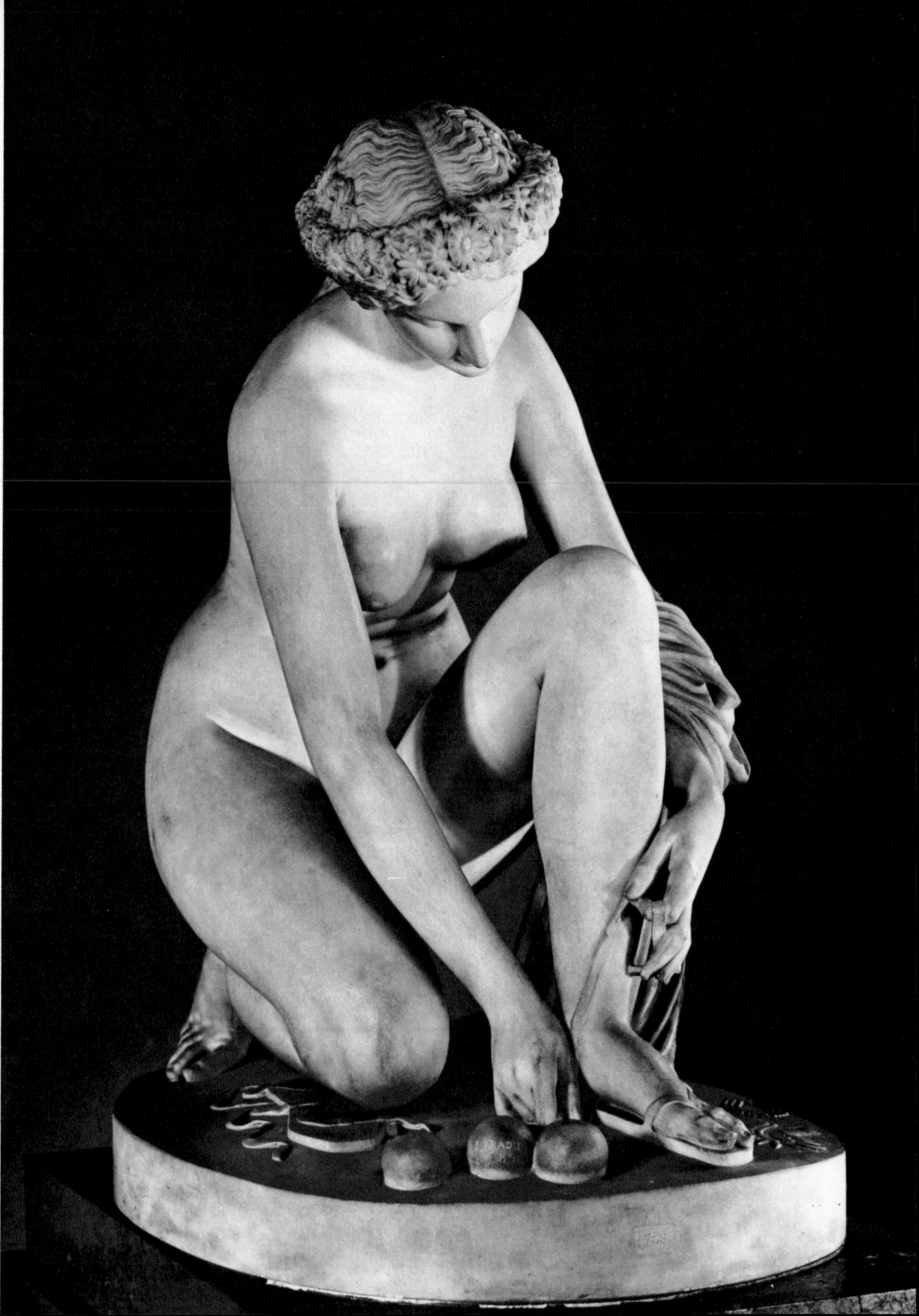

extent of this concern was such that when commissioned to do a portrait of Pauline Borghese, he represented her as Venus. Similarly, his large marble statue of George Washington transforms his subject into a Roman emperor seated with a sword at his feet.

Plate
36

This attraction to antiquity seems more natural in Canova, a Latin, than in Thorvaldsen, a Dane of Norwegian and Icelandic descent. Nevertheless, Thorvaldsen's work was also steeped in mythological tradition and his sole aim was to revive the virile style of the Greek school, as one of his contemporary admirers put it. This brought him great fame in his own country, as well as in Italy, where he spent many years, and in Germany, where he worked for Louis I of Bavaria, but he was never greatly appreciated in France.

In the almost regal mausoleum in Copenhagen where he was buried (in the museum which bears his name), Thorvaldsen is surrounded by all his marble gods and heroes: *Hercules, Jupiter, Minerva, Prometheus, Nemesis,* and *Ganymede* stand side by side in their icy dignity with a *Satyr Dancing with a Bacchante* and *Love Complaining to Venus of a Bee Sting,* inspired by a stanza of Anacreon. But he was also asked to glorify the great men of history; witness his colossal statues of *Copernicus* in Warsaw, *Pius VII* in Rome, *Schiller* in Stuttgart, *Maximilian I* in Munich and *Gutenberg* in Mainz, among others.

In a *Letter on Thorvaldsen,* published in 1856, a fellow sculptor, David d'Angers, judged him accurately: "a stiff, careful artist, infallibly well-behaved. He is always calm, sometimes to the point of somnolence, always severe, sometimes to the point of heaviness."

Canova's example and great fame spread, first through his own country and then throughout Europe. Italy produced many disciples of a neoclassicism heightening the parody of ancient sculpture with a conventional sentimentalism to which marble lent an illusion of nobility. We find this in the work of Lorenzo Bartolini (1777–1850), a student of David's and a friend of Ingres', the creator of *Educative Charity,* of the monuments to *Demidoff* and *Neipperg,* and above all in the work of

Giovanni Dupré (1817–1882), a maker of solemn monuments, sometimes accused Plate 38 of duplicating reality, a tendency more clearly apparent in his *Death of Abel* than in his *Cavour* in Turin or his *Giotto* in Florence. But the naturalistic style which characterizes the Lombard school was intensified to the point of sentimentality by Vincenzo Vela (1822–1891), the sculptor of *Desolation*, the *Dante* monument and Plate 39 a far too graceful *Spring*.

The work of James Pradier (1792–1852), though somewhat more sensual and mannered, takes its place within this same tradition. The Louvre possesses a *Psyche, Three Graces, Atalanta at her Toilet*, and the Hôtel des Invalides boasts Plate 40 twelve marble *Victories* made for Napoleon's tomb. These have a certain grace and nobility, but Pradier popularized his work through treatment of the small decorative themes, the motifs for bronze clocks and fireplace ornaments which had an immense influence on the taste of the Bourgeoisie Triumphant.

Through Pradier, the "noble art" of Canova and Thorvaldsen found its natural inclination toward the form known as genre sculpture. It is amusing, in this connection, to note the subject classification established by a chronicler of the time: "Classical subjects. Biblical and Christian subjects. Philosophical subjects. Social dramas. Modern or genre subjects." The list does not include the historical subjects which had found their interpretation in Meissonnier's painting.

An Epidemic of Monuments

By limiting their ambitions to a neoclassical ideal, sculptors of the younger generation were in large part conforming to the demands made by architects at the beginning of the second half of the century. The artists were most generally characterized, in this particular period, by lack of imagination. The architects transformed this poverty into a virtue by endowing it with a respectable ideology based on "the return to the great traditions of the Renaissance." Unable

41 Albert Wolff. Monument to Friedrich Wilhelm III, 1868. Bronze. Berlin (destroyed).

42 Alfonso Balzico. Monument to the Duke of Genoa, 1860–70. Bronze. Turin.

to provide Greek and Roman temples for all the *Venuses* and *Apollos* produced by the sculptors, society offered them monuments which expressed, through the neo-Renaissance style, the search for that which the Renaissance, so many years before, had derived from Greece and Rome.

If we bear in mind one of the basic postulates set forth in the preceding chapter, that of sculpture as idea-becoming-object, we observe that the ideas expressed by sculpture of this period did not correspond to the artist's inner feelings, but rather to an exterior motive whose source, the State, is easily located. The State initiated or approved the construction of all public monuments, and it was in the official schools that sculptors were trained with an eye to future work on the construction of monuments. By thus stimulating the hope of eventually receiving a government commission, the State oriented the artist's taste toward an art which was designed above all to please the juries.

Now, when we consider that the nineteenth century represents the first important stage of that development of industry and capital which strengthened the power of the State, it seems logical enough that each nation should have felt it had reached an important moment in its history. In effect, Europe suffered from an attack of historical pride. It was necessary to prove publicly that this moment in national life was the result of a long past to which the present was strongly tied; throughout the cities of Europe, the exhibition of a glorious past constituted a way of glorifying the present.

The construction of neo-Renaissance, neo-Gothic and even neo-Byzantine edifices (such as the cathedral built in 1855 by Léon Vaudoyer in Marseilles) was accompanied by a proliferation of commemorative monuments. Each nation was bent on celebrating the great names of its past. These statues still form part of the décor of our urban life. But, although they are with us in public places and squares, they remain unnoticed—they are too ugly—and the names of their makers are all but forgotten. For instance, every Englishman or tourist is familiar with *Nelson's Column* in Trafalgar Square. But very few know that it is the work of Edward

Baily, who was also responsible for the decoration of the façades of Buckingham Palace. The same is true for *Wellington's Monument* in Saint Paul's, the work of Alfred Stevens, a pupil of Thorvaldsen's. The fame of such monuments exceeds that of their creators, and even the fame rests on their real meaning, which is historical, not artistic.

Plates 41-44

The same situation holds true for innumerable statues set up all over Europe. The titles of a few, chosen from the repertoire of the most celebrated sculptors of the period, suffice to indicate the main preoccupation: in France, *Vercingetorix* by Aimé Millet, who also did the bronze *Apollo* on the roof of the Paris Opera House; *Jeanne Hachette* by Jean Bonnassieux, the sculptor of the gigantic *Virgin* of Le Puy; *Henri IV* at Fontainebleau, by Auguste Ottin, whose *Polyphemus,* part of the Medici Fountain in the Luxembourg Garden, is his best work; *Marceau,* by Auguste Préault, the *Duke of Nemours,* by Auguste Clésinger, *Charlemagne* by Antoine Etex. The reputation of Etex was very high and lasted for quite some time. Sculptor, painter, architect and engraver, he had studied with Pradier and Ingres, and exhibited in all the Salons from 1833 on. He died in 1888. The list of his works exemplifies the taste of the time in that it is divided between mythological subjects and heroic scenes. In 1861, he composed a group whose title admirably sums up the spirit of official sculpture: *The Spirit of the Nineteenth Century.*

To continue with our rapid survey of historical sculpture, an inventory of which would require several volumes, we note, in Germany, Christian Daniel Rauch's *Queen Louise* in Charlottenburg, Ernst Rietschel's monuments to *Luther* in Worms and to *Goethe* and *Schiller* in Weimar, Johannes Schilling's *Germania* in Niederwald, Albert Wolff's equestrian monument to *Friedrich Wilhelm III,* done for the Lustgarten in Berlin and destroyed during the war. In Belgium: *Leopold I, Gretry* and *Rubens,* all by Guillaume Geefs. In Berne, Switzerland: the equestrian statue of *Rudolph von Erlach* by Joseph Volmar. In Italy: the tomb of *Pius VIII* by Pietro Tenerani and the monument to the *Duke of Genoa* by Alfonso Balzico. In

44

43

42

43 Albert Carrier-Belleuse. Sleeping Hebe, 1869. Marble. Louvre, Paris.

44 Aimé Millet. Ariadne. 1857, Marble. Hôtel des Invalides, Paris.

45 François Rude. Mercury Fastening his Heel-Wings, 1834. Bronze. Louvre, Paris.

Sweden: *Charles X Gustavus* by Johann Peter Molin. In Poland: *Napoleon, Mickiewicz* and *Chopin* by Jacob Tatarkiewicz. An entire race of great men forever imprisoned in their bronze dignity.

We shall see that the official conformity which more or less characterized all these works was to continue for a long time. Nevertheless, three or four names stand out amid a multitude of sculptors who added no luster to this belated classicism and romanticism. The fame of these exceptions is linked to a style which died out at the end of the nineteenth century.

The Last of the Classicists

The biographies of the most celebrated sculptors of this period follow an almost invariable pattern. Most of them were sons of artisans, acquiring, during apprenticeships in their fathers' trades, a taste for manual work. If born in the provinces, they generally, upon the advice of a neighboring artist, studied drawing and then went to Paris to work at the Ecole des Beaux-Arts. They studied with well-known teachers, then, following the traditional path toward "a career in the arts," as soon as their natural aptitudes had been somewhat disciplined, they began to exhibit in the Salon. To be admitted to the Salon was the ambition of every painter and sculptor, quite understandably, since for a long time there was no other way to become known or to be seen.

The really official establishment of an artist's reputation came with the winning of the Prix de Rome. A first prize, even a second prize, immediately made him a candidate for state commissions. Even the best and most original sculptors of this period, Rude, David d'Angers, Barye, did not escape this routine of professional development. It proved fatal for many sculptors who were too weak to resist the constraints of academic training or not bold enough to oppose the orthodoxy of the official juries.

François Rude (1784–1855) did not turn to sculpture until he was twenty years old. As a small child he was made to learn the trade of his father, an iron-monger and locksmith in Dijon, specializing in the construction of ceramic stoves. At sixteen, Rude began to abandon his father's forge to take drawing lessons, but this led, at first, no further than a job with a house painter. Nevertheless, he developed a taste for modeling and in 1804, began to work on his first heads. In 1807 he went to Paris where he soon entered the studio of Pierre Cartellier, an academic sculptor. He was to leave some traces of this period of apprenticeship in his work on the pedestal of the *Vendôme Column*. Finally, he studied seriously at the Beaux-Arts, obtaining, in 1809, the Second Grand Prize in Sculpture and, in 1812, the Grand Prix de Rome for a statue of *Aristaeus Lamenting the Loss of His Bees*.

In 1821, Rude left for Brussels, where he remained for six years. Louis David, the painter, who was living in exile there, had taken a liking to him and obtained for him a series of jobs on city monuments. Thus Rude designed the pediment of the Treasury Building, a number of bas-reliefs for the castle of Terwueren, and the caryatids for the Grand Theater.

He returned to Paris in 1827 and began to exhibit in the Salon. He first submitted a *Mercury Fastening His Heel-Wings,* and a *Virgin,* done for the Church of Saint Gervais. In 1833, his *Neapolitan Fisherboy* attracted attention and re-established him as a classical sculptor of delicacy and great technical skill. He was then asked to compose one of the groups for the Arch of Triumph in the Place de l'Etoile. The subject of this high-relief was inspired by a scene which he had witnessed as a child in 1792: *The Departure of the Volunteers*. Rude had lived through that exciting moment in which an entire nation had been seized by the impulse to freedom; he evoked it in a synthesis which is harmoniously appropriate to the style of monumental constructions. Classical in its use of allegorical elements integrated into the group of marching men, the composition is quickened with a movement whose dramatic character is not attenuated by its romanticism.

Plate 45

Plate 47

46 François Rude. The Prophet Jeremiah, ca. 1850–55. Terra-cotta sketch. Museum, Dijon.

47 François Rude. The Departure of the Volunteers, 1836. Stone. Arch of Triumph, Paris.

In this movement, whose rhythm seems to come from the chant that pours from the stone mouth of the *Winged Victory,* Rude attains the peak of his art.

Plate 46In the main statues and heads done later (many of which have been assembled in the Museum of Fine Arts in Dijon), he was unable to avoid a certain coldness. His restraint in rendering the human generally reveals more intelligence than sensitivity. Certain smaller sketches, however, such as that of *Jeremiah,* suggest that somewhere between the romanticism of his major works and the classical style in which he also continued to work, there might have been some place for that greater stylistic freedom which seems briefly to have tempted him. In spite of a few state commissions, he had more success with art lovers than with the authorities, and we may note in his favor the fact that he never became a member of the institute.

The work of David d'Angers (1788–1856) displays imaginative and technical powers of a considerably more limited kind. He was, above all, a portraitist, and his main ambition was to leave for future generations the bronze images of all the celebrities of his time. This was the chief source of his own fame. His actual name was Pierre-Jean David, to which he added that of Angers, his birthplace. His father was a sculptor of wooden ornaments whose taste and remarkable ingenuity are apparent in a few pieces belonging to the Angers Museum. Although the young David began at the age of twelve to study drawing in Angers, his father, while initiating him into his own work and training him as a sculptor's assistant, did not wish him to pursue an artistic career. His first work, done when he was eighteen, was merely a signboard modeled for a shoemaker. A painter who recognized genuine gifts in him convinced his father to allow him to go to Paris. The young artist arrived there in 1807 and was hired to work on the cornices of the new wing of the Louvre (at twenty sous a day) and on the ornaments for the *Arch of Triumph* of the Carrousel.

Roland, a sculptor, who had studied with Pajou, admitted him to his atelier and David was finally able to satisfy his passion for sculpture. Like Rude, he obtained a Second Prize, followed in 1811, by the Grand Prix de Rome, for a bas-relief representing *The Death of Epaminondas*. He left for Rome with an introduction to Canova, but was never influenced by him. In 1815 we find him taking part in a rebellion in Italy, and later, living for a while in England. Soon after his return to Paris, he began to enjoy real success; important commissions flowed in. He was elected to the Institute in 1826 and, in 1828, he was appointed to a teaching post at the Ecole des Beaux-Arts in Paris. His work for French towns includes, among others, statues or busts of *Condé, Fénelon, Racine, King René, General Foy, Maréchal Lefèbvre,* and *Talma.* He did a colossal bust of *Goethe* for Germany, one of *Jeremy Bentham* for England and another of *James Fenimore Cooper* for the United States. In 1834, his bronze statue of *Thomas Jefferson* was financed by public subscription in Philadelphia. (It has since been transferred to the Capitol in Washington.) In 1837 he finished the pediment of the Pantheon in Paris.

David d'Angers left almost a thousand works of sculpture, most of which are now in the collection of the Museum of Fine Arts in Angers. Their quality is uneven and his austere classicism is often very rigid. This did not prevent one critic from writing to him at the time of the 1834 Salon: "You lapse into absurdity, you verge upon complete decadence." His statues were really mediocre, but some of his 150 busts—particularly those of *Paganini* and *La Mennais*—and certain bas-reliefs, are not without interest and talent. His technical solidity is, however, most successfully combined with minute observation in the many medallions— he made more than 500—which constitute the best part of his work. They form a unique collection of extremely varied personalities: scientists, writers, politicians, whom David met throughout Europe. He put a generous passion into this work, but owing to the fact that he usually presented each illustrious model with the resulting medallion, he never grew rich from his sculpture.

The last years of David d'Angers' life were curiously active. In 1848, he threw himself into politics, was elected Mayor of the eleventh *arrondissement* of Paris and a member of the Constituent Assembly. His activity as a fierce and

Plates 48-50

48

49

48 David d'Angers. Bust of Paganini, 1830. Bronze. Museum, Angers.

49 David d'Angers. Bust of Lamennais, 1839. Marble. Museum, Rennes.

50 David d'Angers. Napoleon I, 1833. Bronze. Museum, Angers.

advanced Republican was punished by exile, first in Belgium then in Greece, after Napoleon III's *coup d'état*. When he was able to return to France he stopped in Nice to recover from an illness, but died of a paralytic stroke in Paris on January 6, 1856.

In order to understand the dying gasps of a style whose influence upon sculpture was to persist for some years, we must add to the names of Rude and David d'Angers that of a third artist: Antoine-Louis Barye (1795–1875). Barye owed so much of his fame to his representations of animals in combat that Théophile Gautier called him "the Michelangelo of the menagerie."

He was born in Paris, the son of a goldsmith and first worked as apprentice to a metal-engraver. At twenty, he began to study sculpture with Bosio, a maker of rather pompous monuments. He then studied painting with Gros. In 1818, he entered the Ecole des Beaux-Arts, but hesitated for several years between the careers of goldsmith and sculptor. Later in life he was, on several occasions, to combine these two activities in compositions of human figures or of animals in gold or silver plate, as, for example, the centerpiece made for the Duke of Orléans. One senses that Barye by no means considered these to be minor works, for their distinction and purity of style recall those of the great artists of the Renaissance. His contributions to the Salon from 1827 on, nevertheless quite rapidly established his reputation as a perceptive observer of animal life. He actually spent a great deal of time at the zoo in the Jardin des Plantes making very forceful sketches. The titles of Barye's works (some of his sculpture is in the Louvre, others are in the Bonnat Museum in Bayonne) indicate his passion for animal subjects: Plates 51-53 *Tiger Devouring a Gavial, Lion Fighting a Snake, Elk Surprised by a Lynx, Panther Devouring a Gazelle, Young Lion Overpowering a Horse,* etc. Despite the strength and skill animating these bronze pieces, which were later to be so widely and so badly imitated, subjects of this sort now seem rather dull. Barye's technical skill and sense of movement were later admired by younger sculptors (Rodin, in particular), but one regrets the waste of so much knowledge on the creation of this rather monotonous zoology. The monotony was occasionally broken by compositions such as *Centaur and Lapith* or *Theseus and the Minotaur*, and four stone groups that he executed for the Louvre: *War, Peace, Force,* and *Order*. In these and in some admirable sketches we sense that his achievement might have been utterly different.

In his own time, however, Barye's art was described in terms of "romantic frenzy," for he had, in his way, loosened the conventional stiffness characteristic of the sculpture of his day. For this reason he has a place in our analysis of an art which was still struggling to emerge from the rut of tradition. From our twentieth-century vantage point, Barye's influence upon this movement may surprise us, but it was unquestionably important.

52

51 Antoine-Louis Barye. Study for a Monument to Napoleon I,
ca. 1863. Bronze. Petit Palais, Paris.

52 Antoine-Louis Barye. Lion Vanquishing an Ibex. Bronze.
Museum, Marseilles.

53 Antoine-Louis Barye. Thesus Fighting the Centaur Bienor,
1850. Bronze. Museum, Le Puy.

53

III. A BREATH OF FREEDOM

Honoré Daumier

A first glance at the main trends in mid-nineteenth-century sculpture revealed no premonitory signs of a new technical orientation in the plastic arts. It has, however, enabled us to define somewhat more precisely the aesthetic climate surrounding the last stages of development in traditional sculpture. This sculpture continued to be produced for a few years more; its end was hastened by the mediocrity of the very artists who believed it to be eternal. It is essential that we understand their tenacity in order to understand the base from which modern sculpture sprang.

Surprisingly enough, the first man to break with this tradition was not a sculptor, but rather a painter and draftsman who produced a certain number of works of sculpture: Honoré Daumier (1808–1879). As we shall see, the great upheaval which led to a complete renewal of sculptural form was started by the painters.

Daumier owed his fame mainly to his drawings and lithographs, and to his many years of work for illustrated newspapers. His personality far transcended that of a satirical illustrator, but this was recognized belatedly, and it is only now that we appreciate the clearsightedness of Baudelaire in considering him "one of the most important figures, not only in the field of caricature, but in modern art." Although Daumier was known as a great draftsman, his sculpture remained almost unknown during his lifetime, and even the greatness of his painting was slow to be appreciated.

Daumier was the son of a Marseilles glazier who probably considered himself a bit of an artist, since he also did framing and suddenly took to writing verse as well. Daumier came to Paris with his father in 1816 and at the age of twelve, began to earn his living first as a bailiff's errand boy, then as clerk in a bookshop in the Palais-Royal. He started drawing lessons in 1822 with Alexandre Lenoir, acquired some practice in lithography and studied at the Académie Suisse.

The revolution of 1830 had a considerable influence upon Daumier's life and work, for his republican sentiments immediately placed him in opposition to

54

55

54 Honoré Daumier. Bust of Jean Fulchiron, 1830–32. Bronze.
Museum, Marseilles.

55 Honoré Daumier. Bust of an Unknown Man, 1830–32.
Bronze. Museum, Marseilles.

56 Honoré Daumier. The Burden, ca. 1850. Terra cotta. The
Walters Art Gallery, Baltimore.

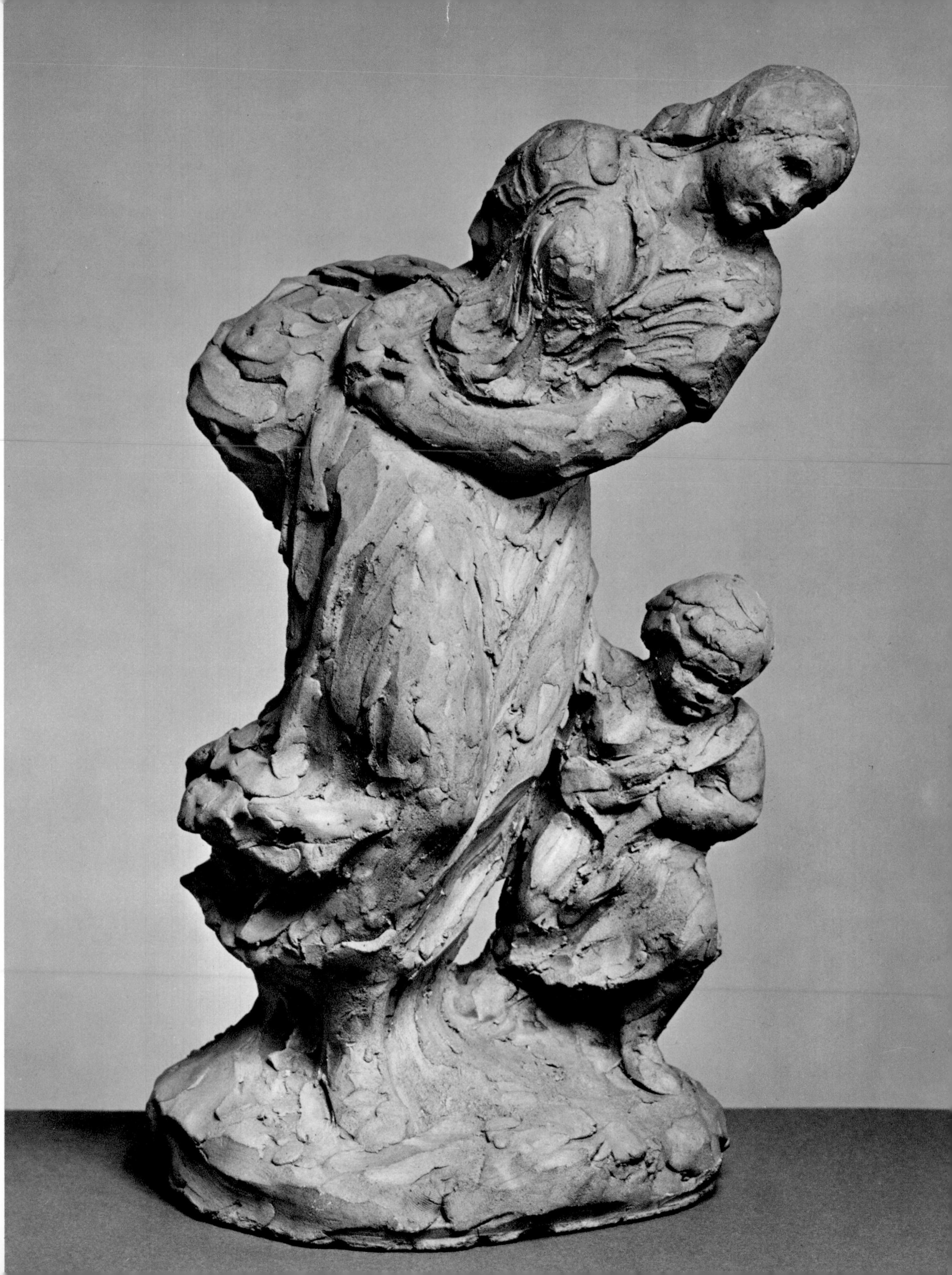

the government and transformed him into what we would now call a "committed" draftsman; he used his pencil as a weapon and threw himself into political satire with a fear-inspiring verve. It was not long before he began to reap the consequences. After his first drawings appeared, in *La Silhouette*, the earliest of the illustrated satirical weeklies to appear in France (to which Balzac also contributed), he published his drawings in *La Caricature*, Philipon's violently liberal paper. In 1831, a drawing representing Louis-Philippe as Gargantua devouring fat budgets and donation-stuffed pies brought him a six-month prison sentence.

It was then that Daumier, who had for some time been modeling in clay, satisfied Philipon's request to model a series of small busts, caricatural portraits of right-wing deputies, senators and ministers of state observed during parliamentary sessions. The series, which probably included more than 40 such busts, was finished in 1832. Thirty-nine were still identifiable in 1878, but today only 36 remain, and some of these are in bad condition. Fortunately, a casting in lost-wax process was made, thus facilitating reproduction in bronze. This admirable series was almost entirely destroyed, for Daumier displayed an extraordinary negligence in the care of his own sculpture. For him, they were simply a means of perfecting his lithographs; he actually used them as models for the savage portraits published in *La Caricature* and *Le Charivari*.

Gifted with a visual memory of unusual power, Daumier rarely worked directly from nature. After he had closely observed a face, he could, upon returning home, unhesitatingly bring it to life in clay. He was not very concerned with firing and almost all his sculpture remained in the fragile state of raw clay, occasionally colored by him. Furthermore, the clay he used was rather coarse, mixed with bits of limestone which did not react well to firing. There is, nevertheless, a story to the effect that he gave some of his pieces to a simple baker to be fired in his oven.

The limited number of Daumier's sculptures which have been preserved is consequently understandable, more so because he never even bothered to ex-

Plates
I, 54, 55

hibit them. Only in 1878, a year before his death, did they become available to the public, in a large exhibition organized by Durand-Ruel. Daumier, who by that time was blind and had recently undergone an unsuccessful operation on his eyes, was unable to attend. He undoubtedly considered his lithographs from which he earned his living and to which he devoted most of his activity for over forty years, the most important aspect of his work. We may, however, presume that part of his sculptural *oeuvre* was destroyed and lament the fact that although we have some 4,000 lithographs, 1,000 wood engravings and 94 paintings, only 60 or so pieces of sculpture have been preserved.

When one remembers that the first series of heads was done when Daumier was only twenty-four years old, one is amazed by their technical boldness and expressive power; indeed, these portraits reveal the first signs of what was later to be termed an "Impressionist" conception of sculpture. Only a few suggest that the artist considered them purely as an expression of caricature. Most of them clearly show that Daumier's genius lay in his power to strip his models, to bare the essentials of character, to go further than caricaturist's cleverness (such as that of Dantan). He created a new style of modeling which he was to illustrate twenty-five years later, even more brilliantly in his *Self-Portrait*. Freedom and energy of style of this kind were not to be seen again equaled until Rodin.

Plate 58

Although Daumier turned to sculpture only intermittently, he did work at it throughout his life. The small busts of politicians were followed, between 1835 and 1838, by a *Head of a Man Smiling* and a *Head of a Man in a Top Hat*, the original dried clay versions of which are in the Glyptotek in Copenhagen. Somewhat later, in 1844, he did the *Man in a Full Wig* and, in 1848, a small terra-cotta figure, *Le Pitre Aboyeur*. His *Ratapoil*, a fine silhouette done in mockery of the Bonapartist propaganda agents, can be dated approximately at 1850. Because of its somewhat seditious character, this work remained hidden for a long time in a straw bottle-case where Madame Daumier concealed it. From that same period, we have *The Burden*, a small terra-cotta statue now in the Walters Art Gallery in

Plate 56

57 Honoré Daumier. The Emigrants (First Version). Plaster. Louvre, Paris.

58 Honoré Daumier. Self-Portrait, 1855–58. Bronze. National Library, Paris.

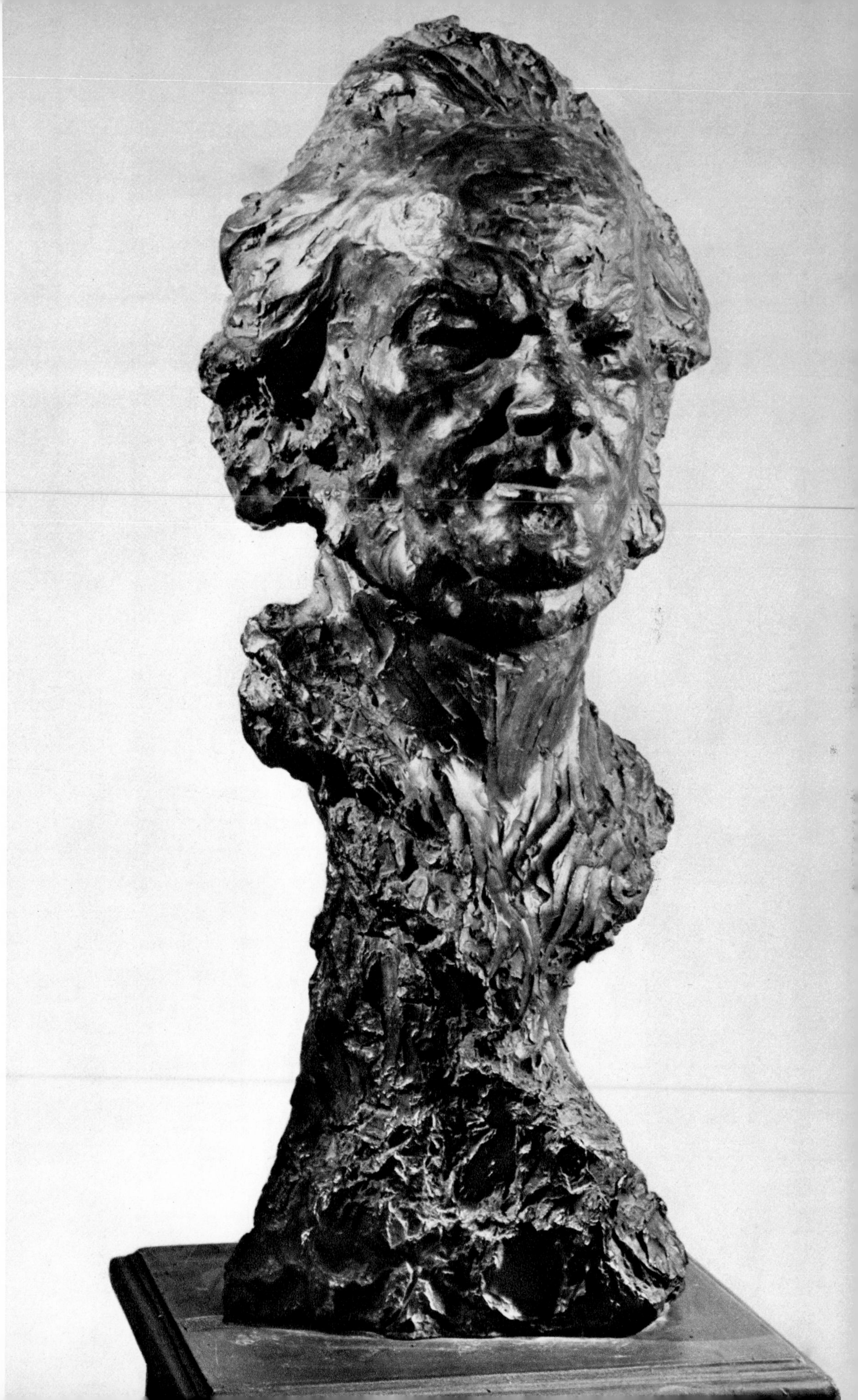

Baltimore. This, too, in the almost "pictorial" character of its modeling which already anticipates Medardo Rosso, shows how far ahead of his time Daumier was. The Louvre possesses one of two versions of a small plaster bas-relief, *The Emigrants,* which cannot be dated with precision and which, like *The Burden,* was also used as subject for a painting. These represent Daumier's major works in sculpture, for if he also executed a series of figurines of Parisian types, these do not display the same originality. They are, for the most part, more facile, more carelessly done.

Plate 57

Daumier's method of using his busts as models for his portraits strongly influenced his graphic style. One can rightfully speak of the "sculptural style" of the lithographs done after 1832.

When, in order to avoid censorship trouble, *Le Charivari* temporarily dropped political satire, Daumier exercised his critical spirit at the expense of the middle class and the magistracy, treating a number of subjects pertaining to mores and current events. The series entitled *Les Bons Bourgeois, Les Gens de Justice, Robert Macaire,* the innumerable types observed in the streets, theaters and trains, and later, his *Saltimbanques* and *Don Quixote,* assured him considerable fame, a renown which needed no reinforcement through a reputation as a sculptor. But it is easy to see that if he had concentrated on sculpture he would have completely upset the traditional techniques then in use. His sculpture remained without influence because it remained unknown. Nevertheless, it is Daumier the Revolutionary who appears as the real precursor of the first aesthetic revolution which was soon to liberate sculpture from its bonds with a past which had grown sterile.

Jean-Baptiste Carpeaux

When we consider Carpeaux' life (1827–1875), we realize once again that the artist's career was, at that time, governed by definite rules; to break them would have been foolhardy for an artist who wished to acquire any reputation. The artist's independence of schools, official awards and standard critical judgment is a victory only won by the twentieth century. Although Jean-Baptiste Carpeaux began by following each stage of the path traveled by his elders, we nevertheless sense in his work a strong impulse of freedom which won him, on more than one occasion, the hostility of officialdom.

The son of a mason from Valenciennes, Carpeaux arrived in Paris to study sculpture at an early age. He enrolled in the Royal School of Mathematics and Design, worked for a few months with Rude, and struggled for years with poverty. To earn a little money, he worked as a market-porter and was frequently forced to live for a whole week on a single pot of boiled potatoes. These difficulties were partly responsible for his choice of a teacher capable of helping him on the traditional road to success. He thus entered the atelier of Francisque Duret, a very conventional sculptor and a member of the Institute who had designed the fountain for the Place Saint-Michel in Paris.

In 1844, Carpeaux began to work desperately hard at the Ecole des Beaux-Arts for the Prix de Rome. This he finally won in 1854 with the statue of *Hector Imploring the Gods for his Son, Astyanax*. In this success lay danger, the risk of the young sculptor stagnating in the narrow field of vision which was that of conventional sculpture. It was, however, soon apparent that even to subjects of the most classical sort, the *Neapolitan Fisherboy with Shell* for example, he brought grace and sensibility of a personal kind.

In Rome, inspired by Dante's description of the torture of Ugolin imprisoned with his children in the Tower of Hunger, helplessly watching their slow death, Carpeaux began to work on a composition which was subsequently to cause many difficulties with officials of the Beaux-Arts and the Institute. The first models of his *Ugolin* show how his original idea for this tormented group was much freer and more striking than the final version to which he finally resigned himself. But, even in its final form (1861), the statue was greatly appre-

Plate
60

65

59

59 Jean-Baptiste Carpeaux. Temperance, 1863. Wax. Masséna Museum, Nice.

60 Jean-Baptiste Carpeaux. Study for Ugolin, ca. 1859. Terra cotta. Louvre, Paris.

ciated in Rome, whereas it met with severe criticism in Paris. The Institute was opposed to its execution in marble which was delayed until 1867 when it was undertaken by private initiative for the Universal Exhibition.

Plates 63, 64

Nevertheless, his contributions to the Salon in Paris, beginning in 1853, marked him as an admirable portraitist. His busts are among his most accomplished works, particularly those of *Vaudemer, the architect* (1859), *Anna Foucart* (1860) (whose face he was later to do again for his *Laughing Woman*), the *Marquise de la Valette,* the wife of the French ambassador in Rome who helped introduce him to the court of Napoleon III (1866), *Charles Garnier* (1869), *Eugénie Fiocre,* a dancer at the Opéra (1869), *Dr. Flaubert,* the brother of Gustave (1874), and *Alexandre Dumas Fils* (1874).

Plates 59, II

To these portraits, full of life and delicacy, should be added the very lovely woman's head known under the title of *Temperance* and *The Violinist;* the former a sketch for the statue commissioned in 1863 by Baron Haussmann for Trinity Church in Paris and the latter a portrait of his brother, Charles Carpeaux. In these two sculptures we sense the freedom with which Carpeaux molded his plaster when he was not concerned with pleasing the public. The studies done for his statues are often more interesting and beautiful than the finished works. He seems to have let himself dream his forms with his fingers, later resigning himself to abandoning part of this dream, yielding to the more rational demands of the perfect technique that was expected of him.

Plate 61

Such was the case with the monument to *Watteau* which was erected in Valenciennes, the painter's birthplace. The first studies have spontaneity, charm and a poetic quality which disappeared in the final version. It was in sketches such as these, in the emotion which seems to animate plaster, that Carpeaux revealed himself as a sculptor of genius, the precursor of a new style.

The friendly interest of Napoleon III, invitations to all the festivities in the Tuileries and the receptions at the castle of Compiègne, brought Carpeaux more than the status of "portrait painter to the Emperor, the Empress, the Imperial Prince and the Princess Mathilda," for the honors showered upon him at court gave him access to the most brilliant social circles of the Second Empire. He was soon overwhelmed with commissions and his statues, busts, statuettes, drawings, and paintings, like the work of Constantin Guys, constitute a valuable document of the splendors of that period.

In 1863, Lefuel, the architect in charge of the new wing of the Louvre, commissioned him to do the exterior decorations for the wing known as the Pavillon de Flore. The work included a group of reliefs, a pediment presenting an *Allegory* of Imperial France, cornice ornaments in which the artist placed little sprites bearing palms, and, as the main subject, the *Triumph of Flora*. Carpeaux worked at this for three years, but the volume of his relief of Flora shocked Lefuel who wanted him to start the work all over again. The sculptor nevertheless stuck to his idea, defended it, and it was accepted only after the Emperor had personally intervened in his favor. Carpeaux' obstinacy was undoubtedly justified, for his *Flora* remains one of the Louvre's loveliest ornaments.

Unfortunately, these difficulties were a small thing to those created by his masterwork, a group known as *The Dance*, which Charles Garnier, architect of the Paris Opéra, had commissioned in 1865 for the façade of the new building. Carpeaux developed a passionate interest in this project. For two years he worked on a series of models, often carried far beyond the imposed limits of the commission by his imagination. (One model included no less than 17 figures.) In this way, through the research, innumerable studies, and work of his assistants, he managed to bankrupt himself, far exceeding the allotted budget. *The Dance* was finally completed in 1869 and, thanks largely to Garnier's affectionate understanding, was placed on the façade of the Opera House. It was then that the scandal broke. Carpeaux' work was considered unbearably indecent!

This may seem strange to us now, as allegorical sculpture had always abounded in representations of the nude figure. No one would have dreamed, during the Renaissance, of reproaching Giovanni da Bologna for having repre-

Plates
65

61 Jean–Baptiste Carpeaux. Study for
   Watteau, ca. 1860–62. Plaster. Petit
   Palais, Paris.

62 Jean–Baptiste Carpeaux. The Three
   Graces, 1874. Terra cotta. Petit Palais,
   Paris.

sented Virtue in the form of a female nude. Nevertheless, the sight of Carpeaux'
female dancers entwining the Spirit of *The Dance* aroused enormous indignation,
so much so that the grace of these lovely stone bodies, their careless gaiety, the
rhythm suggesting the movement of music, went unnoticed. A blindness of this
kind indicates the profound gap between Carpeaux' work and the fashionable
sculpture of the period. The public, accustomed to an academic tradition which, as
we shall later see, was to reach its apogee, no longer realized how conventional its
aesthetic was, how poor its technique was. It was not the subject of *The Dance*
which shocked the public, for another sculptor would have had no difficulty in presenting a group of female nudes dancing about a winged, allegorical figure; it was,
rather, that the life and sensibility with which Carpeaux had modeled his figures
testified to a vision which no longer conformed to academic rules. This vision dis-
turbed the chaste beholder because it revealed a fresh and direct observation of
nature. Carpeaux' great contribution to the sculpture of the nineteenth century
was his ability to transmit, with moving honesty, the nuances of his own sensibility to his materials.

Shortly after the installation of *The Dance,* a certain C. A. de Salelles published a short work entitled *Monsieur Carpeaux' Group, "The Dance," Considered
from the Moral Point of View*. In it, the charming dancers are described as "the
personification of lewdness at its most corrupt. Are not these Maenads drunk?"
asks the author. "They reek of wine and vice . . . their lascivious postures and cyn-
ical expressions provoke the beholder." Finally, after describing this "masterpiece
of immorality" as a "base Saturnalia," and denouncing it as "an insult to public
morality," the philanthropist carries his absurdity to the point of demanding the
elimination of *The Dance* from the Opera House, protesting vigorously in favor of
"the honor of decent womanhood, of my conscience, and of our time!"

Thus incited, on the night of August 27th, 1869, a sacrilegious hand
smashed a bottle of black ink against one of the main figures of *The Dance*. The
large stain which spread over the dancer's belly bore witness to the fanaticism of

stupidity acting in the name of outraged morality. Not unexpectedly, the directors of the Beaux-Arts did not distinguish themselves by good judgment, and it was decided that Carpeaux' fine group should be replaced by one which was "treated with decency." But the Franco-Prussian War was approaching and war, generally so destructive of art, for once had a protective effect: the disputes provoked by the moralists were forgotten, and *The Dance* remained permanently where it belonged.

Another monumental work by Carpeaux, the *Fountain of the World's Four Corners* was erected in Paris in 1874, in the gardens of the avenue de l'Observatoire. Four female figures symbolizing the races of man support an armillary sphere poised above their heads. The style of the bronze version is not entirely suited to that of the horses which were added by Frémiet, and the original plaster conveys much more powerfully the artist's talent for infusing life into everything he touched. This piece will become visible to the public when the Louvre recovers exhibition space in the Pavillon de Flore, for the sculpture is now confined to the reserves in the cellar, where, thanks to the kindness of the museum staff, I was able to see it.

Shortly thereafter, Carpeaux was condemned to suffer a long and painful illness, without, however, abandoning his work. The joyful serenity which informs a work such as *The Three Graces*, one of the most exquisite small statues ever to emerge from his hands, belies the terrible threat which hung over a life already laden with so many professional, personal, and emotional difficulties. He was only forty-eight years old when he was finally delivered from the slow, cruel agony of cancer.

Plate 62

Carpeaux thus takes his place with Daumier as one of the two precursors of a new approach to sculptural technique which was not to be given final form until Rodin. This approach is visible in only those few of Carpeaux' works which retain a private character, as it were: in the few statues which show a renunciation of his own semiclassical habits of technique and in the adoption of a treatment where spontaneity suddenly becomes evident. As with Daumier, his tools—his fingers—

63 Jean-Baptiste Carpeaux. The Betrothed, 1869. Plaster. Louvre, Paris.

64 Jean-Baptiste Carpeaux. Bust of Eugénie Fiocre, 1869. Plaster. Petit Palais, Paris.

65 Jean-Baptiste Carpeaux. The Dance, 1865–69. Stone. Opera House, Paris.

63

64

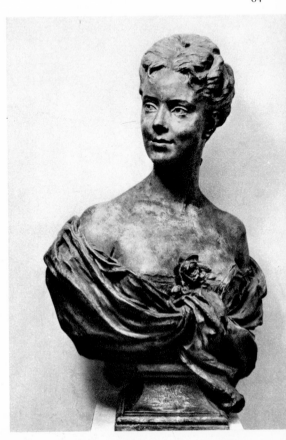

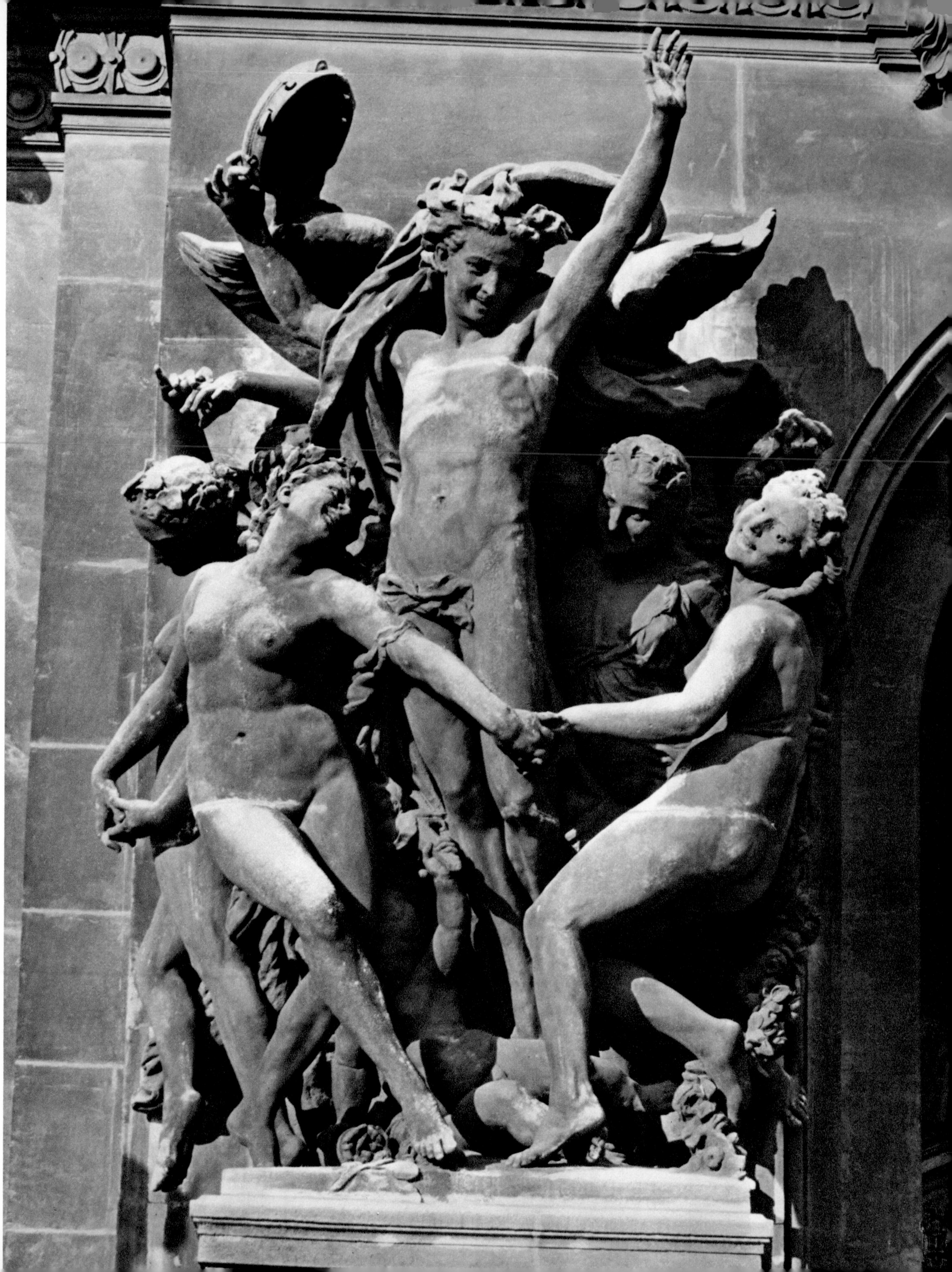

no longer sought to hide their gestures, wishes, discoveries, skill, or personal awkwardness. The sculptural process acquired, for the first time, the inner revelatory value of an almost spontaneous signature. However, whereas a face modeled by Carpeaux remained, beneath its animated surfaces, classical in its construction, those of Daumier implied a far more disruptive approach to the representation of forms. The character which he wished to express forced him, in a way, to destroy his model, then to reconstruct it in accordance with his penetrating and often savage vision. In this, Daumier went much further than Carpeaux, and his busts contain the germ of a conception of sculpture which was to be used much later and in quite another style.

IV. THE AGE OF THE ACADEMICIANS

Mannerism and Solemnity

The last quarter of the nineteenth century witnessed the beginning of the movement which was to uproot and, eventually, to bury all the prejudices and conventions to which for so long art had remained subservient. But no period was more impervious to the value of its own discoveries. A certain perspective was essential for the understanding of Impressionism's decisive role in painting. We shall shortly be considering the repercussions of this movement upon sculpture. At the time of its appearance, however, it commanded only an ironic attention.

Even before Impressionism, however, sculpture had made noticeable progress—if the replacement of one academic tradition by another can be termed "progress." Although the subject might change, techniques remained obedient to traditional rules. The sculpture which dominated the Salons, expanded into the monuments and entered the museums, was anecdotal in character and considered to be realistic; it was roughly a sculptural equivalent of the painting of Bonnat, Bouguereau, Chocarne-Moreau, or Roybet. When we consider that Roybet, the painter of strutting musketeers and jolly cavaliers, was hailed by certain critics as "one of the best new realists," we get some notion of the singular idea of realism which then prevailed.

Courbet's teaching had been completely misunderstood, and his influence proved to be unfortunate; the attempt at naturalism, which began to be visible in the work of many artists, inclined them, not to an intelligent observation of nature, but rather to a choice of subjects which, though drawn from everyday life, were nonetheless treated in a style representing the worst possible combination of mannerism and academicism. Sculpture now revealed the distressing poverty of its aspirations.

The taste for "natural" anecdote, however, had not eliminated the taste for mythology: antiquity made a solemn entrance into the embryonic Art Nouveau, and sculptors, encouraged by architects, abandoned themselves to the extravagance of allegory. Hippolyte Maindron (1801–1884) worked on the Pantheon.

66

67

66 Alfred Boucher. Thought, ca. 1900. Marble. Prayssas (Lot-et-Garonne).

67 Léon Gérôme. Tanagra, 1890. Marble. Louvre, Paris.

68 Laurent-Honoré Marqueste. Perseus and the Gorgon, 1876. Marble. Villeurbanne (Rhône).

69 Augustus Saint-Gaudens. Victory, 1903. Bronze. Metropolitan Museum of Art, New York.

70 Louis Barrias. Nature Unveiling Herself, 1899. Marble and onyx. Conservatory of Arts and Crafts, Paris.

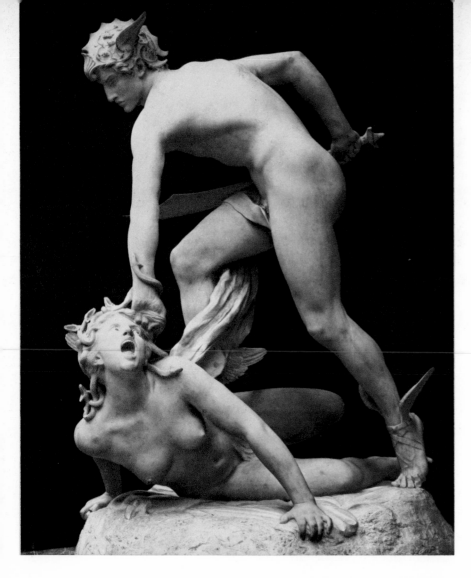

68

69

70

Plate
43

Albert Carrier-Belleuse (1824–1887), a pupil of David d'Angers and portraitist of presidents of the Republic, decorated the new wing of the Louvre and the Opéra, while his terra cottas had great success in the Salon. Paul Dubois (1827–1905), elected to the Institute in 1876, won fame with his *Florentine Singer,* reproduced in countless copies, whose bronze mandolin cast a long-lasting spell

Plate
1

on the good bourgeois living room. Jean-Alexandre Falguière (1831–1900), another member of the Institute and Professor at the Ecole des Beaux-Arts, was an indefatigable producer of monuments; with a *Gambetta* in Cahors, a *La Fayette* in Washington, *Switzerland Welcoming the French Army* and *Pegasus Wafting the Poet toward the Realm of Dreams,* he scattered the evidence of his bad taste and conventional style over a wide area. Like Emmanuel Frémiet (1824–1910) and Henri Chapu (1833–1891), he also produced an inevitable *Joan of Arc.* His pupil, Antonin Mercié (1845–1916) gave the city of Paris the *Spirit of the Arts* which revealed a rather alarming idea of Art and the Spirit.

The statues of this official school, invading cemeteries and public places, resembled each other in their lack of style and sensitivity and in the theatrical aspect of their gestures and attitudes. These figures hoisted onto their pedestals— the abandoned Psyches, Sleeping Hebes and solemn frock-coated gentlemen— look like bad actors, petrified in climactic moments of their roles. Elements of these huge allegorical compositions seem interchangeable; someone like Carrier-Belleuse needed very little imagination to represent *Peace Spreading Her Blessings in Industry* once he had finished *Industry Bringing Peace and Light to the World.*

Similarly, Frédéric-Auguste Bartholdi (1834–1904) also had a fondness for grandiose subjects. Having studied architecture, then painting, with Ary Scheffer, he exhibited in the Salon of 1857, and his first monument, done in 1861 for his home town, Colmar, was commissioned in honor of Martin Schongauer. After the Franco-Prussian War of 1870–1871, the French Government presented the City of New York with Bartholdi's *La Fayette Arriving in America.* He then undertook a gigantic work measuring 33 feet by 66 (1875–1880): a *Lion* carved from a red sandstone block at the foot of the fortress of Belfort. But it was with his *Liberty Illuminating the World,* known as the *Statue of Liberty,* constructed of strips of beaten copper and erected in New York in 1886 to commemorate the hundredth anniversary of the signing of the Declaration of Independence, that Bartholdi managed to achieve world fame.

At this time, the United States too had its celebrated sculptor: Augustus Saint-Gaudens (1848–1907), the son of Franco-Irish parents who had emigrated to America. In Paris, where he studied at the Beaux-Arts until the outbreak of the Franco-Prussian War, and in Rome, where he studied the masters of the Italian Renaissance, Saint-Gaudens acquired the solid technique which upon his return to the United States quickly brought him an immense reputation. His Plate 69 principal works, *Admiral Farragut,* the *Monument to Sherman,* a relief of *Robert Louis Stevenson* and his busts, including one of *Abraham Lincoln,* represent the culmination and the end of a style which had been introduced into the United States by John Quincy Adams Ward (1830–1910), whose statue of *General Thomas* in Washington and *The Puritan* in Central Park are still American landmarks. This style was also represented, though less capably, by Paul Wayland Bartlett (1865–1925), the sculptor of *Michelangelo* and of the *Christopher Columbus* in the Capitol.

The sculptors who had chosen this tone of solemnity and used it with an impressive mediocrity, contrasted somewhat with those whose baroque affectation reflected the visual style of the turn of the century. So it was with Léon Plates 67, 70, 68 Gérôme (1824–1904) as in the *Tanagra* and the polychromed marble *Sarah Bernhardt,* with Louis Barrias (1841–1905), who mixed onyx and jasper with white marble, and Laurent-Honoré Marqueste (1848–1920), creator of *Perseus and the Gorgon,* whose absurd *Cupid* was later to amuse the visitors to the former Paris Museum in the Luxembourg Garden.

As a Frenchman, I have chosen these examples mainly in France, and only because they were more accessible to me. Every nation, however, had its acade-

71

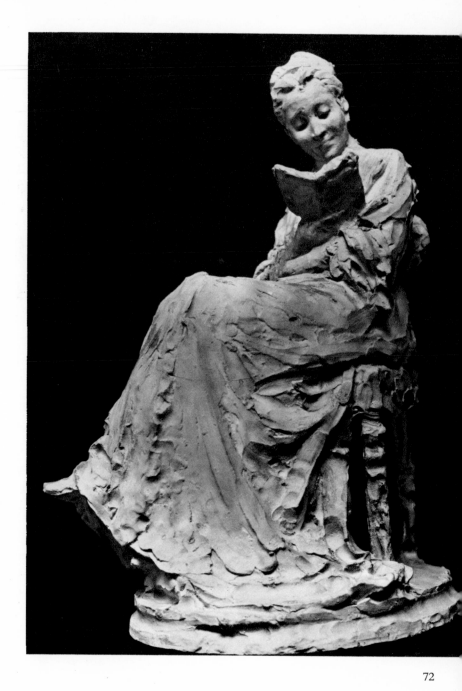

72

71 Jules Dalou. Woman Sewing, ca. 1870–80. Terra cotta. Petit Palais, Paris.

72 Jules Dalou. Woman Reading, ca. 1880. Plaster. Petit Palais, Paris.

73 Jules Dalou. Woman Taking off her Stockings, ca. 1870–80. Terra cotta. Petit Palais, Paris

micians, frivolous or austere. A detailed consideration of their work would be tiresome and would teach us little, for the art of this period was much the same everywhere.

Some Isolated Experiments

The work of these sculptors gave little reason to hope for a redefinition of the problems of form. Not all of them, however, were so unquestioningly obedient to the canons of official art, and a few undoubtedly possessed qualities which, in another period, might have found a freer expression. We cannot know whether the artists, themselves, were aware of this, or whether they merely doubted that a greater boldness would have assured more lasting fame.

The very uneven work of Jules Dalou (1838–1902) reveals, apart from the lack of any real originality of inspiration or execution, in such sculptures as *The Triumph of the Republic* or the *Monument to Delacroix,* traces of effort more directly inspired by close observation of life. This observation is visible mainly in his terra cottas and his work in plaster. His sketches, like those of Carpeaux, his teacher, reveal the sculptor spontaneously and lovingly working out *the idea of a form* rather than the detailed form itself, and they are frequently finer than the too meticulous final stone versions.

Plates 71-73

This quality is very striking in Dalou's *Lavoisier,* and his *Woman Reading,* for the first plaster versions of both display a vivid sensibility, but, in their final versions, both became work of mere technical skill. Dalou liked to carry pieces of clay about in his pocket, modeling forms of workers and peasants from life, making brief notations of gestures which show the precision of his eye and of his fingers. The Museum of Fine Arts of the City of Paris (Petit Palais) possesses a large collection of these statuettes; they enable us to measure the distance between the sculptor's first vision of the object and its final transposition in the finished work.

Constantin Meunier (1831–1905), a Belgian, carried this study of working-class life much farther. His entire work is a hymn to labor, and reflects, in its austere and sometimes overly sentimental lyricism, the social preoccupations of the turn of the century: workingmen, fishermen and peasants, miners, peddlers, hammersmiths, dockers, ploughmen and reapers. These figures, invariably portrayed in labor and under stress, are imbued with power, nobility, and grandeur, but also with a certain monotony which betrays Meunier's rather limited means of expression. His large bas-relief, which unites industrial workers, farm laborers and seamen, constitutes a rather melancholy synthesis of the themes which haunted him throughout his life. Meunier lived in the black regions of the coal mines, a lifelong witness to that hard labor which reduces human energy to those few gestures he chose to celebrate.

Plates 75, 76

In Germany, on the contrary, Adolf von Hildebrand (1847–1921), refusing to concede to the growing taste for realism, attempted to revive in a more humanized form some of the canons of classical sculpture. After attending the School of Fine Arts in Nuremberg, he made his first trip to Rome which impressed him so that he soon returned for a stay of many years. It was not, however, in Florence, where he had his studio, but in Munich that he finally settled for the remainder of his life. Here he did his best-known pieces, including the equestrian statue of the *Prince-Regent Luitpold* and the *Hubertus Fountain*. In 1893, Hildebrand, who had developed a theory of visual forms which corresponded to his architectural preoccupations, published an essay on *The Problem of Form*, which helped to confirm his already considerable reputation. According to Hildebrand, the technique of stone-cutting should be determined by the general aspect of the monument. Bourdelle was to use similar principles some years later. Although in no way revolutionary, some of Hildebrand's works, particularly his busts, are superior to most German sculpture of that period.

Plate 74

74

75

74 Adolf von Hildebrand. The Net Carrier, 1874–75. Stone. New Picture
    Gallery, Munich.

75 Constantin Meunier. The Reaper. Bronze.

86 76 Constantin Meunier. The Soil. Bronze.

At that same time, in Italy, the sculpture of Vincenzo Gemito (1852–1929) proved astonishing, at least partly because of its sheer abundance. His subject matter and varied techniques give his work an aspect of such diversity that one wonders as to the nature of his real personality. This is undoubtedly the source of his major weakness. He was incapable of distinguishing between good and bad, between the sensitive restraint of a portrait like that of *Michetti* or of *Signora Duffaud* and the melodramatic naturalism of a statue such as *Winter*. His somewhat ironical treatment of certain subjects, as in the statue of *Meissonnier*, is counterbalanced by the dull imitation of classical antiquity, as in *The Philosopher*. Nevertheless, in spite of all his contradictions—or rather because of them—Gemito was an effective transitional figure. He was partly responsible for the outbreak of Italian naturalism so abundantly represented by the style of the tombstones in the Genoa cemetery (a real museum of turn-of-the-century sculpture) and he was also one of the first in Italy to begin working, between 1872 and 1880, toward a freer handling of planes and surfaces.

V. REVOLUTIONARY VISIONS

Impressionism and Sculpture

The relationship between Impressionism and sculpture introduces a problem of basic interest for the study of the origins of modern sculpture. Because the role played by painting during this period really extends beyond the framework of Impressionism, we are tempted to consider the influence of certain painters, such as Manet, Redon, Toulouse-Lautrec and Van Gogh, who never belonged to the Impressionist group, or those, such as Seurat and Signac who joined it only in time to participate in the eighth, and last, exhibition of 1885. Nevertheless, we must limit our discussion to what was eventually loosely grouped around the name of Impressionism, for its content already far transcended its theoretical significance.

Impressionism involved a new theory of the painter's vision, of his subjectivity, a new mode of expression based on an equivalence of color and light. It cannot be strictly defined in terms of a direct relationship between aesthetics and technique as expressed in the work of all the painters of the group, for in several ways, these painters differed distinctly from one another.

At the time of the first exhibition in 1874, which included the work of Monet, Cézanne, Renoir, Degas, Sisley, Pissarro, and Berthe Morisot, the word "impressionist" was really most precisely appropriate to the painting of Monet and, though somewhat less so, to that of Renoir, Sisley and Pissarro. Cézanne, whose influence was later to be of the greatest importance, had not yet developed that very personal technique which would evidence itself a few years later, about 1877, in canvases such as *Madame Cézanne Sewing,* in which a construction in planes begins to take shape. Thus, apart from Renoir who had exhibited in the Salon of 1870 (a *Bather* and his *Woman of Algiers,* which already revealed a new tendency), the Impressionists did not exhibit their first characteristic paintings, generally painted after 1869, until 1874. These historical details are necessary to settle the problem of what has, rightly or wrongly, been called "Impressionism" in sculpture. The term, as first used, applied only to two sculptors whom we shall shortly be considering: Auguste Rodin and Medardo Rosso.

Plates 77, 78

89

77 Medardo Rosso. Child in the Sun, 1892. Wax. Kröller–Müller
Rijksmuseum, Otterlo (Holland).

78 Auguste Rodin. Study for Balzac (Detail), 1893. Bronze.
Rodin Museum, Paris.

The application to sculpture of a definition used for a technique basically related to an approach to color is, of course, surprising. However, if we consider the consequences of this technique for landscape drawing, we must admit that it also implied a revolution in the representation of form. If we limit ourselves to the pre-eminence given, by the most theoretically explicit of the Impressionist painters, to the idea of light, then Rosso must be considered the most "Impressionist" of sculptors. On the other hand, we can use the word in its more general sense, that of a more direct and open adaptation of the artist's sensibility to his technique of expression, and this in complete opposition to academic tradition. We then conclude that Rodin, Carpeaux (in whose atelier Rodin worked as a young man) and, long before them, Daumier, had already begun to handle the medium with an unprecedented freedom and freshness, with an approach to reality which was stronger and more intimate, thus anticipating the first signs of pictorial Impressionism.

The Impressionist movement, with which Rodin claimed kinship, undoubtedly encouraged him in the revolutionary direction he had already begun to follow. We cannot, however, say that Rodin's sculpture was born of Impressionism. His personal treatment, his forms and the power with which he animated

Plate 79

his materials had already been visible in the mask of the *Man with the Broken Nose* which was refused by the Salon of 1864, ten years before the first Impressionist exhibition and five years before the group produced their first characteristic canvases.

We should not, on the other hand, forget that the first Impressionist exhibition provoked not only the jeers of the general public and the hostility of the critics, but also the opposition of almost all contemporary artists of any repute. The bitter attacks on Manet ("Monsieur Manet," wrote a critic in 1873, "may be a clever man attempting to fool an ignorant public; he is certainly no painter.") were nothing compared to the insults thrown at the Impressionists. To the press they were madmen, sometimes even with criminal tendencies, accused of "leading younger artists astray." Their influence was, therefore, not immediately established, nor was it immediately apparent in sculpture. The Impressionist painters, however, developed a new position on aesthetic problems, and sooner or later, the sculptors, in their own way, turned this lesson to account.

Auguste Rodin

The traditional image of the sculptor somewhat resembles that of the athlete: a man whose exceptional strength is tamed by a methodically acquired skill, a man with powerful and efficient hands, whose energy is in keeping with the hard labor of kneading and carving. Although in many cases this traditional image has proved false, it does, nevertheless, hold for Rodin, for the strength which radiated from his face and character. This strength was inseparable from the great moral force he displayed throughout the life-long struggle to defend his art. We should also see him with the shades and nuances of a verbal portrait drawn by his close friend, Gustave Geffroy in 1893: "He is small, stocky and calm. . . . Between the short hair and the long beard which flows in blond waves to his chest, the expression of his fine-featured face passes from distraction to anxiety, from anxiety to laughter; it is masked with preoccupation, then illuminated with tranquil joy and silent serenity."

Auguste Rodin was born in Paris on November 12, 1840, at 3, Rue de l'Arbalete. His father, Jean-Baptiste, first an employee in a Police Station and later a detective inspector, apparently disapproved of the boy's passion for drawing. Although he could not stand in the way of his son's natural inclination, he undoubtedly hoped, by enrolling him at the age of fourteen in the School of Mathematics and Design (later to become the School of Decorative Arts), to make him a good craftsman in some branch of applied art, to teach him some sensible trade at which he might earn his living. However, young Rodin was

80

81

79 Auguste Rodin. The Man with the Broken Nose, 1864. Bronze. Rodin Museum, Paris.

80 Auguste Rodin. Bust of Falguière, 1897. Bronze. Rodin Museum, Paris.

81 Auguste Rodin. Bust of Dalou, 1883. Bronze. Rodin Museum, Paris.

more ambitious even before he had thought of becoming a sculptor. He loved, above all, to draw, and knew this was the best way to become a real artist. Draftsmanship always remained a passion with him and his drawings constitute one of the most original forms of his expression.

Rodin's first attempts at modeling revealed an irresistible affinity for the medium of sculpture. After a few lessons from Carpeaux, he tried to enter the Ecole des Beaux-Arts but failed three times and was forced to earn his living by working for ornamentalists and on theater decoration. His first bust, a portrait of his father, done in 1860, shows that at twenty, he could express character with power and restraint. A religious crisis, following the death of his sister, impelled him to spend a few months with the Eudist Fathers. The *Bust of Father Eymard*, which dates from this period (1863), still betrays the influence of classicism, but his mask of *The Man with the Broken Nose*, the portrait of an old street porter, done the following year, reveals a very personal rendering of facial planes.

Barye's courses at the Museum of Natural History were extremely helpful to the young sculptor and Rodin attached great importance to this study of animal anatomy; it gave him an understanding of the fundamental importance of internal structure. The combination in Rodin's training of Barye's austere discipline and the frivolity of Carrier-Belleuse, who was known as the "Clodion of the Second Empire," seems surprising, and yet it was the studio of Carrier-Belleuse which Rodin finally chose to enter. He remained there for six years, from 1864 until 1870, assisting the sculptor in his work, certainly to no great profit. "He had given me some lessons," Rodin was later to say, "and I had to return them." He admired the gracefulness of eighteenth-century sculpture, however, and found traces of it in his teacher's work. With great loyalty, he never let an occasion pass, later in life, to describe himself as "a student of Barye and of Carrier-Belleuse."

On the other hand, he was impervious to the pressure of academic tradition and even his teachers could not alter his very personal ideas. He might not have been able to explain them very clearly at the time, for he was not a well-educated man, but he seems always to have known that he had to follow his natural inclinations and, when he later turned with passionate eagerness to the study of ancient and Renaissance sculpture, he rediscovered for himself principles which were basic for his own work.

In 1871, Carrier-Belleuse, who had received a number of important commissions in Belgium, took Rodin to Brussels, where they remained for several years. While there, Rodin worked for his employer and his associate, Van Rasbourg, on decorations for a great many monuments, among them caryatids, allegorical figures and trophies for the Stock Exchange and the Palace of the Academies. It was at the end of his stay in Brussels that he began the sketches for his first important work which was initially entitled *Primeval Man*, then *The Awakening of Humanity*, and, finally, *The Bronze Age*. Before finishing it, he wished to improve his knowledge of the great Italian Renaissance sculptors, but the Belgian and Dutch museums were richer in painting than in sculpture, and he began to feel the need for a trip to Italy.

Plate 87

In 1875, therefore, we find him wandering through Rome and Florence, discovering Michelangelo and Donatello. Rodin's study of Michelangelo was to have a deep influence upon his work; his influence is tempered, however, by his own particular form of realism, by a poetry and drama of an entirely personal kind. In his *Talks on Art* edited by Paul Gsell, Rodin analyzed Michelangelo's style and the way in which it differed from that of the Greek sculptors. "The quiet charm" obtained by a movement through four planes in a Greek statue was, according to Rodin, expressed in Michelangelo's style "through a reduction to two planes, transformed into a movement which gives the gesture both violence and constraint." This torment, this "anxious energy," Rodin often sought to express in his own work.

Upon his return to France, he completed his *The Bronze Age*. It should have established his reputation, for it displayed technical mastery and an ability to combine sensitive modeling with an almost classical rigor. However, when he

82

83

82 Auguste Rodin. Drawing. Collection Madame Dufet–
Bourdelle, Paris.

83 Auguste Rodin. Head of Sorrow, 1892. Bronze. Rodin
Museum, Paris.

84 Auguste Rodin. The Martyr, 1885. Bronze. Rodin
Museum, Paris.

85 Auguste Rodin. Head of Jacques de Wiessant, 1884–86.
Bronze. Rodin Museum, Paris.

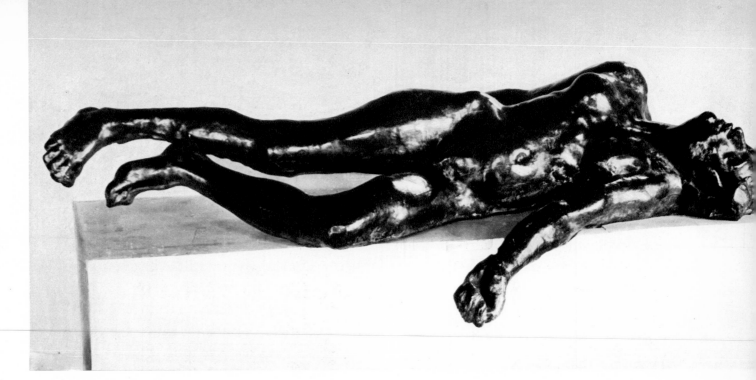

84

85

99

exhibited it in the Salon of the Palace of Industry, in 1877, he was immediately accused of having modeled his statue directly upon a live subject. Rodin was very frequently to meet with this lack of understanding, this hostility, and it was only after several years, thanks to the protests of some indignant technicians, that justice was done to *The Bronze Age* and to its creator. In 1880, the work was finally purchased by the government.

The time was not yet ripe for Rodin's success, and he was forced to solve his financial problems (in a limited way) by doing work of relatively little interest. He thus worked for the Sèvres porcelain factory, which was then directed by Carrier-Belleuse, composing small decorative figures. At night when he returned home, he worked with all the vigor at his command on the first studies for *Saint John the Baptist Preaching*, a statue which was also to provoke critical sarcasm.

He submitted a group for a competition organized for a monument for *Defense*, but the jury chose a conventional work by Barrias. Rodin was firmly resolved, however, never to let a jury's taste influence his work and, during his entire lifetime, received only one official prize: a Third Prize medal awarded in 1880 by the French Artists' Society. Deeply preoccupied by the new form and expressive power he wished to bring to sculpture, he pursued his work, indifferent to the opinions of those about him.

His *Eve* (1881) represented an important stage in the steady development of that sensitive, powerful style which was to produce seven years later, one of his
Plate
92
masterpieces, *Man Walking*. The two legs and armless, headless torso sufficed to provoke the haughty scorn of his enemies! He was accused of being unable to finish a sculpture. They did not perceive the remarkable way in which Rodin had conceived the representation of the movement of walking: the two contrasting attitudes of the legs suggesting two different periods of time, future and past, in illustration of a theory of movement which was frequently used in his sculpture and which we shall again have occasion to consider.

An analysis of Rodin's development, year by year and sculpture by sculp-

86

86 Auguste Rodin. The Thinker (Detail), 1880. Bronze. Rodin Museum, Paris.

87 Auguste Rodin.
The Bronze Age
(Detail), 1876.
Bronze. Rodin
Museum, Paris

ture, enables us to trace the main conceptual directions and varying technical expressions of his work. This analysis is facilitated by the existence of the Rodin Museum, housed in the Hôtel Biron, that lovely eighteenth-century dwelling in the Rue de Varenne where Rodin took up residence, in 1907, when his name had begun to acquire the halo of world fame. The Museum contains most of his work, and we can easily observe, to begin with, a division into two main categories of technique.

The first, involving the modeling of clay or plaster directly with his hands, reveals the freedom and sensitivity of touch which make each surface, as Rodin himself expressed it, "the natural outcome of an inner form." This powerful handling and the astute deployment of planes, create a play of light which attracts the spectator's eye at every angle; the vitality of each corner, each interstice, establishes a relationship between the figure's movement and its thought.

This category includes Rodin's finest work: *Man Walking*, the study for *Fugit Amor, Large Head of Iris, The Burghers of Calais, The Martyr, Head of Sorrow, Earth, Crouching Woman, The Helmet-Maker's Wife.* It also included many busts, notably those of *J.-P. Laurens, Gustave Geffroy, Henri de Rochefort, Octave Mirbeau, Falguière, Dalou* and *Clemenceau,* all fine portraits, even though they were not always to the taste of the sitter. Clemenceau, among others, took some time to accustom himself to his. These pieces, which generate a real electric current, transmitted by the sculptor's hands to his materials, suggest that for Rodin, sculpture was not only an idea which assumed concrete form, but a physical thing, the achievement of a deep and indissoluble harmony between his hands —the creators—and the object created. The history of sculpture boasts few examples of such clearly apparent harmony; we do know, however, that it already existed in the work of Daumier.

The second group, which found its ideal medium in marble, is grounded in an entirely different aesthetic. Apparently, Rodin wanted to leave the bodies which emerged from marble half-imprisoned in the medium; they appear to us

Plates
83, 84, 88
90, 92, 121

Plates
80, 81, 96

88 Auguste Rodin. The Burghers of Calais, 1884–86. Bronze. Rodin Museum, Paris.

89 Auguste Rodin. Paolo Malatesta and Francesca da Rimini in the Clouds, 1905. Marble. Rodin Museum, Paris.

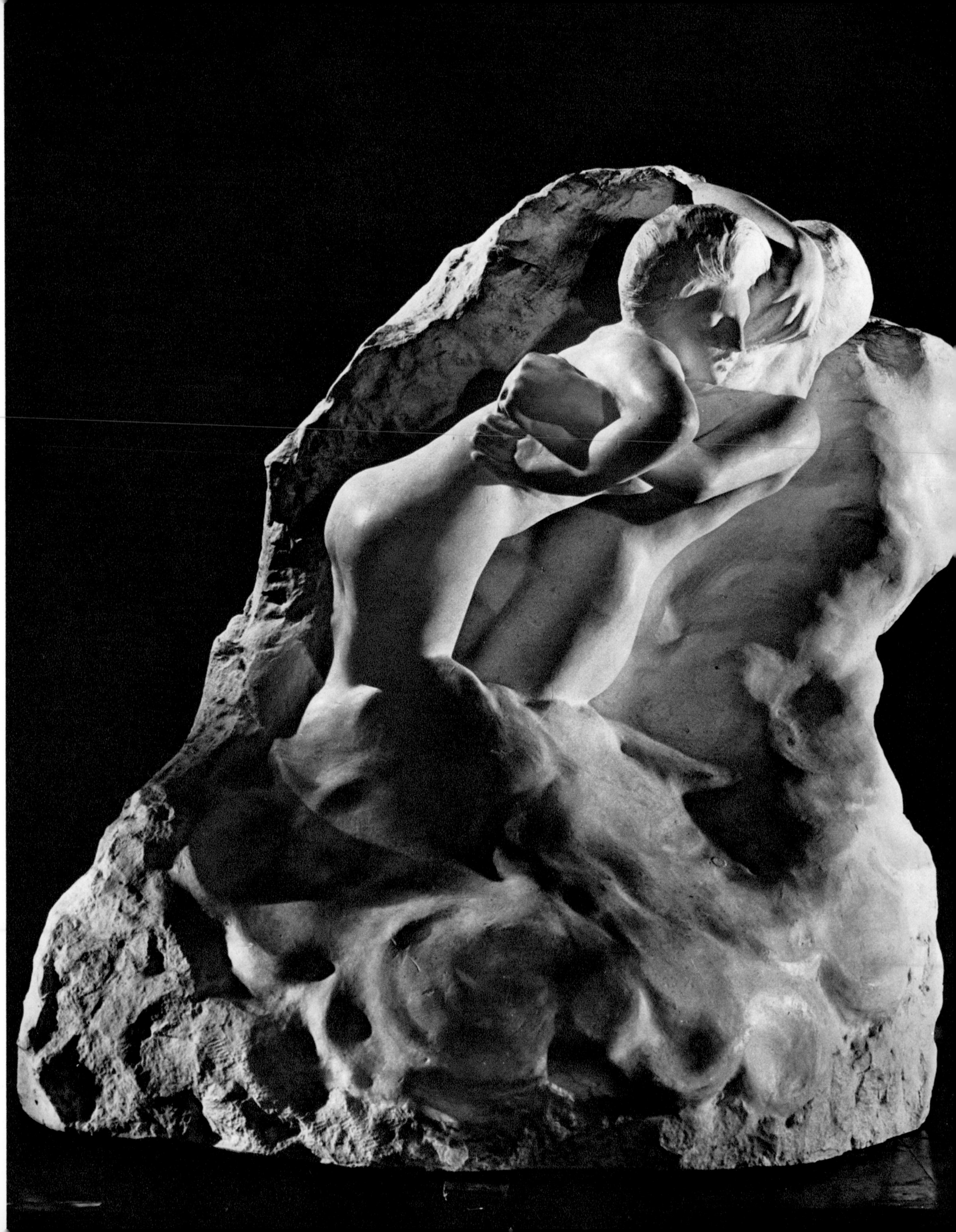

only as a bare flowering of marble. Their gestures are no longer released in space; there is no circulation of air around them. These human forms half melt, like snow, into the snow of the marble block. The work seems incomplete; the polished surfaces give us only a half-veiled image of the dramatic or sensual scene evoked by the sculptor. Most of the sculpture in this style—and there are about 30 pieces—was done between 1887 and 1910. The most important are *The Wave, The Dove and the Sparrow Hawk, Orpheus and the Furies, The Ocean Nymphs, Paolo Malatesta and Francesca da Rimini in the Clouds, Love and Titon, Psyche, The Creation of Woman, Man and his Thought, Ariadne, Mother and her Dying Daughter,* and a few busts including those of *Lady Warwick* and the head of *Puvis de Chavannes* which is so oddly engulfed in the huge, shapeless supporting mass of marble.

Plate 89

How are we to explain Rodin's taste for a style of this kind which was, in its calmness and, often, in a certain softness and tameness, so far removed from his usual tension?

The reasons are complex. On the one hand, Rodin had memories of Michelangelo's uncompleted figures for the *Tomb of Jules II,* which remained partly embedded in the marble. We also know of Rodin's rather surprising admiration for Eugène Carrière. He owned and hung many of Carrière's paintings (including *Motherhood*) in the Hôtel Biron. These canvases, which were invariably composed of figures shrouded in shadow or seen as through a fog which obscured their outlines, suggested the possibility of a similar expression in sculpture. Whereas in Carrière's work the vagueness creates an aura of a dim light diffused throughout the canvas, in Rodin's sculpture, the vagueness is transformed into light. This light, accentuated by the marble's whiteness, seems completely to obliterate the form's precision and to absorb all surface relief. Carrière's subjects seem to retreat into a dreamy melancholy, while Rodin's struggle under the weight of nightmares toward the sunlight of life. This metamorphosis which transforms the mineral kingdom into a loving and suffering humanity seems also to express the sculptor's attachment to that ever-miraculous instant of creation in which raw matter and the embryonic work of art maintain an opposition while, at the same time, they unite under the act of sculpting. Thus, Rodin was led, through quite separate types of work in marble and in bronze, to follow two divergent paths. He seems to have wished occasionally to minimize this opposition by treating the same subject successively in two different media. Examples of this are *The Man with the Broken Nose, Fugit Amor, Danaïd* and *The Kiss,* which he created in at least two versions, one in marble, another in bronze. The comparison between the two media demonstrates that Rodin's strength and sensitivity were far better suited to bronze than to marble.

Plates 79, 95 IV 121

Although certain titles suggest that Rodin did not always disdain the allegorical subject, nothing was further from his preoccupations than allegory as such. He detested "sculptured literature" and he wished, above all, to express in work which was unfailingly based on direct observation of nature those passions which may inhabit an individual—never passion transposed into a "general idea." Suffering, desire and tenderness interested him only in so far as they were expressive of an individual existence, and this meaning was, in Rodin's view, visible, not only in the human face, but in the body's structure, as well. "I have always tried," he said, "to render inner feelings through muscular movement." In this he took his cue from the art of antiquity. "The palpitating muscles of the Greek statues are animated and warmed by life; the empty dolls of academic art seem frozen in death." If the emotional power of this life which Rodin imparted to his media—with a sensuality which was frequently held to be scandalous—seems so intense, the reason lies in his technique which was new and very different from that of classical sculpture.

The irrational manner in which he established those mysterious correlations between thought and gesture constitutes one of the most striking aspects of his genius. It enabled him to achieve immense tragic tension—not in the theatrical sense of the word, but in the sense of a clear-sighted revelation of the human

90

90 Auguste Rodin. Large Head of Iris, 1891. Bronze. Rodin Museum, Paris.

91 Auguste Rodin. Torso of Adele, 1882. Plaster. Rodin Museum, Paris.

Plate
88
condition. The scene composed in *The Burghers of Calais* provides the most remarkable example of this. Rodin had read in Froissart's *Chronicles* the story of the sacrifice of these six men of medieval Calais who, in order to save their city, voluntarily surrendered themselves, clad in sack cloth, with ropes tied about their necks, to Edward III of England. Rodin did not wish to erect a "commemorative monument," and he represented the characters separately, individuals standing beside one another, on the cobblestones of the town square. He would even have preferred—but this wish was not granted—to set them directly on the ground.

The various attitudes which express, for each figure, a particular form of resignation and anguish, reveal how Rodin had studied the sculptural technique of movement. Movement was never, for him, "caught on the wing," that is, arrested in a moment of impetus inexpressible in solid form; rather, it was revealed as a traditional state between two attitudes which were simultaneously suggested.

For Rodin, everything was movement; every feeling, every passion had its corresponding gesture. The state of rest, in contradiction to the expression of life, could contribute nothing to his art. For this reason he liked to let his models, male and female, move about freely and in the nude through his studio while he worked. Man, in Rodin's sculpture is, therefore, essentially man-in-movement. Rodin's humanity is swept by the wildest and most excruciating passions, by movement chosen for its ardor, tension, and violence, so that gesture becomes a sort of language dominated by the cry. Rodin thereby developed his style to its utmost possibilities; in many of his creations, the almost acrobatic gesticulation of his figures, the curious contortions of their bodies, go so far as to defy the laws of balance. In this he was not a stranger to the baroque style of the turn of the century.

But Rodin was never a sculptor of monuments in the usual sense of the word. He did not have an architect's vision of sculpture. Those bodies quivering with life, those sensual lovers, those tormented groups, everything that emerged from his hands, found its justification in its evident truth. The statues can be

92 Auguste Rodin. Man Walking, 1888. Bronze. Rodin Museum, Paris.

93

93 Auguste Rodin. Detail of Tympanum of the Gates of Hell, 1880–1917.
Bronze. Rodin Museum, Paris.

seen from any angle, lighted in various ways, as Rodin himself was wont to do with a lamp or candle: each facet is interesting, so that we demand of the face, the hand, or the belly, no other reason for being than that of having been sculpted for itself.

Nevertheless, Rodin dreamed of a monumental work. He had begun the study of a grandiose project, a *Tower of Labor*, for which he had made a model in 1899. Around a column, tipped by two winged figures, spiraled groups of figures representing workers, ranging from the common laborer shown at his most arduous tasks, to the artisan and the artist. Apart from the winged figures which, under the title of *Benedictions* were given separate, final form, the *Tower of Labor* was never completed. The simplicity of the gestures and rhythms of humanity at work in industry may not have greatly inspired Rodin, whose gifts lent themselves to the interpretation of basic human instincts, repressed or released.

He therefore eagerly accepted a commission to create a great door for the Museum of Decorative Arts, for this project suggested the possibility of creating a universe on his own scale. The subject of the work proposed is summed up in its title: *The Gates of Hell*. Rodin planned to have two panels topped by a tympanum which would assemble, in an interlocking movement of convulsive scenes, all the obsessions, carnal frenzies, all the despair of a humanity tormented by desire—eager, troubled, ecstatic and doomed to suffer. Inspired by Dante's descriptions and by the bitter sensuality of Baudelaire, Rodin was to work for more than twenty years on the composition of more than 186 figures which cover a surface 18 feet high.

Cast in bronze, as we see it today at the Rodin Museum (for it never occupied the place for which it was planned), *The Gates of Hell* represents a synthesis of all the major themes which dominate Rodin's creative expression. He reworked many of its subjects separately and on a larger scale, including *The Three Shades* which project out above the *Gates, The Thinker*, which constitutes a kind of thematic center, *Ugolin, Paolo and Francesca,* and the *Prodigal Son*. In

Plates 93, 86, 89

95

94 Auguste Rodin. The Cathedral, 1908. Stone. Rodin Museum, Paris.

95 Auguste Rodin. The Kiss, 1886. Marble. Rodin Museum, Paris.

94

96 Auguste Rodin. Bust of Clemenceau, 1911. Bronze. Rodin Museum, Paris.

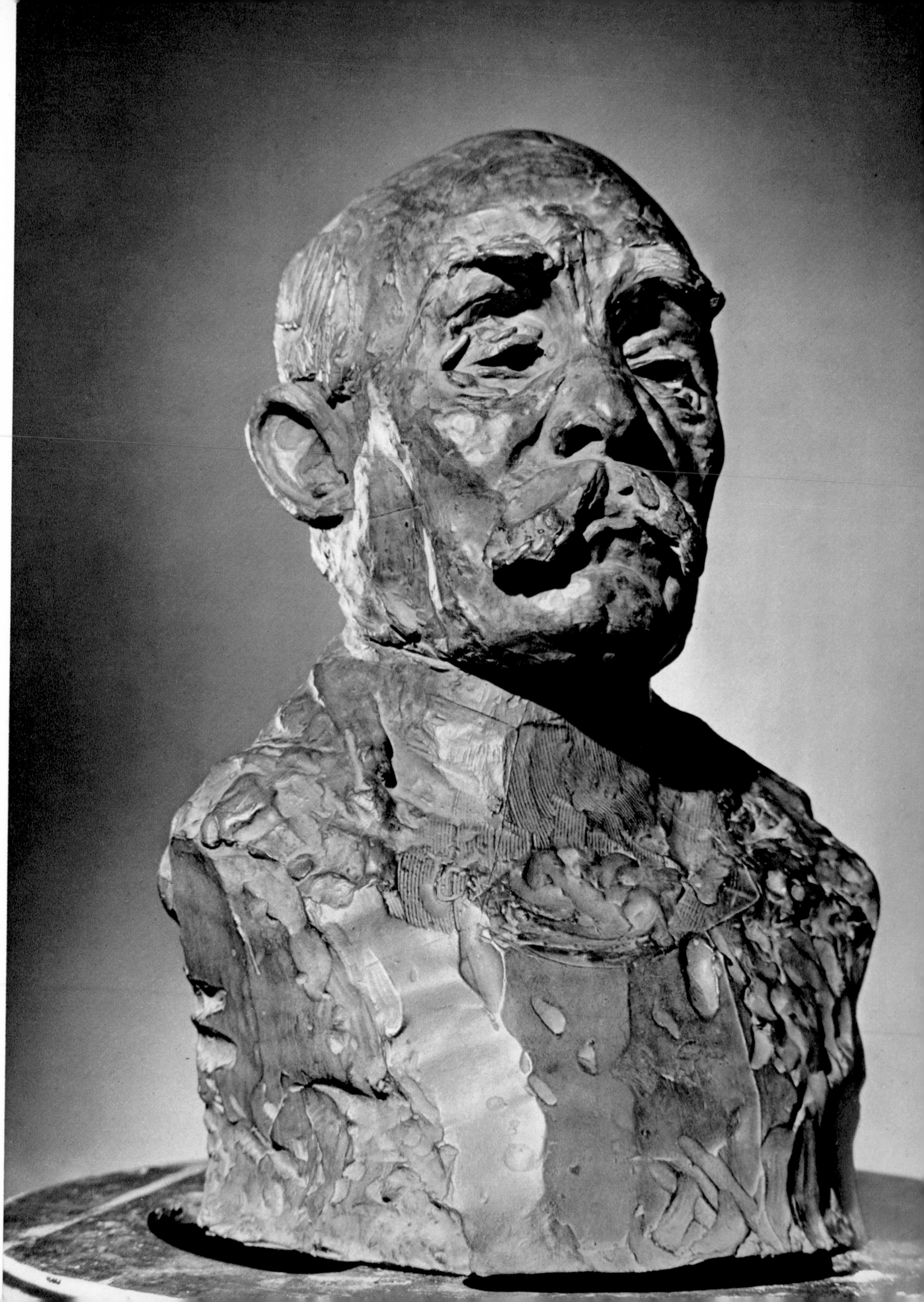

spite of the beauty of certain parts and the tragic movement which animates the work, the composition as a whole lacks unity; it remains dominated by a baroque spirit which has not found its own style and it is not completely integrated into the vertical surfaces. Rodin was aware of these flaws. Eventually he wearied of *The Gates of Hell,* abandoned it for other works better suited to a talent which was ill at ease within the constraints imposed by architecture.

Rodin's difficulties with the problems of the monument were renewed in his various attempts at a *Victor Hugo*. But it is with the statue of *Balzac,* in which he attempted with supreme audacity to explore the nature, the somewhat monstrous quality, the creative voraciousness, of a fascinating character, that Rodin attained the height of his daring and his powers. This work had been commissioned by the Society of Men of Letters whose President, at the time, was Emile Zola. Plate 78 For it Rodin made a number of sketches, his first study (1892) was a nude *Balzac,* but he did not wish to stop there. By 1894, he was working on his fourth model, and the Literary Society began to show signs of impatience—to Rodin's complete unconcern. He continued with his work, becoming more exacting as time passed, and did not exhibit his statue until the Salon of 1898, when it was greeted by an explosion of sarcasm from the outraged critics. The City Council was challenged to name a site for the erection of this "monstrosity" and, once again, the great sculptor was faced with the blindness of officialdom. As we have seen, however, he was not a man to make concessions. He took back his statue, refused to make any changes and declared it would not be set up anywhere at all. Forty years passed before it was recognized as a masterpiece. It was actually not until 1939 that the *Balzac* took its place in Paris—at the Vavin crossing in Montparnasse—twenty-two years after Rodin's death on November 17, 1917, at his villa, "Les Brillants," in Meudon.

Rodin's work and, undoubtedly, his personality were responsible for an enormous upheaval in the development of sculpture. In his time, sculptural expression was stifling in an exhausted academicism and an unauthentic realism.

The *Balzac* is a supremely important work because in it, all the sculptor's capacities are deployed, with an impressive power and restraint, in a determination to find new forms to express what Rodin termed "the inner truths which lie beneath appearances." A close look at the *Balzac*, that amazing volcanic mountain, convinces one that this is the work with which Rodin virtually carried sculpture into the future.

Plate III

Medardo Rosso

Medardo Rosso's singular theories place him outside the mainstream of sculpture. He was born in Turin in 1858 and, although his father wished him to prepare for an administrative career, he began at a very early age to study painting, particularly landscape painting. While working for a marble-mason, he developed a taste for that sumptuous material. Although he was later to prefer plaster and wax, because they were more malleable, he claimed that "the important thing is to make the public forget the medium."

Rosso's beginnings as a sculptor were quite unrelated to the preoccupations which later formed the basis for his very personal style; they were limited to subjects handled in the style of Lombard naturalism, a kind of pale and "finicky" expressionism. In this manner he treated a number of anecdotal subjects, a study for a monument to Garibaldi and some portraits of army officers. At this same time, however, during his military service—from 1880 to 1882—he hit upon a new conception of sculpture, inspired by a passage from Baudelaire's review of the Salon of 1846, published in the *Aesthetic Curiosities*. In this text Baudelaire expressed an aversion to sculpture, in reaction, most probably, to its then current poverty of expression. The central lines of this passage, which throw some light on Rosso's intentions, stated that "sculpture has several disadvantages, necessarily deriving from its techniques. Sculpture, though real and brutal, like nature, is also vague

98

99

97 Medardo Rosso. Bust of Yvette, 1895. Wax. National Gallery of Modern Art, Rome.

98 Medardo Rosso. Laughing Woman, 1890. National Gallery of Modern Art, Rome.

99 Medardo Rosso. Woman with Veil, 1893. National Gallery of Modern Art, Venice.

and undefinable, because it presents so many aspects at once. The sculptor attempts in vain to adopt a single point of view, for the beholder walking about the figure is free to choose a hundred different ones—all except the right one. Frequently, to the artist's humiliation, a lamp or a chance lighting effect reveals a beauty which is not that which the artist had conceived. A picture is limited to that which the artist has willed; it can be seen only in its own light. A painting contains only one point of view; it is tyrannically exclusive. The painter's form of expression is consequently far more powerful."

Rosso then undertook to work toward a form of sculpture which would correct one of these "disadvantages." He wished, through a modeling which would limit the absorption of light to a given side of the sculpture, to force the spectator to look at his figures from a single angle. "One does not walk around a statue," he writes, "because one doesn't walk around a form in order to get an impression of it." In this he was completely opposed to Rodin. Still, a certain fluidity and the slightly mysterious character of all Rosso's sculpture relates them to some of Rodin's marbles, although we cannot really speak of influence in either direction.

This primary importance given to light, not only through the orientation of the surface but also through a very subtle style of modeling, brought him closer than any other sculptor to the Impressionist painters, who directly influenced him some years later, in 1884, during his first period in Paris. Nonetheless, Rosso's approach to Impressionism was an entirely personal one.

The first pieces done according to his "anti-spatial" theory date from 1882, when he was studying sculpture at the Brera Academy, from which he was expelled for instigating a movement of rebellion against traditional teaching methods that he quite rightly considered outdated. That same year in Milan and the following year in Rome, he exhibited a few of his sculptures: *Birichino* (or *Street-Arab*), *The Unemployed Singer*, the *Concièrge* (a small bust which is already quite characteristic of his new technique), and *Impression of an Omnibus*. This word *impression* (which Monet had launched by exhibiting, in 1874, his famous canvas, *Sunset*,

Impression) was frequently to recur, with an obvious intention in Rosso's titles: *Impression of Woman beneath Umbrella, Impression of Boulevard, Impression of Child* (the last two dated 1892). In this way he emphasized the subjective character of his vision and was the first to express awareness of the poetic value of spontaneity, a value too often destroyed by the classical preoccupation with "perfect" finish.

Rosso's stay in Paris in 1884 had been more than disappointing; it was disastrous. Extreme poverty and privation had eventually led to hospitalization, and he returned to Milan, with his pockets as empty as the day he had set out, but convinced that he must persevere in his chosen form of expression. In 1885, he spent some time in Vienna. In 1886, he submitted a piece of sculpture to the Salon in Paris, and exhibited several in London. His work was discussed in a few of the English papers, but there, as in France, he was reproached with doing "sculptured painting."

It was not until 1889, the year of his return to Paris, and after exhibiting in the Salon des Indépendants, that Rosso began to have some degree of success. Attacked by several critics, he was also defended by artists and men of letters—including Degas, Rodin and Zola—who had formed a small clan of admirers. Rodin, who had taken a liking to Rosso, exchanged one of his own *Torsos* for the *Laughing Woman*. Sometime later, however, a rather childish controversy over which of the two artists had been the first to use Impressionism in sculpture was responsible for a misunderstanding between them.

Plate 98

Rosso's most important pieces—those in which his singular sensibility found its boldest and most personal expression, were done between 1889 and 1906. *The Hospital Patient* and the *Portrait of Henri Rouart,* in which the modeling recalls the movement of lapping water so characteristic of the modeling in Carpeaux' *Violinist,* already prefigures the still greater freedom with which Rosso later treated the figures in his *Conversation in a Garden.* In this small group which was shown together with the *Woman with Veil* in his 1893 exhibition, the forms are reduced to

Plates 100, II

101

100 Medardo Rosso. Portrait of Henri Rouart, 1890. Bronze. National
Gallery of Modern Art, Rome.

101 Medardo Rosso. Portrait of Madame Noblet, 1896. Plaster. National
Gallery of Modern Art, Rome.

Plates
103, 97, 99 such an allusive minimum of figuration that they suggest the beginning of an abstract sculpture. Although such was not Rosso's intention, he carried this even further in his portrait of *Yvette Guilbert* (1895). In this piece, figuration is obliterated in expression, or, rather the bare hint of an expression. In the *Bust of Madame X* (1896), the features disappear almost entirely and we discern only the existence of the nose in the center of an oval haze. With a slight geometricization and a smoother surface, we would almost have a Brancusi.

If Rosso really believed his sculpture would make the viewer "forget the medium," he was mistaken. In pieces such as the *Portrait of Monsieur M.M.* (also known as *The Bookmaker*), the medium is made conspicuous by the sculptor's treatment. Far from forgetting it, we are particularly struck by the deft reconciliation of form and the formless. The figure, leaning to one side, seems driven by the wind, as if emerging from a stormy sea. Actually, it emerges from the lump of clay in which it has been modeled and from which it is not in any definite way distinguished. The plainly visible fashion in which matter assumes human shape—coming to life, as it were, beneath our very eyes—constitutes one of the most Plate
V moving aspects of the metamorphosis performed by art.

The importance for us of Rosso's work lies not in the theory behind it but rather in his entirely new way of obviating certain problems of representation; he used only those aspects of figure which he considered strictly necessary for the expression of character. This principle far transcends that of the "single point of view." For the first time—and the *Portrait of Madame Noblet* constitutes a partic- Plate
101 ularly striking example of this—the methods traditionally used for producing a resemblance were discarded.

In this respect, Rosso went considerably further than Rodin who had, nevertheless, written, "I am reproached for not finishing my sculptures and for presenting the public with sketches. The essential modeling is done; I consider it unnecessary to linger over the polishing of toes and curls; those details do not interest me. They comprise the general idea, the main line of my work." Although some of Rosso's sculptures (*Conversation in the Garden,* for example) may, even more than any of Rodin's work, seem like sketches, this technique of "the unfinished" as it was thoughtlessly termed, should not be confused with the work usually involved in the making of a sketch. A face as modeled by Rosso did not presuppose an imaginary complement with a more explicit meaning. On the contrary, through the elimination of certain features, Rosso kept the human face within the limits of a decipherable essence, thus giving it the poetic density of the inexpressible, forcing us to linger before it, in a dreamlike state of wonder. These faces put questions into our eyes, instill us with an attitude which many future sculptors were, in entirely different ways, to demand of the viewer.

Plate 103

Rosso had settled in Milan and lived there until his death in 1928. For a long time he remained forgotten, except in his own country, where he had acquired a great reputation; a museum which bears his name was founded in Barzic. The strange originality of his work was slow to gain recognition. It is rather curious that a sculptural *oeuvre* of this kind had no direct influence on other artists, but Picasso's early busts are the only sculpture related to Rosso's. The principles underlying Rosso's art, it is true, imposed rather severe limits upon his work. The complete transformation of sculptural technique through a work of such limited character is, however, by no means the least of Rosso's singularities.

102

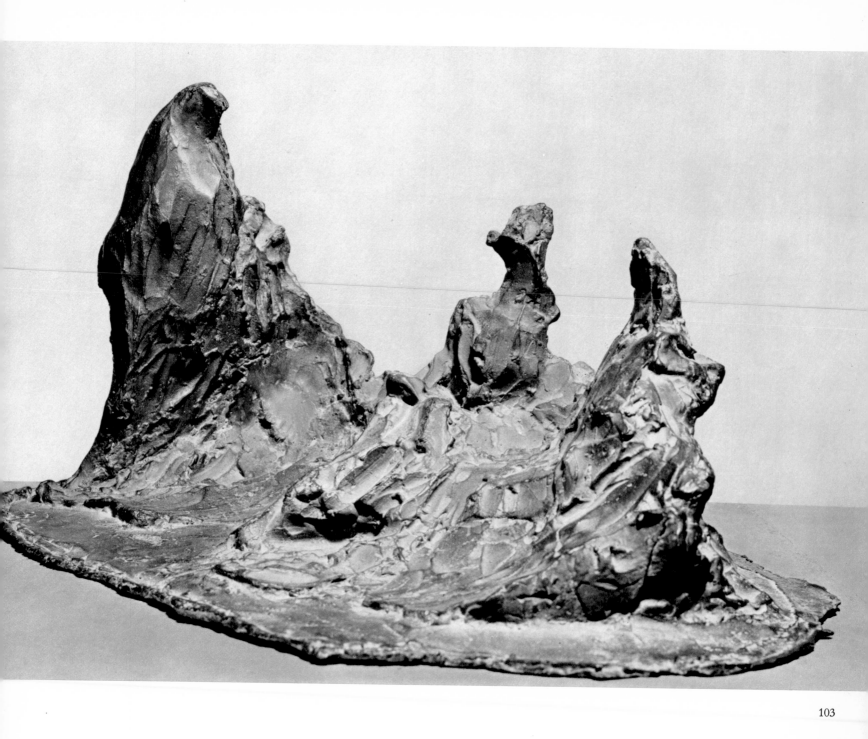

102 Medardo Rosso. Sick Child, 1892. Bronze. National Gallery of Modern
Art, Rome.

103 Medardo Rosso. Conversation in a Garden, 1893. Bronze. National
Gallery of Modern Art, Rome.

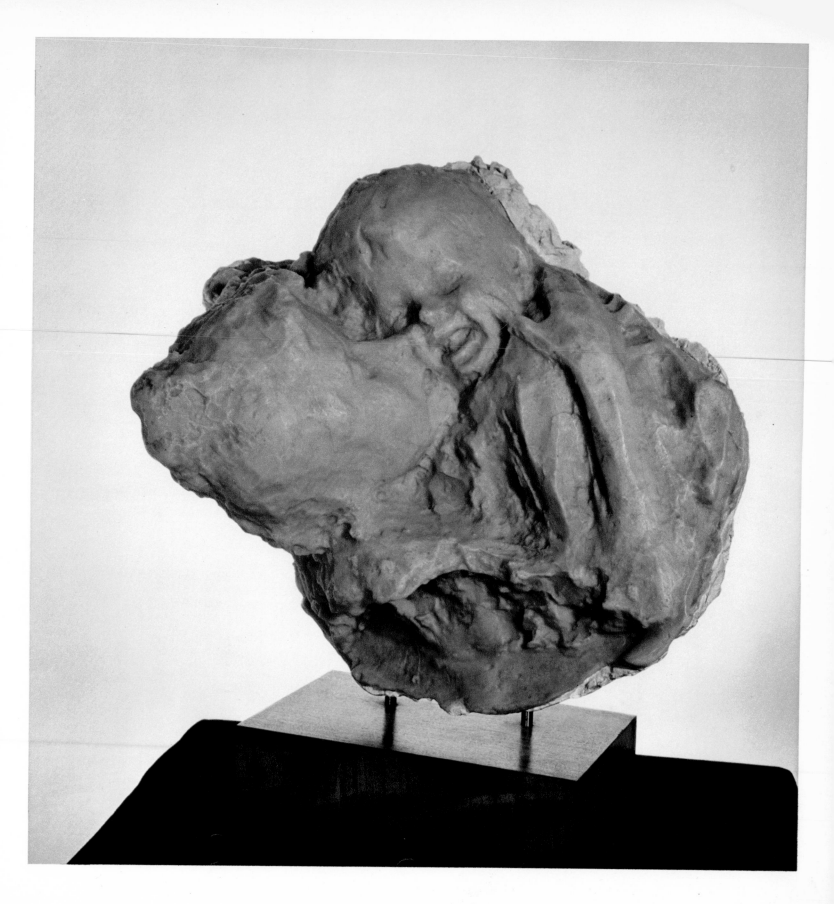

V Medardo Rosso. The Golden Age, 1886. Wax. The Joseph H. Hirshhorn Collection, New York.

VI Antoine Bourdelle. Study for
Monument of Beethoven on
a Rock, 1903. Plaster.
Bourdelle Museum, Paris.

VI. CONTINUITY AND CHANGE

Rodin's Influence

It was no longer possible to work in the style of Rodin's predecessors, but many sculptors were unaware of this. Academic sculpture, with its artificial allegiance to classical tradition, went right on disfiguring public squares and cemeteries with armies of bombastic statues and melodramatic monuments. Still, Rodin's work made artists sit up and take notice of problems which called into question the very function of sculpture. The most important new discovery in painting and sculpture alike, was that the artist was independent of the Academy and could rely on himself to develop his own style. The far greater freedom and subjectivity which were now possible eventually produced a new sculpture, but it took some time for Rodin's example to sink in. Before examining the repercussions of Rodin's teaching upon aesthetic concepts which were far removed from his own, we must turn to the work of some of the many sculptors who, either directly or indirectly, came under his influence.

Strictly speaking, Rodin never had any pupils, but he made great demands on the young sculptors who assisted him and they learned their calling in his studio. When the time came for them to strike out on their own, it was logical that they should have some difficulty in shaking his influence. This did not prevent some, such as Bourdelle and Despiau, from becoming fine sculptors in their own right. Similarly, Pompon, although he worked for Rodin longer than most, always managed to keep his work free from his master's influence. Others, like Camille Claudel, the sister of Paul Claudel, and Judith Cladel never completely succeeded in effacing the traces of their overzealous admiration. Indeed, it is surprising that Rodin should have allowed Camille Claudel to model her work so closely upon his own, and one wonders to what extent he might have been flattered by this imitation. For Rodin was vain; he insisted on his son's calling him "Master." Camille Claudel was, however, an intelligent artist and a remarkable technician. The forcefulness of her work, which includes a *Bust of Rodin,* is exceptional for a woman.

Perhaps the most famous of Rodin's "students" was Bourdelle, who was

104

105

104 Antoine Bourdelle. Love in Agony, 1886.
Plaster. Bourdelle Museum, Paris.

105 Antoine Bourdelle. Study for Monument on
Mount Montauban, 1893–94. Plaster.
Bourdelle Museum, Paris.

106 Antoine Bourdelle. Pallas with Drapery, ca.
1889. Bronze. Bourdelle Museum, Paris.

107 Antoine Bourdelle. Head of Eloquence, Study
for Alvear Monument, 1917. Bronze.
Bourdelle Museum, Paris.

thirty-two when he went to work for Rodin. He was no longer a beginner, yet his contact with Rodin had a decisive effect upon his work. He left a voluminous collection of writings in the spontaneous, lyrical style peculiar to him, dealing with his life, tastes and aspirations. They also contain the main lines of his lectures at the Academy of the Grande-Chaumière, where he taught for twenty years. Filled with an enthusiasm that never left him, even in old age, these writings provide insight into the peculiar development of his sculpture.

Like David d'Angers, Bourdelle (1861–1929) was the son of a cabinet-maker (or, as he himself put it "carpenter, cabinet-maker and carver"). His first attempts at sculpture were the ornamental carvings on sideboards done for his father. Later in life he liked to recall his childhood in Quercy and the sunny days spent herding his uncle's goats—an experience reflected now and then in his sculpture. At school in Montauban, his home town, he was not a very hard-working pupil, but spent most of his time drawing. His parents were forced to recognize an irresistible vocation and were wise enough to encourage it. After attending the local art school for a while, he entered the Toulouse School of Fine Arts where he won a scholarship for the Beaux-Arts in Paris.

Falguière's courses there were probably not well suited to him. He stayed there only a few months and finally left the Beaux-Arts thoroughly disgusted with its teaching methods. He then went to work with Dalou, whose more humanistic approach was better suited to his temperament. The personality of Rodin had already begun to fascinate him, with the result that he became Rodin's assistant in 1893 and remained with him until 1908. Rodin quickly came to value his assistance, and they always remained the closest of friends. For a thorough understanding of the part played in Bourdelle's development by his fifteen-year stint with that extraordinary master, we must now examine Bourdelle's work. It is, intriguingly enough, divided between two tendencies which are so different as to appear contradictory.

It is obvious that Bourdelle's "first period" was strongly influenced by

Rodin, even before he went to work for him; Bourdelle himself was the first to acknowledge this. In view of the fact that by 1893 he was already an accomplished sculptor, with some of his best work already behind him—*Mask of a Young Girl* and the first studies of *Beethoven* (1888), *Pallas with Drapery* (1889) and *Bather Crouched on the Rocks* (1891)—one wonders why he felt the need to become Rodin's assistant. The modeling of these works already showed strong traces of Rodin's technique; Bourdelle himself could not fail to realize that. Was it not, therefore, rather dangerous for him to work for Rodin? Bourdelle felt he still had much to learn about technique and that he could find no better teacher than Rodin. Then, too, Bourdelle already seemed to sense that he was moving toward a conception of sculpture quite different from that of his master. Perhaps he felt strong enough not to fear Rodin's influence and even to accept it temporarily.

Plate 106

Some of Bourdelle's sculpture, such as *Love in Agony* (1886), the first studies for *Sappho* (1887) and of the *Torso of Pallas* (1889), reveal a concern with problems which, though they do not give a very clear picture of his later style, are in any case, quite foreign to the art of Rodin. Even his splendid *Pallas with Drapery*, which might never have been done had Rodin not existed, bears his personal stamp. Nevertheless, the great sculptor's influence was to persist in Bourdelle's work for several years. It is especially noticeable in *The Cloud* (1905), *Motherhood* (1906) and in some of the new versions of the bust of *Beethoven*, as well as in the *Draped Beethoven*, which is reminiscent of Rodin's *Balzac*.

Plate 104

Plates 108, 110

There came a time, however, when Bourdelle needed to shake off this influence. This prompted his adoption of a new style which grew more distinctive as time passed. Its underlying principle had been revealed in the *Head of Apollo* (1900), a splendid work, in which the artist managed with great technical economy to concentrate all the head's inward intensity in a contrast between the almost anguished sensuality of the mouth and the severely intellectual look about the eyes. However, in this piece, Bourdelle was probably less concerned with the expression of sensitivity than with the achievement of a synthetic style. This

Plate 109

109

110

108 Antoine Bourdelle. Tragic Mask of Beethoven, 1901. Bronze. Bourdelle Museum, Paris.

109 Antoine Bourdelle. Head of Apollo, 1900. Bronze. Bourdelle Museum, Paris.

110 Antoine Bourdelle. Head of Beethoven, 1902. Plaster. Bourdelle Museum, Paris.

would seem to explain why he regarded it as the point of departure for a style which actually became quite unlike that of this head. No doubt he had his reasons for considering it "the work through which I discovered my basic principles." But just what principles did he have in mind?

Bourdelle's various explanations on this subject are not very clear to the uninitiated. "I abandoned the perforated, accidental plane, to find a permanent one. I sought the essence of structure, leaving transient waves in the background; I sought a universal rhythm." These lines are indicative of the sculptor's technical concerns and theoretical ambitions. He was often obsessed with the notion of "relating [things] to the universal." In a lecture delivered to his pupils on February 10, 1910, entitled "Art Is the Harmonization of Numbers," he said: "Add to each particular being the general tide of things, give to accidental planes and outlines the amplitude, the peace, the respiration of the universal plane." And in another lecture, delivered on January 9, 1914: "If you wish to broaden your work and build it fuller, construct it from within, in all the truth of universal structure, from within your inmost soul, then seek out the soul of the universe."

Statements of this kind were probably rather puzzling to the master's pupils. I, for one, have not the faintest idea what the "soul of the universe" is. One thing is sure, for Bourdelle it corresponded to the conception of that "monumental style" which he had developed and to which he was fervently attached, since it allowed him to express what he probably regarded as his true personality.

It was through this style that he saved himself, so to speak, from Rodin, whose monuments he had correctly diagnosed as his one weak point. For Bourdelle, however, monumental sculpture was not a matter of mere size. He wanted to gear facial expression and the rhythm of attitude to the basic concepts and over-all harmony of his composition. Unfortunately, the excessively literary intentions of the resulting synthesis were not always free of an exaggerated lyricism. For this reason, he did not limit his use of this style to large monuments, such as *The Virgin with Offering,* also known as the *Virgin of Alsace* (1921), the eques-

VII Aristide Maillol. Night, 1905. Terra cotta. Collection Dina Vierny, Paris.

VIII Henri Matisse. Decorative Figure,
     1903. Bronze. The Joseph H. Hirshhorn
     Collection, New York.

111

112

111 Antoine Bourdelle. Study for Monument to Mickiewicz, 1909. Plaster.
Bourdelle Museum, Paris.

112 Antoine Bourdelle. Tolstoi, ca. 1906. Bronze. Bourdelle Museum, Paris. **141**

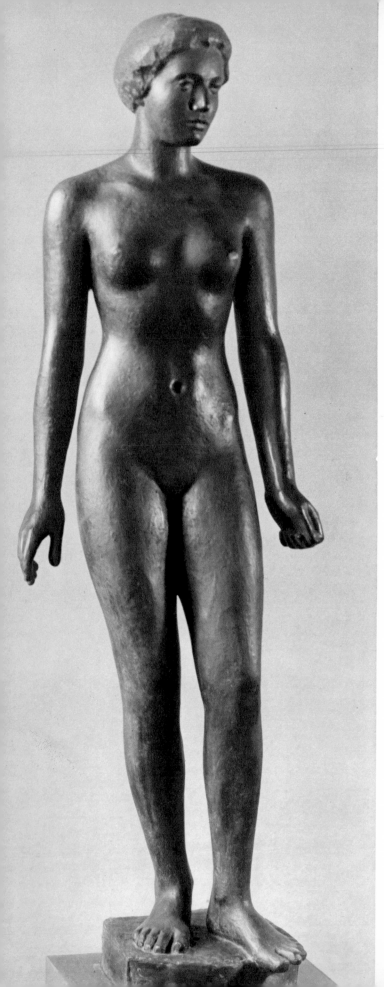

113 Georg Kolbe. Young Girl Standing, 1915. Bronze. Art Gallery, Mannheim.

114 Lucien Schnegg. Bust of Jane Poupelet, 1897. Bronze. Municipal Museum of Modern Art, Paris.

114

113

trian statue of *Alvear* in Buenos Aires (1923), the *War Memorial* at Montceau-les-Mines (1924) and the *Mickiewicz Memorial* (1927). He also applied it to smaller works such as *Herakles Archer* (1909), the reliefs for the Champs-Elysées Theater, inspired by the dances of Isadora Duncan and Nijinsky (1912), and the *Dying Centaur* (1914). Plates 107, 111

These sculptures, which include elements of real power, form the basis of Bourdelle's reputation. They reveal a certain nostalgia for Roman sculpture and an odd mixture of medievalism and romanticism. They also display a tendency toward a form of decorative stylization which both influenced, and was in turn influenced by, its periods.

One feels that Bourdelle went out of his way to avoid being accused of imitating Rodin but, in fact, was far too great a sculptor to fear any such accusation. Many splendid pieces, done in a manner very different from that of his "monumental" style, display a freedom of vision and technique which owes little to Rodin, and which would have sufficed to establish him as one of the most original sculptors of the early twentieth century. The daring side of his character was always somewhat repressed, but was handed down to his pupils, some of whom, including Germaine Richier and Alberto Giacometti, went on to become great sculptors.

In order to grasp Bourdelle's *true* personality, which he himself did not, apparently, quite dare to acknowledge, one must visit the Bourdelle Museum on the Paris street which now bears his name. The 800 pieces preserved there include his preliminary plaster and terra-cotta studies and such little-known masterpieces as the model for his *Beethoven on a Rock* (1903), *Carpeaux at Work* (1909), *Tolstoi* and *Rembrandt As an Old Man*. Sculpture of this quality makes us forget the dry theories and the cosmic aspirations which weakened Bourdelle's work. One is struck by the creative force of the hand grappling with matter transforming it into a torrent of invention; one is moved by the artist's creative hunger. Plates VI, 112

Bourdelle influenced a great many artists, but only through his best-known

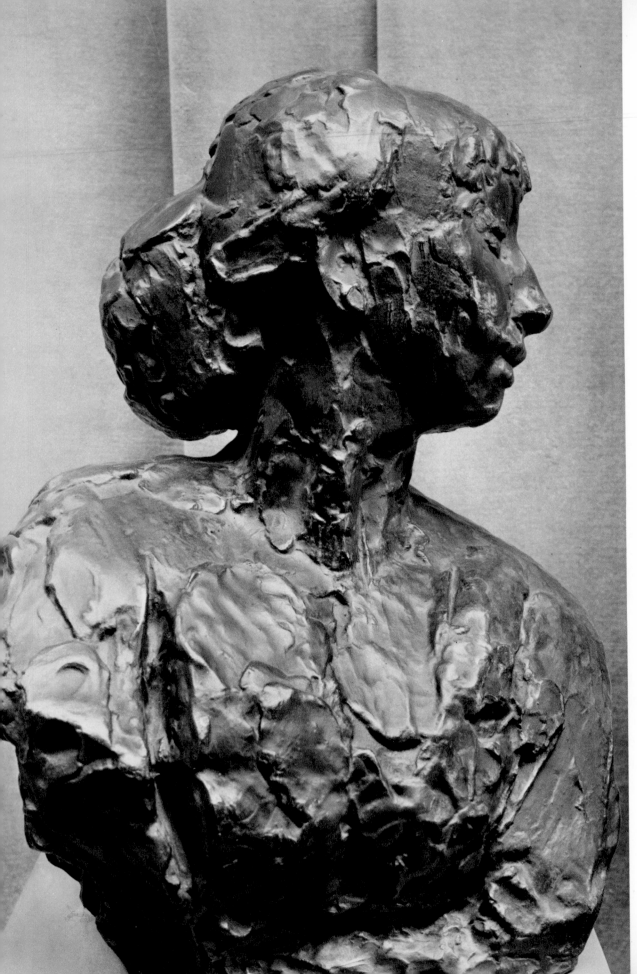

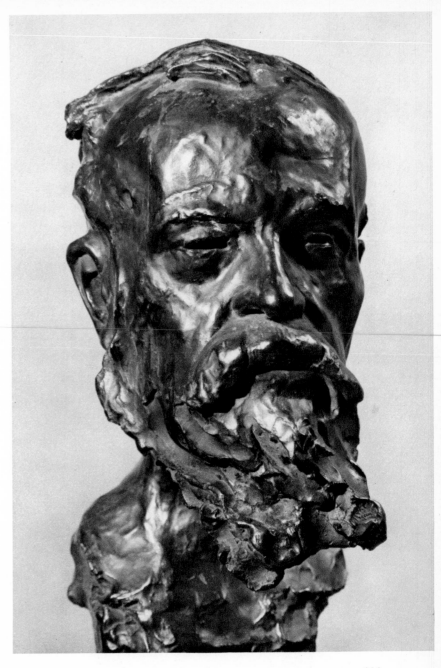

116

115 Rik Wouters. Nel with a Chignon, 1909.
Bronze. Collection Madame de Carnière-
Wouters, Overijse (Belgium).

116 Max Klinger. Bust of Wilhelm Wundt, 1908.
Bronze. Art Gallery, Mannheim.

work, his "monumental" style. This influence is strikingly apparent in the work of Rik Wouters (1882–1916), a Belgian sculptor who was also a very engaging painter. Reminiscences of Cézanne, Renoir and Bonnard are often strangely mingled in his painting, but the highly personal, sensual handling of color makes one regret his death in Amsterdam at the age of thirty-four. Premature though it was, however, this death delivered him from the most terrible affliction that can befall a painter: blindness.

Wouters began to sculpt at an early age; his father was a wood-carver and taught him the secrets of his trade. By the time he was twenty-five, he was already an impressively deft and intelligent craftsman. His *Mask of Edgar Tytgat, Smiling Peasant Girl* (1907), *Leaning Torso* (1908) and the various portraits of his wife, Plate 115 Nel, seemed to foreshadow a significant body of powerful works which was cut short by death. However, his *Foolish Virgin,* inspired by Isadora Duncan (1912), his busts of *Nel* and *James Ensor* (1913) and some of the little statues which constitute a kind of disciplined extension of Impressionist sculpture, reveal Rik Wouters as the most interesting Belgian sculptor of his day.

Rodin's influence was thus felt, either by artists who had worked for him, like Bourdelle, or by those to whom it was transmitted through Bourdelle's teaching. Although academic sculpture had received a severe blow, it is important to note that most of the sculptors inspired by Rodin remained much more faithful than their master to a certain kind of classicism. Such was the case with Lucien Plate 114 Schnegg (1864–1909) and Léon Ernest Drivier (1878–1951).

The work of Charles Malfray (1887–1940), on the other hand, is more anguished and impressive. Malfray had a hard life and for many years his work was unjustly neglected. His family were stonecutters in Orléans. He began his studies in the local School of Fine Arts and at the age of twenty entered the Beaux-Arts in Paris. Malfray was gassed during the First World War and the newspaper attacks against his *War Memorial* erected in Orléans so discouraged and bewildered him that he gave up his own work almost completely, earning his living for many years as a sculptor's assistant. He later taught for nine years at the Ranson Academy and died at the age of fifty-three, leaving a somewhat uneven body of work. His studies of motion were sometimes influenced by Rodin; for instance, *Two Swimmers* is clearly related to the great sculptor's *Fugit Amor*. (In this connection, it is interesting to note that this kind of horizontal movement, fairly rare in sculpture, recurs with striking similarity in an abstract piece by Stahly, *Serpent of Fire*.) Much of Malfray's work, done with power, sensuality and grace, is quite lovely, and he certainly deserves a more prominent place in the history of twentieth-century sculpture than is usually allotted to him.

Plates 118-121

In contrast, the influences that shaped the work of the Belgian sculptor, Georges Minne (1866–1941) are harder to detect. Rodin's influence alternates with that of the more realistic Constantin Meunier. Minne's work was ultimately dominated by a tormented mysticism, a deep melancholy, and symbolist tendencies which were reinforced by his relations with certain poets. He was especially influenced by Maeterlinck, evidenced by his illustrations for *Hot-Houses*.

Minne's earliest work dates from 1885. Following a stay in Paris, where his encounter with the works of Rodin encouraged him to follow his own bent, he enrolled in the Brussels Academy of Fine Arts. In 1898 he went to live in Laethem-Saint-Martin where he soon came to be regarded as the spiritual leader of the first artists' colony founded there. He nevertheless underwent a long period of struggle and uncertainty which lasted until 1912, when he was given a chair at the Academy of Fine Arts in Ghent, where he had begun his studies as a boy. His influence was strong, especially on German sculptors. The style of Lehmbruck's work between 1911 and 1914 may be traced to Minne's slim *Young Boy Kneeling* (1897). His major works include several pieces on the *Mother and Child* theme, the *Rodenbach Monument* at the Grand Béguinage in Ghent, several *Pietàs*, a *Prodigal Son* and *The Relic Bearer*, representative of his soberest style. Georges Minne died during World War II at Laethem-Saint-Martin where he had spent some of his most intensely creative years.

Plate 117

118

117

117 Georges Minne. The Relic Bearer. Bronze.

118 Charles Malfray. Torso of a Swimmer. Bronze.
Collection Dina Vierny, Paris.

119 François Stahly. Serpent of Fire, 1956. Bronze.
Galerie Jeanne Bucher, Paris.

120 Charles Malfray. Two Swimmers, 1940.
Bronze. Collection Dina Vierny, Paris.

121 Auguste Rodin. Fugit Amor, 1882. Bronze.
Rodin Museum, Paris.

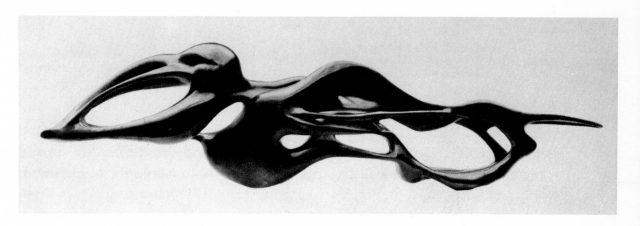

119

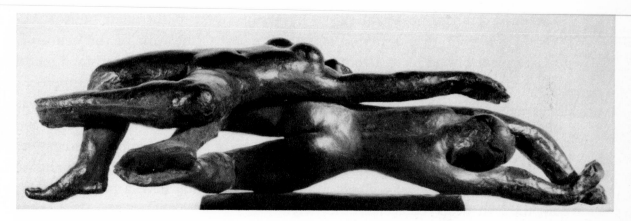

120

121

One of the first German sculptors subject to Rodin's influence was Max Klinger (1857–1920) whose manual dexterity of modeling technique constituted a reaction against the idealistic sculpture made fashionable by Hildebrand. He worked in Karlsruhe, Berlin, Paris, Rome (1888–1898) and Leipzig as a painter and engraver as well as a sculptor. His large graphic output influenced many artists, especially Alfred Kubin.

Like other sculptors of the period, Klinger made several attempts to revive the chryselephantine technique. The results were unfortunate. His statue of *Beethoven,* done over a period of several years at the turn of the century, is a masterpiece of bad taste. Beethoven's head is carved of white marble; a mantle of black onyx is draped over his shoulders and he is seated, like an emperor, on a throne of bronze adorned with angels' heads carved in polished ivory and a black marble eagle with eyes of yellow amber! It took the shock of Rodin's work and his personal example to free Klinger from the grip of this deplorably gaudy style. He then produced some fine heads, including one of *Nietzsche* (1902) and another of

Plate 116

the philosopher *Wilhelm Wundt* (1908), both of which have a power responsible for the well-deserved acclaim they won.

Another German, the painter Georg Kolbe (1877–1947) discovered Rodin while visiting Paris in 1898 and decided to take up sculpture. Kolbe was deeply interested in rendering movement, and did a number of figures of dancers. The delicate simplicity of his delightful early work (1907–1915) is, however, most

Plate 113

apparent in his nudes and in certain figures of adolescent girls. The bombastic style which became fashionable in Nazi Germany had an unfortunate effect on Kolbe's work, although he returned, later in life, to the use of a more delicate technique.

Excessively widespread dissemination automatically causes the decline of any style. It was not until Rodin's tremendous influence began to wane that his importance became truly apparent. His contribution was not really a style bequeathed to posterity, but a preparation for new developments, new ideas. Before

122

123

122 Aristide Maillol. Woman with a Dove, 1905. Bronze. Private
Collection, Paris.

123 Aristide Maillol. Bather with Drapery, 1905. Bronze. Collection
Dina Vierny, Paris.

124 Aristide Maillol. Pomona, 1910. Bronze.
Private Collection, Paris.

these new ideas could find expression, figurative sculpture, which had now been liberated from its conventions, received a new lease on life; there was a return to classicism on the part of certain artists, some of whom had been influenced by Rodin. In reaction to his work and to the craze for movement which had been released by it, they illustrate a search for more static, formal, purity. They were far less daring than Rodin, of course, but the clean, sober lines of their work indicated an increasingly urgent need for simplicity which soon appeared as a reaction against the turn-of-the-century baroque—that very factor with which Rodin himself had never completely broken.

An Advanced Classicism

Foremost among those sculptors whom we may consider "advanced classicists" stands Aristide Maillol (1861–1944). Probably no other young sculptor has ever found his style so quickly and varied it so little throughout his life. This explains both the impressive unity of his work and its limitations. His late *Nudes* differ from his first *Bathers* and *Young Girls* only in their greater strength and in the skill of their modeling.

Plates 122-126

The speed and sureness with which Maillol chose his path is probably due to the fact that he came to sculpture at the age of thirty-four. His talent had matured in the long practice of other arts; for he had spent his youth preparing for a career as a painter. Born in Banyuls-sur-Mer, a small town in the Pyrenees to which he often returned in later life, he came to Paris in 1881 to study under the famous teachers at the Beaux-Arts, still respected at that time. However, he was not very satisfied with his experience in Gérôme's classes and was eventually expelled. He attended the School of Decorative Arts for a while, then returned to the Beaux-Arts, this time to study under Cabanel, whose huge, ridiculous historical paintings had earned him in 1863 a seat in the Institute. Clearly, these so-called masters had nothing to teach Maillol.

125

126

127

125 Aristide Maillol. Young Girl Sitting, 1900. Terra cotta. Collection Dina
   Vierny, Paris.

126 Aristide Maillol. Study for Monument to Cézanne, 1912. Bronze.
   Collection Dina Vierny, Paris.

127 Charles Despiau. Paulette, 1907. Marble. Museum of Modern Art, Paris.

He needed a great deal of courage to bear up under the hardships of his life in Paris; his only source of income was a monthly allowance of twenty francs from his family. His meeting with Gauguin and the Nabis was responsible for a crisis in his career: his intense admiration for a form of painting which corresponded to his own aspirations so discouraged him that he turned to another art form. His next enthusiasm was for tapestry-making, an enthusiasm which included such delight in beautiful materials and a flair for handicrafts that he dyed his own yarn with herbs gathered in the mountains. Similarly, he was later to build his own kiln to fire clay statues and he made his own paper for his first set of woodcuts, illustrations of Virgil's *The Georgics* (1912).

Maillol's first tapestry, *Music,* met with such success when exhibited in 1893 that, after moving his workshop from Banyuls-sur-Mer to a Paris suburb, he devoted himself solely to this craft. A serious eye disease, which deprived him of his sight completely for six months, forced him to give up the painstaking tasks of cartoon designing and weaving. When he was cured, he turned his attention exclusively to sculpture.

Until then he had made only a few modest attempts at wood carving—a few statuettes, a small relief and *Woman with a Mandolin* (1895), a mirror frame (1896) and decorations for a cradle (1897). His first serious efforts to find a style of sculpture were also in wood. However, it was in work with clay and plaster that he ultimately found himself. For many years Maillol derived all his inspiration from the young girls of southern France—strong, fleshy maids from the Roussillon with that mixture of innocence and sensuality which was his ideal in womanhood. (He had married one of the local girls who worked in his Banyuls tapestry shop and often used her as a model.)

Though he did a few fine busts, including one of *Renoir* (1907), Maillol was not a master of the portrait. His statues' faces are generally expressionless. It was not the face nor the thought or feeling expressed in the face, that Maillol wished to render in his *Eves, Venuses, Pomonas* and *Nymphs.* Their names hardly

marginal
Plate
124

mattered; Maillol's perpetual glorification of the female body in full bloom was merely his way of striving to communicate, with ever increasing strength and perfection, his vision of happiness. Whatever the subject (*Night, L'Ile-de-France, The Mediterranean, The Air, The Mountain, The River* or *The Harmony*, on which he was working just before his death), the bronze invariably assumed the form of a curved, healthily muscular, adolescent girl, a joyous image of relief from the stress and strain of life. This was his principal, almost his only subject. The designs for monuments to Blanqui, Cézanne and Debussy, though not very successful, were also primarily celebrations of womanhood.

Plate VII

Plate 126

The words "balance," "quiet joy," "serenity" are immediately suggested by Maillol's work. His sculpture may seem somewhat monotonous, and even at times, heavy and unimaginative, but in his case the stubborn repetition of a single theme may be regarded as a dedicated, fervent, almost religious worship of the eternal goddess. The simplicity of his vision, utterly unliterary and devoid of allegoric complication, is often deeply moving in its grace and stateliness. The Grecian tone of Maillol's placid modeling has often been ascribed to a trip to Greece which was made possible by a German patron, Count Kessler. While Greek sculpture undoubtedly offered him an eloquent, encouraging example, Maillol had a rockbound "Athenian balance" of his own, and the gentle strength of his style was altogether natural to him.

Charles Despiau (1874–1946) was another sculptor who loved serenity. He was one of Rodin's most active assistants, however, and he owed much of his knowledge to his master. Natural inclination, or perhaps a fear of becoming too deeply involved in Rodin's aesthetics of movement, limited him to a cautious, static form of sculpture, neither daringly experimental nor exaggeratedly monumental. His work thus resembled Maillol's, and though less imposing, it was sometimes more refined. His masterpiece remains the head of *Paulette,* which brought him to the attention of Rodin in 1907. The sensitivity and slightly secretive intensity of this girl's face are not always to be found in his later work. Although his

Plate 127

129

130

128 Wilhelm Lehmbruck. Young Man Seated, 1918.
Bronze. Art Museum, Duisberg.

129 Carl Milles. Bust of Ferdinand Boberg, 1906. Bronze.
Millesgården, Lidingö.

130 Joseph Bernard. Girl with a Jug, 1910. Bronze.
Museum of Modern Art, Paris.

131 Wilhelm Lehmbruck. Bather, 1914. Stone. Art
Gallery, Mannheim.

131

sculpture as a whole seems rather disappointing today, some of his nudes, torsos and busts of women and young girls—especially those of *Antoinette, Madame S.* and the child, *Dadi*—as well as his lovely statue of *Assia,* contain a quiver of life which, however faint, attests to the artist's constant concern with human values and his refusal to transpose the inner truth of his model's character in terms of an aesthetic synthesis or lyricism.

Plate 130

On the contrary, Joseph Bernard (1866–1931), worked toward a stylization of both form and movement. His style was originally sober enough to give his statues grace and rhythm, and was regarded at the time as a new departure in sculpture. This was true of his two best works, *Water Carrier* (1910) and *Young Girl with Drapery* (1914), but Bernard yielded to the temptation of a superficial, decorative style, which was common to the sculptors of that period; his originality was unmistakably impaired.

Plates 129, 133

Something of the same sort happened to the Swedish-born, naturalized, American sculptor, Carl Milles (1875–1955). Influenced at first by Rodin during a visit to Paris in 1897, he adopted Hildebrand's theories while staying in Munich in 1904. These very different influences were reflected in contradictory aspects of Milles' work, the best of which did not always seem to win his most whole-hearted approval. Most of his voluminous output is housed in a museum in Lidingö, near Stockholm, which bears his name (Millesgården). The pieces which deserve singling out have a classic grace that seems refreshingly simple when compared with the complicated, involved style of his monuments, a rather in-articulate combination of expressionism with a high-flown, neo-Baroque lyricism.

The name of Milles recalls that of a Scandinavian contemporary, the Norwegian sculptor, Gustav Vigeland (1869–1943). For Vigeland, Rodin's influence was also decisive, but rather than prompting him to develop a personal technique, it merely intensified an obsession with the portrayal of human passions in a grandiose manner. Some forty years of Vigeland's life were spent working on the 150-odd statues which adorn the Frogner Park in Oslo, creating an undeniable sense of unity but also an overwhelming impression of monotony. I remember my stupefaction as I entered the huge park (its sculpture is more abundant than its shrubbery) and came upon a swarm of human bodies. Men, women, and babies are detached in small groups or bunched together in fantastic clusters, gesticulating madly. Some of them seem about to turn somersaults. All are frozen in a convulsion of stone and bronze. They line the sides of staircases or railings, disappear into mazes, revolve upon the *Wheel of Life*, clamber up a gigantic fountain, or submerge themselves in the inextricable tangle which forms the centerpiece of this strange spectacle: *The Monolith*, a 97-foot obelisk covered with a hundred or more figures who look quite annoyed at having to hold such uncomfortable poses.

Plate 132

Vigeland was not really devoid of ideas. Some were wild enough to have qualified him as a surrealist, had they been differently expressed, but he had no style of his own. For want of it, his ambitious undertaking remains a literary project of very dubious quality. It does not touch us.

Another sculptor who came to the fore prior to the First World War was Wilhelm Lehmbruck (1881–1919). His early work, which wavers under the successive influences of Rodin, Constantin Meunier, and Georges Minne, reveals an evolution from realism to a very discreet form of mysticism. It was not long before Lehmbruck developed his own style, however, and the postures he devised for his long, slender figures were preserved from the danger of a superficial stylization by his keenly sensitive modeling. Their grave and often careworn faces, both anxious and elegant, have a moving dignity. His many statues of adolescent boys seem to contain some of the dark fire that burned within him, he who suffered from severe depression and committed suicide at the age of thirty-eight.

Plates 128, 131

It was becoming increasingly apparent that the sculptors of this generation were of two kinds and that they differed less in their choice of subject matter than in their techniques. One group felt the need for a directly manual expres-

132

133

132 Gustav Vigeland. The Monolith. Stone.
Frogner Park, Oslo.

133 Carl Milles. Study for Monument of the
Resurrection (Detail). Bronze. Millesgården,
Lidingö.

134 Elie Nadelman. Man in the Open Air, ca. 1915.
Bronze. Museum of Modern Art, New York.

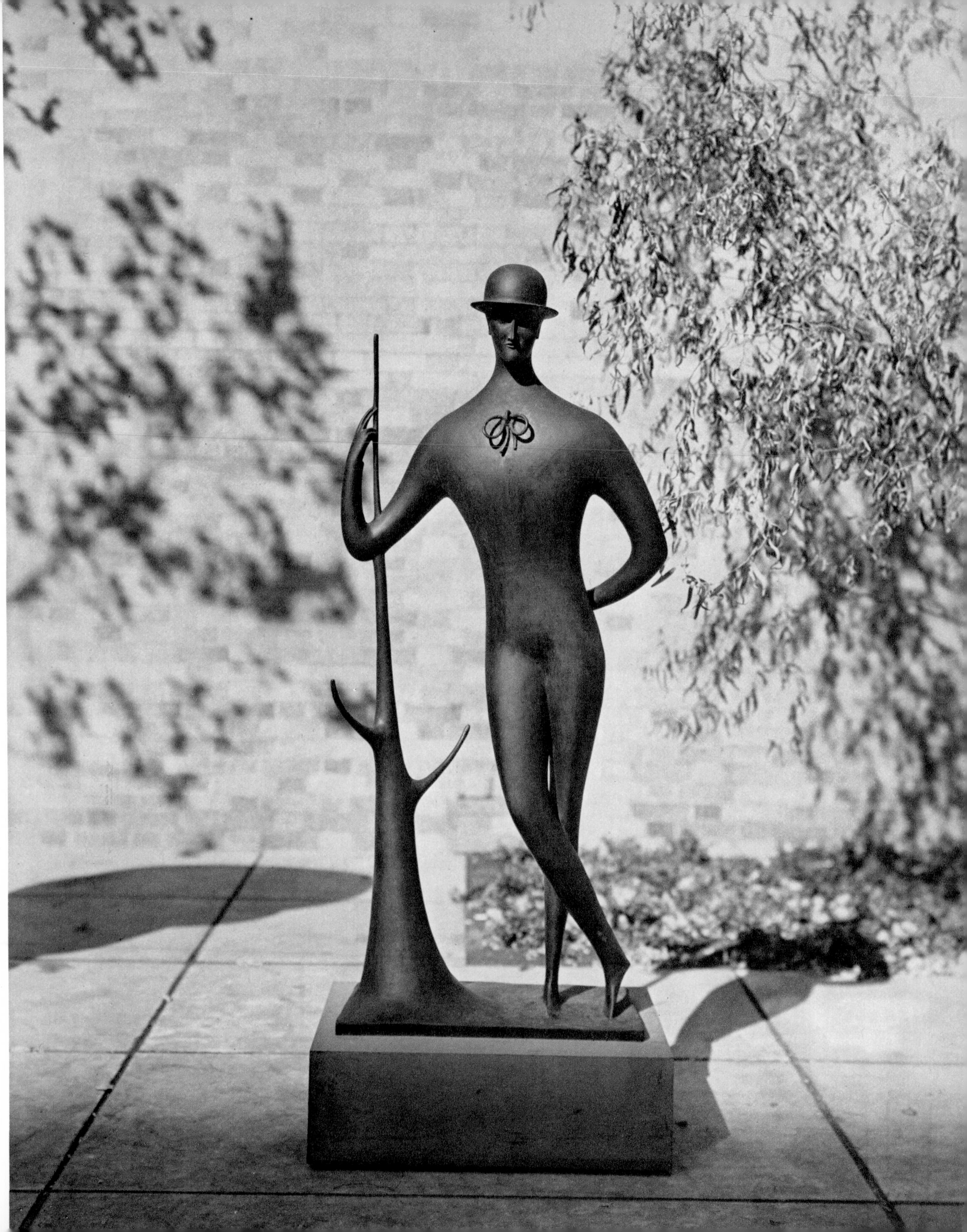

sion, kneading the clay or plaster, leaving no surface in repose. They regarded the malleability of their raw material as the reflection of their own shifting vision, the nervous play of their fingers as a necessary element of spontaneity. This approach has proven the most fruitful as a direct expression of sensibility; it has been preserved to this very day. It recurs in the dramatic compositions of Germaine Richier, in Giacometti's tall, enigmatic figures, in Courturier's world of anguished humanity, and in the delicate reveries of Fenosa. Its appearance in abstract sculpture is more recent.

The other group, on the contrary, did their best to remove any trace of the sculptor's hand; they wished to make pure forms and polished surfaces. In so doing they were paving the way for a schematized style which eventually led to abstract sculpture. This category of artists, who were primarily interested in volume relationships, included the French-born Gaston Lachaise (1882–1935), the Polish-born Elie Nadelman (1885–1946) and the French sculptress, Chana Orloff, born in Russia in 1888.

Nadelman reduced the planes of the human body to a near-synthetic system of curves, giving his statues a fluidity that sometimes seems just a bit too graceful. His men in bowler hats have a shade of humor and indicate his open approach to the problem of subject matter. Nadelman's earliest work, done between 1906 and 1909, includes a number of pieces in plaster which have survived only in photographs, but they show that he was still concerned with slightly broken surfaces. Surfaces later became completely smooth, leaving the eye free to concentrate on the statue's general contours. These were determined by a theory of curves set forth in his book, *Towards Plastic Unity*, published in 1914. Nadelman then left for New York, where his work began to veer toward a form of baroque elegance which, although slightly dated, was not without personal charm. Pieces such as *Wounded Bull* (1915) and *Man in the Open Air* (1915) lead one to think that he would have gone much further had he not become so involved in his own theories. Nevertheless, Nadelman's style is as personal as that of Gaston Lachaise.

Plates
144, 134

Lachaise went to America after completing his studies in Paris. In 1906 he entered the studio of Henry H. Kitson, a Boston sculptor of public monuments. Lachaise found his personal mode of expression in the full-blown female nude, whose athletic abundance, though rather overwhelming, is nevertheless majestic. The experiments in movement and balance of his *Floating Figures* are more curious, but Lachaise's most important work does not fall within the historical scope of this study. They are, nevertheless, fairly typical of an artist who broke with the classical idea of the human figure, yet failed to find a technique adapted to his formal innovations. This would seem to explain why his giant women produce a feeling of false, immature modernity, whereas similar distortions are perfectly acceptable in the work of an artist like Henry Moore.

Plate 141

The work of Chana Orloff, with its mixture of the schematic and the rounded plane, lies halfway between the extreme simplification of Nadelman and the swollen shapes of Lachaise. She came to Paris in 1910 and first showed at the 1913 Salon d'Automne. Her early work was done in wood, and it displays that slightly excessive tendency toward stylization which was carried over into her work in other media. Though a bit ponderous at times, her later work is freer and more interestingly geometrical.

The sculptural world of François Pompon (1855–1933), peopled almost entirely with animals, also thrived on simplification. He had been trained as a marble cutter in his native Burgundy, and after a course in architecture at the Dijon School of Fine Arts, went to Paris (in 1875) to attend evening classes at the School of Decorative Arts. During the day he earned his living decorating the façades of buildings and tombs. He first exhibited at the Salon of 1879 and worked as assistant to several sculptors: Falguière, Antonin Mercié, Saint-Marceaux, and even Sarah Bernhardt, who took up the chisel in her spare time. It was in Rodin's studio, however, where he worked for some fifteen years, that Pompon fully mastered his style, remote though it was from the statues he roughed out at the Hôtel Biron. The 300-odd pieces which became state property after Pompon's

135

136

166

137

138

135 Gustave Moreau. Hercules, ca. 1875–80. Wax. Gustave Moreau Museum, Paris.

136 Gustave Moreau. Lucretia, ca. 1875–80. Wax. Gustave Moreau Museum, Paris.

137 Gustave Courbet. Bust of Madame Max Buchon, ca. 1864. Plaster. Collection Alfred Daber, Paris.

138 Edgar Degas. Trotting Horse, ca. 1879–81. Bronze. Collection Jacques Dubourg, Paris.

death constitute a vast survey of the animal kingdom, in which the hippopotamus, the bear and the cow stand side by side with the marabou, the duck and the snail. Though his work is uneven, Pompon's keen sense of observation enabled him to catch each animal in a characteristic attitude. He brought something new to a difficult form of sculpture which had come to a virtual standstill in the work of Barye's laborious imitators.

Few sculptors avoided this choice between a realism which, whether strict or relaxed, was always accompanied by sensitive craftsmanship, and a schematization which often risked lapsing into set decorative patterns. The Spaniard Manolo —his real name was Manuel Martinez Hugué (1876–1945)—suffered from hesitation between these two very different sculptural conceptions. The work is unassuming, like the man himself, for Manolo led a very retired life. He lived in extreme poverty from the time he came to Paris in 1900; a few years later he retired to Céret, a small town in the Pyrenees. While he can hardly be regarded as a great sculptor, one easily understands why his friends, Picasso, Max Jacob and Apollinaire, were so fond of his work. His small, early statues were partly inspired by folk art, and he remained fond of simple, real-life scenes. His models were local peasants, washerwomen, wine-harvesters, and fishermen. He also did bullfight scenes, sometimes with a half-humorous realism, sometimes in an almost oversimplified style. His small sculptures have a charm of their own, but were never highly original.

Plate
142

Painter-Sculptors

In order to get at the roots of the great revolution in sculpture during the first decade of our century, we must turn once again to the painters. All things considered, it was rather surprising to observe so many painters simultaneously interested in sculpture. For some it was merely a minor

139 Edgar Degas. Dancer Looking at the Sole of Right Foot,
ca. 1896–1911. Bronze. Collection Jacques Dubourg, Paris.

140 Edgar Degas. Grand Arabesque, Second Time, ca. 1882–95.
Bronze. Collection Jacques Dubourg, Paris.

139

140

142

141 Gaston Lachaise. Equestrian Woman, 1918.
Bronze. Museum of Modern Art, New York.

142 Manolo. Crouching Woman, 1914. Bronze.
Galerie Louise Leiris, Paris.

aspect of their work, but others kept at it persistently throughout their lives. Such widespread duality, as a whole, was unparalleled in the history of art.

As we have already mentioned, Gustave Courbet in no way revolutionized the technique of sculpture. The few pieces he modeled are, unlike his painting, conventionally classical. His earliest sculpture seems to have been *The Bullhead Fisher,* a small, skillful, classical statue done after a sketch which is dated 1861. It was exhibited in the Salon of 1862. Mounted on a fountain in the public square of Ornans, his home town, the work was mutilated by Bonapartists in a demonstration against Courbet, whose Republican opinions were notorious. In 1864, during a three-month stay in Salins-du-Jura, he did several portraits in plaster of friends; two were profile reliefs in medallion form: *Madame Max Buchon* (the wife of a poet who had been Courbet's classmate at the little Besançon seminary, of whom Courbet had painted a lovely portrait some ten years earlier) and *Alfred Bouvet.* Madame Buchon also posed for a bust. Her medallion and *The Bullhead Fisher* were the only pieces shown in the one man show of one hundred paintings held at the Rond-Point de l'Alma in 1867. Plate 137

In 1875 Courbet was forced to flee Paris in order to avoid paying a fine for the destruction of the *Vendôme Column* in which he was accused of having taken part. He hid in Switzerland and there took up sculpture again. His state of mind at that time is expressed in a bust of a woman radiant with joy and passion: *Helvetia,* or *Liberty,* erected in a square of Tour-de-Peilz, the small Swiss town in which Courbet lived until his death in 1877. His last piece of sculpture, done in 1876, is a high-relief medallion called *The Lady of the Lake.* In it, a seagull perches on a woman's head with its wings draped about her face. This piece is now in the Vevey Museum in Switzerland.

At the same time that Courbet was working on these few pieces, Edgar Degas was also turning to sculpture. His style was freer, fresher; the differences between these two sensibilities were apparent in the development of a new syntax. Degas' early sculpture was done between 1866 and 1870, at the time of the Impres-

143

143 François Pompon. Little Owl with Sunken Eyes, 1918. Bronze. Museum of Modern Art, Paris.

144 Elie Nadelman. Wounded Bull, 1915. Bronze. Museum of Modern Art, New York.

145 François Pompon. Brown Bear, 1918. Bronze. Private Collection, Paris.

144

145

sionists' first experiments. (It was not until 1869 that Renoir and Monet really began to find themselves, and not until 1872–73 that Sisley and Pissarro achieved maturity.) While Degas belonged to their group, his highly individual goals as a painter set him apart from the other Impressionists. Renoir, too, ultimately drifted away from them, and Gauguin, a latecomer to the group (1880), also was concerned with theories which differed greatly from theirs. It is significant that these same three artists, Degas, Gauguin and Renoir, were the only members of the group to turn to sculpture. This cannot be completely explained by the Impressionists' almost exclusive interest in landscape. For Gauguin and Degas, sculpture was a way of realizing a need for precise construction which most of the Impressionists never experienced. The case of Renoir is more mysterious, and we shall try to analyze it presently.

In his earliest known piece of sculpture, a small bas-relief called *Apple-Picking*, Degas was still feeling his way in a style somewhat reminiscent of Daumier's *Emigrants*. He soon evolved a personal manner which subsequently varied only slightly in the 72 pieces done over a period of more than forty years. All were modeled in wax with a boldness that gives them the look of rough drafts, although they are rigorously constructed. Degas may not have been immediately aware of the value of this rough style, for the only wax statue he ever agreed to exhibit (in 1881) is his now-famous *Fourteen-Year-Old Dancer*. This piece is far more polished and constrained, its realism further emphasized by Degas' rather strange addition of a real gauze tutu, satin slippers, and a pale-blue silk hair-ribbon (which, for some unknown reason, has been replaced by a yellow ribbon on the bronze casting now in the Louvre). A few later attempts to model skirts on his dancers proved rather unsuccessful, and Degas finally decided to portray them in the nude. In any case, he was chiefly interested in the marvelous study of movement to which these models lent themselves.

The subject matter of Degas' sculpture is confined almost exclusively to the two areas also favored in his painting: horses and dancers. He had, in fact, previously treated most of the themes of his sculpture in oils, pastel or pencil. The dating of Degas' sculpture is still only approximate. According to the chronology established by John Rewald, we presume that until approximately 1879, horses were his chief concern: horses in still poses drinking, rearing, galloping or being brought over hurdles by jockeys. Next came the series of dancers, in which all the figures and positions of classical ballet are studied with an accuracy that never impairs the freedom of the modeling. This series also contains a few women, seated or combing their hair: *A Woman Drying Her Neck, The Tub* (ca. 1886), a small group entitled *The Masseuse,* and *A Woman Walking in the Street.*

Plates 138-140

Although he was content to work on a small scale (the 38-inch *Fourteen-Year-Old Dancer* is the only exception), Degas was one painter for whom sculpture was always a major activity. Almost all his statues remained unknown until his death in 1917, but in 1920 and 1921 bronze castings were made from the 70 intact original wax models remaining out of a total of 150. With the exception of three *Dancers* and a *Horse* donated to the Louvre by Paul Mellon, all of the models are now in the United States, and many are in the collection of the Metropolitan Museum in New York.

Degas' work represents a rather limited area of sculpture. It has no intellectual pretentions and cannot be regarded primarily as work of the imagination. It is, rather, the work of a keen observer who set out to find a new solution to a consistently thorny problem, that of stabilizing the unstable: movement. His way of molding the wax, his lack of concern with "finish," his habit of leaving finger marks on the legs of a dancer or a horse, and his emphasis on the expressive quality of a gesture rather than on the beauty of a shape, are as far removed from the idealistic theories of classical sculpture as from the prosaic goals of realism. In this respect, and with due allowance made for its modest proportions, his sculpture belongs to the spiritual family of Rodin. It is worth noting that Degas and Rodin became sculptors at the same time. Even had Degas' sculpture become known during his lifetime, its influence could never have equaled that of Rodin's. It

146

147

148

146 Paul Gauguin. Bust of Madame Gauguin, 1877. Marble. Courtauld
Institute, London.

147 Paul Gauguin. Bust of Madame Emile Schuffenecker, ca. 1889. Plaster.
Louvre, Paris.

148 Paul Gauguin. Adam and Eve, 1891–93. Wood.

149 Paul Gauguin. Head of Tehura, 1891–93. Wood. Otto Gerson Gallery,
New York.

149

nevertheless remains a milestone in the history of modern sculpture, for Degas' vision was utterly free of academic convention; he was the first of a series of major nineteenth-century painters who made significant contributions to the art of sculpture.

Some ten years after Degas had first begun to work at sculpture, Gustave Moreau (1826–1898), known as "the Master of Symbolism," also turned to this form. Moreau's twelve small figures were probably done between 1875 and 1880, but their history is rather strange, for they remained unknown even longer than the sculptural works of Degas. It was not until 1957 that Ragnar van Holten, a young Swedish art historian who was preparing a thesis on Moreau, became curious as to the contents of a locked cupboard in the Gustave Moreau Museum (formerly the artist's Paris home, at 14 rue de la Rochefoucauld). Mr. van Holten asked that the cupboard be opened, but no key was to be found. A locksmith had to be found before it yielded its mysterious secret: the twelve statuettes. This explains why no book published on Moreau since the inventory taken at his death, in 1898, has included any mention of them.

Moreau himself may have regarded them merely as preparatory drafts. The rather bold, vigorous modeling has more in common with his charming sketches and unfinished paintings than with his large canvases which, notwithstanding their elaborate, dreamlike compositions, legendary figures, fantasies, and wild, tinselly ornamentation, were sometimes very badly painted. In any case, these figures testify to a project which, though never carried out—probably for want of time—is nevertheless described in one of Moreau's notebooks for 1874. He intended "to do wax or clay models of one or two figures which, when cast in bronze, will demonstrate, more clearly than any painting, my sense of rhythm and linear skill." Indeed, most of Moreau's wax statuettes were done after earlier paintings or water colors; the *Lucretia* comes from his painting *Lucretia and Tarquin* (1865); *Hercules* was one of his favorite subjects *(Hercules and the Lernaean Hydra* was shown at the Salon of 1876); *Jacob and the Angel* was the subject of a canvas done

Plates 135, 136

150

151

150 Auguste Renoir. Bust of Coco, 1908. Bronze.

151 Auguste Renoir. Mother and Child, 1916. Bronze.

179

152

152 Auguste Renoir. The Washerwoman, 1916. Plaster. Collection Renou, Paris.

in 1878; *Venice,* represented by a nude woman reclining next to a lion, corresponds to various drawings and water colors on the same theme. *Jacob and the Angel, The Argonauts, Autumn* (depicting the rape of Deianara), *Prometheus and the Apparition* (a strange composition showing the head of John the Baptist gazing on a frightened Salomé) all suggest that Moreau had larger-scale works in mind. Another *Salomé* is sketched on a small articulated wooden puppet which was probably used in the study of clothing arrangements for his painting of *Salomé Dancing Before Herod.* When Mr. van Holten showed it to me, he pointed out that the coat of modeling clay which had been spread over it did not hamper the movement of its joints.

Compared with works by Degas and Moreau, the workmanship of Gauguin's sculpture seems rather crude, especially in the wood carvings done in Tahiti and the Marquesas. Not all of Gauguin's sculpture is like this; the lesser known, earlier work (done after 1877) shows that he had not yet developed his "primitive" style, with its Symbolist overtones, that he was still capable of a delicacy which he probably came to regard as too realistic. In any event, Gauguin's interest in sculpture dates from the time of his earliest experiments in painting and it remained with him all his life. He was taught the rudiments of the art by Bouillot, a sculptor's assistant. His contribution to the fifth Impressionist exhibition of 1880 included, together with seven paintings, a small marble bust of his wife *Mette.* At that time he chose his models from his family circle; other known portraits of that period are a wooden statuette of *Mette Gauguin,* a marble bust of his son *Emil* and a wax model of his daughter *Aline.* The bust of *Madame Emile Schuffenecker* was done later (perhaps in 1889), and is more delicate and sensitive, more personal.

Plate 146

Plate 147

Ernest Chaplet, the ceramist, taught Gauguin how to fire earthenware; in 1888 several pieces of ceramics were included in Gauguin's first one-man show at the Boussod and Valadon Gallery. He never lost interest in this medium and produced some curious vases of earthenware and glazed clay, decorated with

153

154

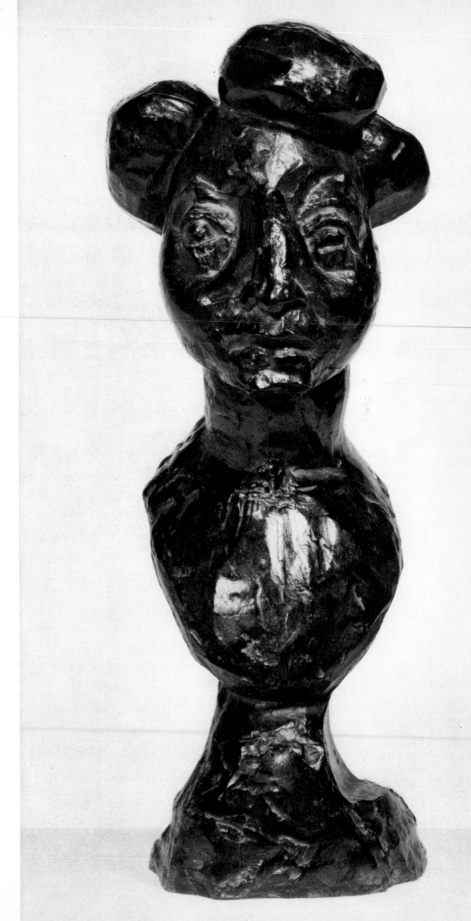

153 Henri Matisse. The Slave, ca. 1900–03. Bronze.
     The Art Institute of Chicago.

154 Henri Matisse. Seated Nude with Arms Behind
     Head, 1904. Bronze.

155 Henri Matisse. Head of Jeannette III, 1910–13.
     Bronze.

women's faces and, in some instances, with Tahitian figures. He also made a to-bacco jar with a relief of a man's hand, thought to be a self-portrait. The small statue, *Noa-Noa* (1894), is one of his best pieces of ceramics.

Plate
148

During his first stay in Tahiti (1891–1893) Gauguin began to carve wood in a crude style copied from primitive idols. Some of his carved wood cylinders are copies of this kind: *Idol with Pearl* and *Idol with Shell*. Though less successful than his paintings, of course, they are sometimes even more violently expressive of Gauguin's discovery of alien spiritual forms which could be incorporated into his personal mythology. Upon his return to Paris, Gauguin exhibited two of these statues at Durand-Ruel's, together with 44 paintings done in Tahiti. When he returned to Tahiti in 1895, he began carving again and did a fine cylinder decorated with Tahitian figures as well as a panel entitled *"What are we?"* In 1901 he moved to Atuana (Dominique) in the Marquesa Islands, where he decorated his hut with wooden statues and large, multicolored panels carved with a knife. These pieces

Plate
149

were more carelessly done; they lack the strength and expressive subtlety of works such as the portrait of *Tehura,* the young vahine who lived with him. On the lintel above his door, two women's heads flanked the inscription *"House of Pleasure."* The phrase has a ring of desperate irony, for this was the wretched hut in which Gauguin, penniless and consumed by a frightful disease, died in 1903.

Our interest in these wood carvings derives from the insight they afford us into the great, agonizing adventure that was Gauguin's life. They were the silent witnesses of his tropical reveries, his anguish and his solitude; as such, they are moving. They also have a curiosity value, for they reveal the tremendous energy expended in the recreation of the mythological environment of Gauguin's dreams. The crude simplicity of their primitive style sometimes radiates a muted spiritual-ity which transcends their sensual content. Of all the painters who turned to sculpture between 1870 and 1914, Gauguin was the least concerned with the new technical and aesthetic problems. However, he was a great painter and an im-portant theoretician, whose ideas were to have widespread repercussions. His

Tahitian statues, on the other hand, played a part in calling attention to the art of Africa and the South Sea Islands as more than mere exotic curiosities.

Renoir's sculpture constitutes a very strange case. About 1878, when he had already painted some of his major works—including his *Bather* of 1870 and the *Moulin de la Galette* (1876)—he began to amuse himself (this would seem the most appropriate term) by modeling the frame for a mirror in the drawing room of Madame Georges Charpentier, the wife of a Parisian publisher. Renoir does not seem to have regarded this small relief of a woman's profile surrounded by drapings and foliage as a first step in familiarizing himself with a new mode of expression. It was not, in any event, immediately followed by any more serious work in this medium. Only thirty years later, in 1907, was he to model a medallion of *Coco* (his son Claude), which was hung on the wall of his house in Cagnes. The following year Renoir did a bust of *Coco*. These works, delightful though they are, would certainly not suffice to establish Renoir's reputation as a great sculptor. They are, nevertheless, the only pieces modeled by his own hands, for these hands were soon almost completely paralyzed. By contracting his fingers in a certain way, Renoir could still hold a brush, but he could no longer sculpt.

Plate 150

Practically all of the 20-odd pieces generally referred to as "Renoir's sculpture"—busts, medallions, reliefs, statues of all sizes and a project for a clock—most of them signed, were done between 1913 and 1918. Obviously, Renoir's actual share in these works was practically nil, even if he did manage to apply a superficial touch here and there. However, it is equally obvious that if not for Renoir, none of them could ever have existed. Ambroise Vollard, the dealer who was to handle most of the bronze castings, took the initiative in this venture. He obtained for Renoir one of Maillol's assistants, a Catalonian sculptor named Richard Guino. The strange collaboration between the great painter and the Spanish sculptor began with a *Small Standing Venus* which Guino modeled after a drawing by Renoir, under his close supervision. Guino was allowed no personal initiative whatever. Renoir's satisfaction with the experiment was great enough to

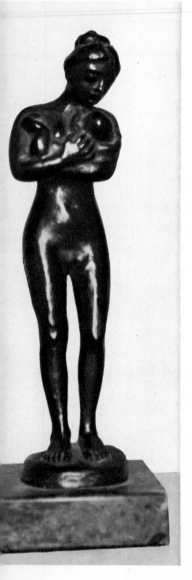
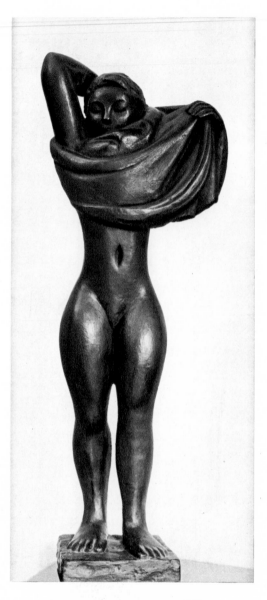

156

157

158

156 Félix Vallotton. Young Mother, 1904. Bronze. Collection Paul
    Vallotton, Lausanne.

157 Roger de La Fresnaye. Young Girl Removing her Dress, 1912. Bronze.
    Galerie Maeght, Paris.

158 Roger de La Fresnaye. The Italian Girl, 1912. Bronze. Galerie Maeght,
    Paris.

159 Pierre Bonnard. Standing Nude. Bronze. Private Collection, Paris.

160 Pierre Bonnard. Sitting Nude. Bronze. Private Collection, Paris.

159

160

187

encourage him to continue with this rather vicarious form of sculpture. He was highly fortunate to have found such a skillful, tractable craftsman, who understood his intentions so well. We have no reason to think that these pieces would have been more personal had Renoir modeled them himself.

One wonders, however, what powerful urge drove that aging, crippled painter—he was seventy-two in 1913—to see the buxom women of his paintings reproduced in three dimensions, for they had already insured his fame on canvas. Possibly Renoir derived a certain compensation for his own inactivity from these more lifelike representations. Possibly, too, the vitality of these sculptured forms consoled him somewhat for the loss of that steady draftsman's hand which had given such beauty to his painting.

Thus, year after year, he continued to supervise the execution of an entire series of sculptures modeled after his paintings or drawings. A variant of the *Small Standing Venus* was followed by a little bas-relief, *The Judgment of Paris* (1916). This was followed in turn by the large-scale *Venus Victorious* modeled after the *Small Venus* and mounted on a pedestal which was intended to be adorned with a larger version of *The Judgment of Paris,* done in 1916. The statuette *Mother and Child* and a head of *Madame Renoir,* done after an 1885 portrait (a bronze casting was placed on her grave at Essoyed), also date from 1916. This was certainly a productive year for Renoir's eye and Guino's hand, for it also produced the *Blacksmith* and the *Washerwoman* (also known as *Fire* and *Water*), two small statues which are among their best. (A larger version of the second is known as the *Large Washerwoman.*)

Plate 151

Plate 152

The series of medallions—portraits of *Ingres, Delacroix, Corot, Monet, Cézanne* and *Rodin*—based on paintings by Renoir and sometimes even on photographs, were much weaker than the previous pieces. Also, when Renoir quarreled with Guino and replaced him with a new pair of "hands" named Louis Morel, in 1918 (one year before his death), the results were not very felicitous. The three small bas-reliefs modeled by Morel, two *Dancers with Tambourine* and a *Piper* prove that "sculpting with his eyes" did not come easily to Renoir and to some extent depended on the hands which must be controlled by his eyes.

Although it is easy to see how Renoir's portraits of women could find a three-dimensional equivalent in a style which is, after all, fairly close to that of Maillol, it is surprising that Matisse, who was so little concerned with volume in his painting, should also have been drawn to sculpture. He did not try his hand at it until he was thirty—his first piece was a *Jaguar Devouring a Hare* (1899) inspired by Barye—but continued to devote a fair amount of time to it thereafter. This does not mean that he always managed to make the difficult adjustment between his free handling of the human figure and the requirements of a medium which forces the artist to respect the existence of the third dimension.

Some of his small, early statues, such as *The Slave* (1900–1903), demonstrate that Matisse could not wholly ignore the example of Rodin, even though it reached him through Bourdelle, whose class at the Grande Chaumière Matisse attended for a while. The sculptural *oeuvre* of Matisse (68 bronzes in all) indicates that he was not quite certain of his intentions. He seems to waver between an impressionistic modeling, resembling that of Bonnard's few little sculptures, and a style of distortion rather like that of Picasso. This hesitation is apparent in the technical differences in the five successive *Heads of Jeannette* done between 1910 and 1913, now in the Museum of Modern Art in New York. The third in his series of *Large Heads* (or *Henriettes*) has, however, a rather unexpected, almost classical aspect. Plates 153, 154 VIII Plates 159, 160 Plate 155

Many of Matisse's smaller figures and especially his nudes (the various *Crouching Nudes* of 1906 and 1908, the *Seated Nudes* of 1909 and 1910, *The Dance* of 1911 and the more recent *Reclining Nudes* of 1927 and 1929) are marred by an uncouth flabbiness which is not counterbalanced by the charm of a deliberately rudimentary modeling technique. The play of volumes and planes lacks that balance, or calculated imbalance, which is the mark of a really great sculptor.

These pieces, however, are interesting in their very rejection of artfulness,

162

161 Pablo Picasso. Crouching Woman, 1906.
     Bronze. Galerie Berggruen, Paris.

162 Pablo Picasso. Head of a Beggar, 1903.
     Bronze. Galerie Berggruen, Paris.

163 Pablo Picasso. Bust of Fernande Olivier,
     1905. Bronze. Petit Palais, Paris.

163

a trait which is equally appealing in Matisse's painting. His sculpture is all the more interesting in this respect; it suggests that Matisse used this medium for empirically conducted investigations of form which were not possible in painting—not in his painting, at any rate. For Matisse, the painter, always remained true to the principles of Fauvism, which gave precedence to color as an almost autonomous entity. Although this does not mean that Matisse always used color at the expense of form, nevertheless, this was sometimes the case. Matisse himself once wrote that "line belongs to the realm of intelligence, color to that of the senses." This is a debatable viewpoint, for it is difficult to see why sensibility—or sensuality—cannot be expressed graphically; it does, however, provide an explanation of Matisse's art. It also reveals a dissociation of the intellect and the senses which endangered that art.

The obvious lack of sensuality in Matisse's sculpture is, consequently, not surprising. Apparently, in tackling a medium which excluded the use of color, he was attempting to compensate, with a somewhat tortured treatment of form, for this loss of power, this absence of what he always regarded as the vibration of life itself. Though the results were uneven, they constituted a vision of the world which was remarkably daring and "off-beat" for the period. A work such as *Madeleine* seems to foreshadow, as early as 1901, the break with even the most advanced forms of classicism which was to occur a few years later. In this respect, Matisse was a precursor and, as so often happens with precursors, his ideas were perfectly embodied only in the works of his successors.

It was logical, moreover, that the first symptoms of this break should appear in the sculpture done by painters. Indeed, something very important was taking place in painting, something which was to affect all the arts far more deeply than Impressionism. For painters were unconsciously but inevitably moving toward Cubism. This development, for which Cézanne was largely responsible, produced an extremely interesting period in the visual arts.

From the standpoint of the development of *forms* in the history of art, the first timid appearance of a geometrical discipline in sculpture may be likened to the transition from Romanesque style to Gothic, marked as it was by a sudden *fold in the stone.* A similar "fold" in the sculptor's stone indicated his acceptance of the constructive principles of Cézanne and his followers. It appeared as early as 1910 in a sculpture by Picasso, to be discussed later, and again in 1912, in *The Italian Girl,* a small statue by Roger de La Fresnaye, a painter with a keen interest in the new Cubist approach to the representation of mass. La Fresnaye had studied sculpture at the Académie de la Grande-Chaumière, and while we have only a very few pieces by him, they have considerable historical significance. Plate 158

Immediately following the death of Cézanne—exactly one year after the Cézanne retrospective at the Salon d'Automne of 1907—a number of painters abruptly changed their styles, from one canvas to the next. In some cases the transition was even more spectacular, occurring within a single picture. In *Les Demoiselles d'Avignon,* for example, which Picasso completed in 1907 and which is now in the collection of the Museum of Modern Art in New York, the geometric distortion of the faces seems merely embryonic on the left side of the canvas, while it is fully developed on the right. This lack of cohesion, which is visually rather unpleasant, perfectly illustrates the break with a recent past which had not yet exhausted its influence, even upon Picasso who took something of a backward step in a Cézanne-influenced period that lasted until 1909.

Picasso was also one of the first to apply Cubist tendencies to sculpture. The small figures and heads done between 1899 and 1906—*Seated Woman, Beggar's Head, The Jester,* the portraits of *Alice Derain* and of *Fernande Olivier, Crouching Woman*—still display an "Impressionistic" technique; their rough, undefined surfaces are reminiscent of Rodin and Rosso. In 1907, however, he began to carve crude, rather totemlike figures which looked unfinished or rough-hewn. In 1906, Derain, who was still a full-blown Fauve, also adopted this form of direct sculpture, shaping three blocks of stone into rather primitive, squat figures. Though perhaps not actually influenced by the Fauves' marvelous dis- Plates 161-163 Plate 169

164 Etruscan God. Hellenistic Period. Bronze. Louvre, Paris.

165 Antoine Bourdelle. Madeleine Charnaux, 1917. Bronze. Bourdelle Museum, Paris.

166 Pablo Picasso. Figure, 1931. Bronze. Collection Mrs. Meric Callery, Paris.

167 Alberto Giacometti. Large Figure, 1958. Painted plaster. Galerie Maeght, Paris.

168 Amedeo Modigliani. Head of a Woman, 1919. Stone. Museum of Modern Art, Paris.

169 André Derain. Nude Woman Standing, 1906. Stone. Collection Mouradian and Vallotton, Paris.

164

165

166

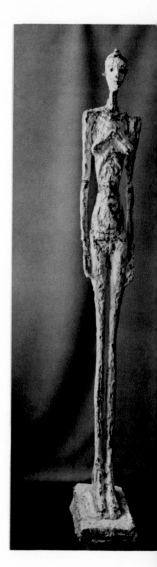

167

169

Plate
X

covery of African art, these figures did indicate a predisposition to that influence, which was again visible in sculptures done by Modigliani in 1909.

Plate
X

In 1910, however, a piece of sculpture by Picasso introduced a style which, though still strongly rooted in Impressionism, was undeniably new. The sharp-edged planes of the face of this *Head of a Woman* have distinct Cubist qualities

Plate
187

and also recall *The Mother* done one year later by Umberto Boccioni. This is most important, for it demonstrates that so far as style was concerned, sculpture was keeping closely abreast of painting, which had already begun the transition from "Cézannism" or pre-Cubism to that analytical Cubism which absorbed Picasso until 1912.

In 1913, during the period described by Daniel-Henry Kahnweiler as that of "superimposed planes," Cubism invaded Picasso's reliefs. In them he used paper and wood and incorporated the concrete elements already introduced into his painting one year earlier. In 1914 he included a real metal utensil in his

Plate
IX

Absinthe Glass, a wax model to be cast in bronze. This device was adopted by sculptors of the next generation and is, of course, now current practice. Another interesting feature of the *Absinthe Glass* was the simultaneous visibility of both the inside and outside of the subject. This was a logical consequence of the Cubist doctrine of simultaneous representation of various aspects of a given subject. It

Plate
188

is only fair to point out, however, that in 1912—one year earlier—Boccioni had already produced the *Development of a Bottle in Space.*

Picasso was not the only Cubist painter to make sculpture. At one point

Plate
171

Juan Gris turned to this form, though only for a short time. His plaster *Harlequin* (1917) was an attempt to apply the theories so staunchly propounded in his painting. Braque, on the other hand, turned his back on Cubism when he took up sculpture in 1920, and Léger had already left it far behind when he did his first pieces, belatedly, in 1950.

Following the First World War, Picasso's sculpture attained such constant inventiveness and technical freedom that it was able to assimilate and exploit the

IX Pablo Picasso. The Absinthe Glass, 1914.
Painted bronze. Galerie Berggruen, Paris.

X Pablo Picasso. Head of a Woman,
   1909–10. Bronze.
   Galerie Berggruen, Paris.

most unexpected materials. It is true that in 1920, at the beginning of his so-called "classical" period, Picasso temporarily lost interest in sculpture. His interest in the rendering of volume was apparently satisfied through the sculptural qualities of huge, monochromatic figures. However, he soon returned to sculpture, and his experiments have continued ever since: smooth-surfaced, tortured figures reminiscent of certain pieces by Henry Moore; iron and wire constructions which may be described as "solid drawings"; open-work sculpture in which the interstices constitute an integral part of the composition; a series of elongated "stick-figurines" carved out of thin shafts of wood in the vertical manner of the ancient Hellenistic tradition. This style, after reappearing in the work of Bourdelle, cropped up again in the work of Alberto Giacometti and some of the younger sculptors of today, including the Englishman, McWilliam. Through it all, Picasso remained in some degree figurative, sometimes fantastically distorting nature, sometimes viewing it realistically, as in *Shepherd Holding a Lamb*. Picasso has explored in half a century every area of investigation except that of pure abstraction; he has never completely discarded the "object." But pure abstraction was opened up to sculptors only after the abolition of traditional limits, a resolution which was the work of Picasso's generation.

Plates 164-167

Of all the painter-sculptors discussed in this chapter, it was Magnelli who, as early as 1914, applied the principles of abstraction most strictly. This is especially curious because at that time his painting was not yet abstract. He was living in Florence, and although on friendly terms with the Futurists, he rejected their doctrine. Magnelli produced only twelve pieces of sculpture. He sometimes incorporated real objects—bottles, utensils or recipients—into the sculptured forms. His mistrust of the *subject* and of any theory justifying it, led him to utterly reject the object. He later used the object with a view to transfiguring it. Reality of the most banal kind was thereby raised to the rank of conscious creation. The invention of the "Ready-made" by Marcel Duchamp later provided a similar demonstration of this principle. Unfortunately, Magnelli's sculpture was done in plaster

Plates 170, 172

170

171

200

172

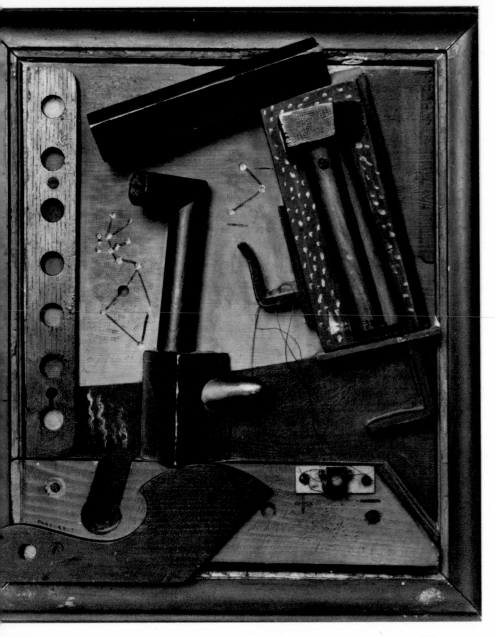

173

174

170 Alberto Magnelli. Rhythms, 1914. Plaster and copper. Collection of the
     artist.

171 Juan Gris. Harlequin, 1917. Plaster. Galerie Louise Leiris, Paris.

172 Alberto Magnelli. Still Life, 1914. Plaster, glass, stone. Collection of the
     artist.

173 Max Ernst. Fruit of Long Experience, 1919. Painted wood and metal.
     Collection Roland Penrose, London.

174 Jean Pougny. Relief, 1915. Colored cardboard.

and did not withstand the journeys imposed by two world wars. The only two known to have survived are reproduced in this volume.

At almost the same time—toward the end of 1913—Jean Pougny, a Finnish-born painter who later became a French citizen, was working on *The Cardplayers*. Despite its title, this was his first abstract relief. In 1915, together with Xenia Bogouslavskaya, his wife, and Malevich, he signed the *Suprematist Manifesto,* a document which protested against all forms of compromise with logic ("2 x 2 equals anything you like *but* 4"), and denied that meaning was the function of art ("The object—the world—deprived of its meaning breaks down into real elements, the bases of art."). In 1915, with the "Streetcar W" and "0.10" groups in Petrograd and in 1916, at the Jack-of-Diamonds Gallery in Moscow, Pougny

Plate 174

exhibited reliefs made of wood, metal, and painted cardboard. Like Magnelli, he sometimes incorporated real objects, such as billiard balls and dinner plates, thus provoking the insults of the entire Russian press. Even after Pougny returned to figurative painting, he continued making completely abstract reliefs until 1919.

Plate 173

They were built into boxes, like those done in 1919 by Max Ernst, whose interesting experiments in sculpture were to become more frequent in later years. This, however, brings us to the final stages of an evolution which must be considered in greater detail. To do so, we must look back and see what the sculptors were doing.

VII. THE NEW AESTHETIC

The Discoveries of Figurative Sculpture and the Road to Abstraction

When we try to define the major tendencies in sculpture beginning with the early years of the twentieth century, we must bear in mind that each tendency implies a certain continuity. We then realize that we must give up the idea of a "major tendency," as it does not cover the many directions and the frequent deviations taken by sculpture. Nevertheless, one main line can be isolated in its perennial obstinacy: that of academic sculpture, which had a long past and a seemingly inexhaustible energy. Still officially endorsed and dominating the Salons, it continued to lead the more conventional forms of figurative sculpture into a blind alley. For a long time these forms continued to distract public attention from the sporadic experiments of a few artists, who were as yet either unknown or held in ridicule.

Although a strong and widespread "Rodin-tendency" existed, it abruptly disappeared from the work of a number of sculptors. Thus, Brancusi, whose earliest work dates from 1901, was influenced by Rodin until 1907, and the face imprisoned in the marble of his first version of *Sleeping Muse* reveals its sources. On the other hand, *The Kiss* (1908), a stone block composed of two embracing figures inscribed within the strict geometry of a parallelepiped, seems more than a rebellious answer to Rodin's *Kiss;* it contradicted Brancusi's own style and heralded a new era in sculpture. Plates 210, 211, 95

This new era was characterized by symptoms of an intellectual and technical nature. It involved, too, a new choice of materials and media. Thus, the growing admiration of the machine had opened up a new domain of aesthetics and was partly responsible for the new interest in the artistic use of iron. The appearance of the machine as a theme in both painting and sculpture, exemplified by Fernand Léger's "mechanical" canvases and Jacob Epstein's *Rock Drill* (1913), was most significant, even though Epstein's temporarily experimental work was later to develop toward a classicism of debatable originality. Plate 175

It is hardly surprising that iron should have been particularly attractive

175 Jacob Epstein. The Rock Drill, 1913. Bronze. Collection of the artist.

176 Jacob Epstein. Bust of Admiral Lord Fisher, 1915. Bronze. Imperial War Museum, London.

177 Pablo Gargallo. Faunesse, 1908. Copper. Collection Anguera, Paris.

178 Pablo Gargallo. Head, 1903. Terra cotta. Collection Anguera, Paris.

176

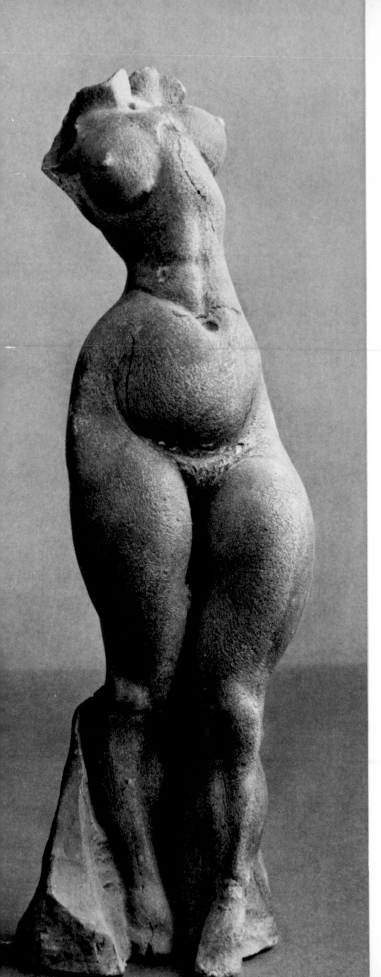

to the artists of Spain, a country which had known a continuous tradition of craftsmanship and ironwork since the Middle Ages. Spain had produced a number of great artists known simply as "ironcutters" whose work, during the seventeenth and eighteenth centuries, had been associated with all the fine monumental enterprises of the Baroque period. Thus, we find the Spaniard Pablo Gargallo (1881–1934), who had studied classical sculpture techniques, discovering, at the age of twenty, his own path in the renewal of metalwork technique. He was born in Maella, a small Aragonese village, near Catalonia. As a child, he began to model in clay and was only twelve when he sold his first bust to a neighbor for one *duro* and a tie. In 1900, or thereabouts, after a period of apprenticeship to an officially recognized sculptor, he enrolled in the Barcelona School of Fine Arts. In 1903, a scholarship enabled him to spend six months in Paris, but he was compelled to return to Spain after his father's death. To support his mother and three younger brothers, he worked for a sculptor in Madrid and for various fashionable architects. In 1906, he exhibited, for the first time, a few sculptures which attracted critical attention, but no public approval. The following year, however, he was commissioned to do four bas-reliefs for a theater façade.

Plates 177, 178

The decisive year for Gargallo was 1911, for at that time he returned to Paris where he quickly made the acquaintance of Modigliani, Juan Gris, Apollinaire, Max Jacob, and Pierre Reverdy. In spite of the bohemian existence to which his obscurity and poverty constrained him, he undertook to develop a new mode of expression, using thin sheets of iron and copper which he cut, twisted, hammered, and fitted. In this fashion he composed his first masks, which were bought by Léonce Rosenberg, one of the most enterprising dealers of the period. Gargallo was thereby encouraged to persevere in the improvement of his new technique.

Plates 179, 180

The First World War took him away from his work for some time, and he reluctantly accepted an appointment to teach sculpture at the Bella Oficis School in Barcelona. In the years which followed, however, he settled permanently in

XI Umberto Boccioni. Unique Forms of Continuity in Space, 1913. Bronze.
Museum of Modern Art, New York.

XII Alexander Archipenko. Carrousel Pierrot, 1913. Painted plaster. The Solomon
     R. Guggenheim Museum, New York.

Paris and there produced the curious works which reveal the sureness and subtlety with which he solved his difficult technical problems. He never completely abandoned modeling, but expressed himself most personally in metalwork.

Gargallo's work is particularly remarkable for the extreme technical economy with which he managed to suggest volume; he gave very little relief to his thin sheets of metal. Sometimes, as in the lovely, small *Motherhood,* he transformed a convex surface into a concave one. He later used this technique on a larger scale, adding to it the use of open space cut into the very body of his figures. In this way, he gave greater lightness and expression to their movements, as in his *Harlequin,* his *Antinous* and the large figure of the *Prophet.*

Julio Gonzalez (1876–1942), another Spaniard who worked in metal, had been familiar with the technique of smith's work since childhood. His father, an artisan and sculptor, was an ironsmith in Barcelona. It was not, however, until many years later that Gonzalez adopted iron as the medium most suited to his rigorous sensibility. Originally a painter, he had arrived in Paris about 1900, where he led the rather difficult life of an artist transplanted far from home and compelled to find his way amid the indifference of a great city. In spite of the Spanish and French friends who formed a congenial group about him—Picasso, Manolo, Roig, Max Jacob, Maurice Raynal and Edgar Varèse—his life remained very sad and lonely for many years. The bronze heads done in *repoussé* between 1910 and 1914—the portrait of *Tia Lola,* the *Inclined Antique Head,* the *Mask, Called Meditative,* whose technique was still hesitant—all reflect this melancholy.

Plates 181-183

During the First World War, Gonzalez was forced to work for a while in the Renault factory. There he gained experience of a technique which was later to play a most important part in his future work: that of autogenous soldering. When, in 1927, he decided to devote himself almost entirely to sculpture (though he always remained very deeply attached to painting), he did his most original work with metal and the soldering iron. In his *Peasant Women* and in the portraits whose surfaces are strangely shaped and simplified, we find Gonzalez' character-

181

182

179 Pablo Gargallo. Small Mask, 1911. Copper. Collection Anguera, Paris.

180 Pablo Gargallo. Portrait of Monsieur de Soto, 1920. Lead. Collection Anguera, Paris.

181 Julio Gonzalez, Tia Lola, ca. 1912–14. Bronze. Collection Madame Roberta Gonzalez, Arcueil.

182 Julio Gonzalez. Mask, called Meditative, ca. 1912–14. Bronze. Collection Madame Roberta Gonzalez, Arcueil.

istic austerity expressed with increasing freedom and violence. His style grew ever more stark, leading him toward abstraction without, however, detaching him completely from nature.

The link with nature grew so tenuous, however, that it was not always perceptible. Metal, as Gonzalez used it, was a medium whose aggressive hardness he no longer sought to attenuate. Even in those light assemblages which traced almost linear figures in space, the metal sheets, rods and points did not hide their industrial origins. In this way, and through the introduction of prefabricated elements, he created a new language, a language of signs which was later used by many other sculptors.

The work of these sculptors cannot be classified with precision, and, indeed, the work of most of those who determined, directly or indirectly, the major movement from which all of modern sculpture was to emerge, is interesting in precisely this respect. With them, we return, once again, to that first fascinating decade of the century during which the path of art was decided. The most curious sculpture of the period, preceding that of Cubism or simultaneous with it, does not fit into any category. The first experiments of Freundlich, Csaky, Gaudier-Brzeska, Archipenko, and Duchamp-Villon testify to the sculptor's need to express himself with greater violence and in a more synthetic manner. Cubist sculpture involved a deformation of this need, as it systematized a vision which could adapt adequately to the individual sensibility only by retaining the possibility of nuance.

Plates
184-186
190-192
196-198

In order to understand why a change occurs, one must always attempt to see to what degree it constitutes a reaction against an already existing condition. Now we have every reason to believe that the *avant-garde* at this particular time was impelled by a need to react against the formal lyricism which architecture and the decorative arts had pushed to the point of the ridiculous. The relationship between painting and what was internationally known as Art Nouveau, Modern Style, *Jugendstil,* or *Stile Liberty,* has never been really satisfactorily established.

The stylization which was somewhat belatedly discovered in the work of certain painters has been stressed; when one considers, however, that the structure of turn-of-the-century Baroque, was, like all Baroque, based on the notion of movement, one realizes that the painting of this period was, to a large extent, related to it.

This aesthetic of movement cannot be dissociated from the fluid, organic style of the decorative arts around 1900, with its sinuous lines and softly flowering plant life, tresses, and waves. One of the main concerns of the painters and sculptors who rebelled against this style seems to have been the elimination of the curved line from the representation of movement. For the idea of movement— far from being abandoned—was, on the contrary, cultivated with methodical application. One of the Cubist revolution's principal aims was, therefore, to cure movement of the evil effects of Baroque.

A revolution of this sort was possible only through a very clear intellectualization of painting. The Fauve movement, which made its first appearance in the Salon d'Automne of 1905 (simultaneously with the founding of *Die Brücke* in Dresden), involved an intellectualization of Impressionism, from the point of view of color. The pre-Cubist followers of Cézanne were to lead painting toward an intellectualization of form, toward that most important transition from the *form-as-seen* to the *form-as-conceived*. Without this change of point of view, without this step toward an increasingly subjective conception of art, formulated, nevertheless, in the name of greater reality, in spite of an apparently natural development of the forms which emerged from Cézanne's painting, the transformation from pre-Cubism to real Cubism cannot be explained.

The notion of movement was also at the heart of the Futurists' preoccupations. In 1909, Marinetti, in the *First Futurist Manifesto,* said: "We declare that the world's splendor has been enriched by a new beauty, the beauty of speed." Giacomo Balla, Carlo Carrà, Luigi Russolo, and Gino Severini, signed the *Technical Manifesto of Futurist Sculpture,* which was written by Umberto Boccioni

183

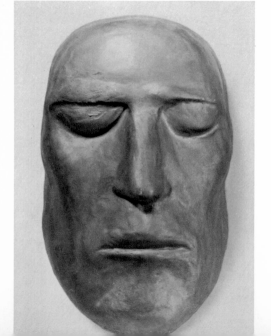

184

183 Julio Gonzalez. Inclined Antique Head, 1910. Bronze. Collection Madame Roberta Gonzalez, Arcueil.

184 Otto Freundlich. Mask, 1911. Plaster. Collection Madame Freundlich, Paris.

185 Otto Freundlich. Mask, 1915. Bronze. Private Collection, Paris.

186 Joseph Csaky. Head, 1914. Bronze. Museum, St.-Etienne.

185

186

and published in Milan on April 11, 1912. In it, Boccioni stated: ". . . If a sculptural composition requires a special rhythmical movement to accentuate or contrast with the static rhythm of the sculptural whole (the work of art's necessity), one can apply a small motor which will provide a rhythmical movement adopted to a given plane or line." This was later done, both with and without mechanical aid, by Tatlin, Gabo (in his "kinetic sculpture"), Moholy-Nagy, Calder, and, more recently, by Tinguely and others.

Plates
188, 189, XI

Boccioni himself did not go quite as far as his theories. However, in 1912 with the *Development of a Bottle in Space* and the *Synthesis of a Human Dynamism* and in 1913 with some of the eleven sculptures exhibited at the Galerie La Boetie in Paris, such as *Unique Forms of Continuity in Space,* he expressed, in a style which was tangential to that of Cubism, this will to express the movement of an object in space, thereby introducing the notion of time into a static construction. Both Balla and Marcel Duchamp, working outside the framework of Cubism or effecting slight theoretical changes, had done this in painting: *Dog on a Leash* and *Nude Descending a Staircase* both date from 1912.

These experiments in movement and Boccioni's ideas on the use of mixed media were to have important consequences. "The supposed nobility of marble and bronze, which is merely a matter of literature and tradition must be done away with," wrote Boccioni in his *Manifesto,* "and the idea that only one medium must be used for a sculptural ensemble must be categorically denied. The sculptor may use twenty or more in a single work, if he so chooses, provided that they correspond to an inner, formal necessity. The sculptor's choice would include, among others, glass, wood, cardboard, cement, concrete, horsehair, cloth, mirrors, electric light, etc." Boccioni's own sculpture was not, however, Futurist to the point of breaking with that lyricism which the Cubists had rejected; in many ways, it remained Baroque. This probably explains why it did not play a very significant role in the development of sculptural form.

In contrast the contribution of Archipenko was considerably more im-

187

188

187 Umberto Boccioni. The Mother, 1911. Bronze.
     National Gallery of Modern Art, Rome.

188 Umberto Boccioni. Development of a Bottle in Space,
     1912. Bronze. Museum of Modern Art, New York
     (Aristide Maillol Fund).

189 Umberto Boccioni.
Synthesis of a Human
Dynamism, 1912. Plaster.

portant. He, too, was for a time interested in real movement; his *Archipentura* was designed as a time-and-space-trap. His work done during the period 1909 and 1910 is most remarkable, however, for a bold and sudden transition from forms which were still realistically descriptive of the human body to forms which were not only schematized, but which also reconstructed the volumes of the human body in quite another type of volume. At this time, he began to substitute the convex surface for the concave, as Zadkine and Gargallo later did. He also began to use open space (the hole) as a constructive element in the representation of the body. (It is interesting to note, in this respect, Henry Moore's later adaptation of this technique.)

The rapid development of Archipenko's work, and his free juxtaposition of constructive principles, provide an insight into the logic of the evolution of one aspect of figurative sculpture: its gradual estrangement from natural forms, its approach to abstraction. A development of this kind was made possible by a constantly intensified refinement of form and by the use of a new formal language. Classical modeling technique was eliminated in favor of the form itself, so that the surfaces always remained clearly defined or, sometimes, even smooth. The first stages of this process can be seen in two works: the *Seated Black Torso* of 1909, which is still strongly checked by a respectful conception of nature, and the *Seated Figure* of 1913, in which the body is a barely human object, reduced to its simplest geometric expression. The tendency toward a colder, or more mysterious, mode of expression was sometimes counterbalanced by the use of polychrome.

Plates
190, 193-195

The tragically early death, in 1918, of Raymond Duchamp-Villon interrupted a work which already had compelled recognition as one of the most singular of its time. Although the Futurist and Cubist theories had a certain influence on Duchamp-Villon's sculpture, the main pieces, done during the last six or eight years of his life, testify to a completely personal style. Each sculpture constituted a new problem for him.

191

192

190

190 Alexander Archipenko. Silhouette, 1910. Chromium-plated bronze. Hessian Museum, Darmstadt.

191 Henri Gaudier-Brzeska. The Red Stone Dancer, ca. 1913. Waxed stone. Tate Gallery, London.

192 Henri Gaudier-Brzeska. Birds Erect, 1914. Stone. Museum of Modern Art, New York (Gift of Mrs. W. Murray Crane).

193 Alexander Archipenko. Médrano, 1914. Painted tin, glass, wood, oil cloth. The Solomon R. Guggenheim Museum, New York.

194 Alexander Archipenko. Torso of a Woman, 1922. Marble. Art Gallery, Mannheim.

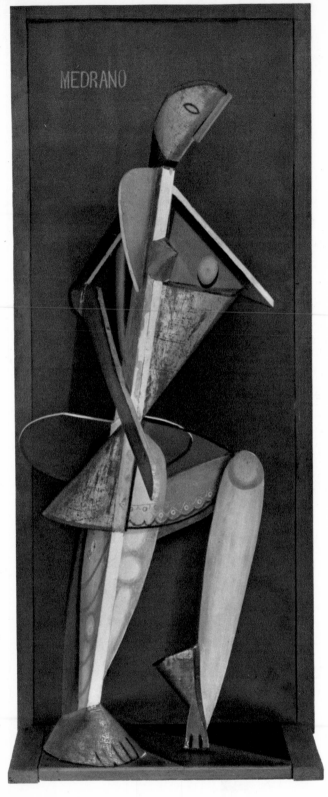

193

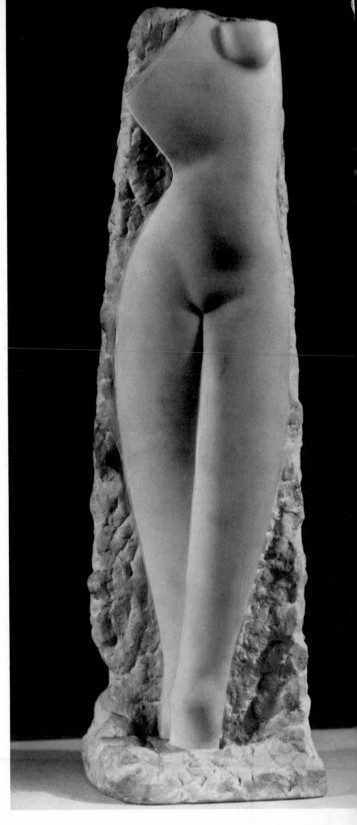

194

Plate
XIII
The bust of *Maggy* (1912) is constructed for the sole purpose of intensi-
fying a face whose forms seem almost caricatured by a deforming mirror. The
beholder's eye glides over surfaces which have been emptied of any detail and
focuses upon the expression which is suggested, in a very simple yet slightly
Plate
197
diabolical way, around the eyes and mouth. In the 1914 *Seated Woman,* it is the
body's movement which counts, the slant of the torso, and the interlacings formed
by the relationship of arms to legs. Here the subject's inner life has been replaced
by the wholly exterior play of volumes reduced to their bare rhythmical elements.
Plate
198
In *Horse and Rider* (1914) all the surfaces are smooth, even though they have
been modeled in a semi-Impressionist style which recalls that of Rosso. The rider
is one with his horse; the rearing animal is hardly articulated in the mass. *Horse's*
Plate
196
Head (1914) is done in a very different manner, geometricized into volumes which
are far removed from natural forms and in accordance with a construction which
Plate
XII
rather resembles that of *Carrousel Pierrot,* Archipenko's polychrome plaster
of 1913.

This tendency to replace real volumes with more powerfully expressive
ones attains even greater purity and strangeness in one of Duchamp-Villon's last
sculptures, the *Portrait of Professor Gosset,* done in 1917.

If Cubism did not assume real importance in sculpture until 1914, when
its second or synthetic period began to draw to a close, this was probably due to a
decline which left sculptors free to solve, in their own way, a problem not basically
their concern. The simultaneous representation on a flat surface of different points
of view, creating a play of contradictory perspectives that suggest volume and
movement, began to lose part of its justification through the construction of real
volumes in the sculptured object. In its use of displaced planes and geometricized
volumes, sculpture began to approach, to a certain degree, the painters' vision,
although it could not totally apply their theories. A certain ambiguity, even a
certain contradiction between suggested and real volumes, begins to be visible in
Plates
2, 201-206
XVI
the first Cubist sculptures done by Lipchitz and Zadkine (1913 and 1914) and in

those of Laurens (1918). One is struck by the compact mass of the block in which the only gestures possible for the figures represented are reduced to constricted attitudes. There is no breathing space in Lipchitz' *Seated Bather*, nor in Zadkine's *Standing Woman* nor in Laurens' *Large Boxer*.

This concern with a painterly problem, moreover, tended to favor the introduction of subjects which had usually been reserved for painting. Lipchitz' *Still Life*, Laurens' *Guitar* and a composition entitled *Bottle of Beaune* are significant in this respect. Zadkine gradually moved, through Cubism, toward the use of open space. In order to attain greater freedom of movement, Lipchitz and Laurens eventually were forced to abandon Cubism. Plate 209

Though painting and sculpture followed related paths, these paths did not always lead in the same direction. It was not Cubist sculpture which led the sculptors toward abstraction. Logically enough, however, Cubist painting, through its first movement of retreat from the real, perceived object and its early use of a dialectic of the visual imagination, did beget abstract painting, even though Kandinsky, who painted his first abstract water color in 1910, had not passed through a Cubist stage. Mondrian's first abstract painting, done in 1912, the same year in which Malevitch developed the theory of "Cubo-futurism," was still visibly influenced by Cubism.

Abstraction made its first appearance in sculpture in 1913, in a form related to that of painting: as a picture, in a box-frame, fixed to a wall. Vladimir Tatlin (1885–1956), who composed these first abstract reliefs, assemblages of geometrical elements, used a variety of materials in their construction: wood, metal, plaster, tar, ground glass, etc. He was also the first to take the reliefs out of their frames, to present them as objects isolated in space, not placed on a pedestal but suspended at the intersection of two walls. He gave them the name of "counter-reliefs" and exhibited them, first in Moscow, in 1915, then in Saint Petersburg. Plate 207

Tatlin's ideas broke fresh ground in sculpture, anticipating a future which

195

196

195 Alexander Archipenko. Struggle, 1914. Painted plaster. The Solomon R. Guggenheim Museum, New York.

196 Raymond Duchamp-Villon. Head of a Horse, 1914. Bronze. Galerie Louis Carré, Paris.

197 Raymond Duchamp-Villon. Seated Woman, 1914. Bronze. Galerie Louis Carré, Paris.

198 Raymond Duchamp-Villon. Horse and Rider (First State), 1914. Bronze. Galerie Louis Carré, Paris.

197

198

few artists could foresee at that time. Tatlin, himself, might have produced a more important body of work, if Soviet hostility to all advanced art had not constrained him, from 1920 on, to limit himself to utilitarian work. The last of his remarkable projects (1919) was a *Monument to the Third International*, an abstract construction consisting of a spiral form in metal, 1200 feet high, encircling two cylinders and a glass pyramid.

Plate 174

The constructions of Jean Pougny, previously referred to, are related to Tatlin's compositions and, like them, are done in the style known as "Constructivism" or "Cubo-Constructivism." Both terms clearly indicate a wish to establish a distinction from sculpture proper. Like Tatlin's, Pougny's work was limited to the principle of the relief. It was finally through the relief, and generally with the use of polychrome, that many sculptors—including Arp, Kurt Schwitters, Csaky, Oscar Schlemmer, Moholy-Nagy, and Sophie Taeuber-Arp—ventured into abstraction.

Plate 208

At this point a theoretical difficulty peculiar to abstract sculpture arises. I have already indicated the contradiction inherent in Cubist theory and its application to sculpture. The use of the term "abstract" for sculpture involves a far greater contradiction, for although painting can justify its abstraction by a refusal to represent any object—even the invented object—sculpture, by its very nature and irrespective of its technique, cannot escape being and remaining an object. For this reason, it can never completely reject its underlying, determining conditions. The result is an ineradicable difference in meaning between the term *abstract* as applied to painting and the same term as applied to sculpture; or, if one prefers, a difference of degree between these two forms of abstraction.

The transition from the figurative to the abstract was frequently accomplished through a process which is, on the whole, quite simple: the methodical, progressive reduction of the object to a synthetic or schematic form, or to a sign. Once the distance between sculpture and object reached the point at which the relation between the two could no longer be spontaneously grasped, there re-

199

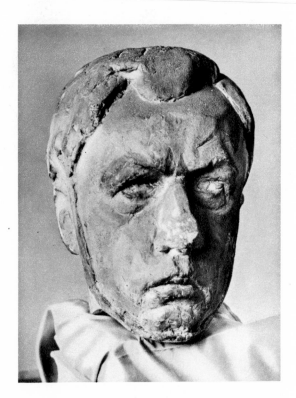

200

201

199 Henri Laurens. Portrait of Marthe Girieud, 1912. Stone. Galerie Louise Leiris, Paris.

200 Ossip Zadkine. Portrait of Georges Annenkof, 1912. Plaster. Collection of the artist.

201 Jacques Lipchitz. Dancer, 1913. Bronze. Museum of Modern Art, Paris.

202

203

202 Henri Laurens. Woman with a Guitar, 1919. Stone. Galerie
Louise Leiris, Paris.

203 Jacques Lipchitz. Acrobat on a Horse, 1914. Bronze.
Private Collection.

228

XIII Raymond Duchamp-Villon.
Maggy, 1912. Bronze.
Galerie Louis Carré, Paris.

XIV Constantin Brancusi. The New Born, 1920 (after a marble of 1915). Bronze.
Museum of Modern Art, New York.

mained only one more step (not in the sense of a new style, which already existed, but in that of a release of intention) toward the elimination of any meaningful detail.

Some of the most remarkable work done during the first two decades of the century is situated on this road which leads to abstraction. For instance, Constantin Brancusi (1876–1957), who made one of the most significant contributions to this development, never quite closed the very narrow gap which separated his work from pure abstraction. By 1907, he had shaken off the direct influence of Rodin and begun his long, slow, gradual, refinement of form—an attempt to express only that which he considered essential. He consequently often repeated his themes, as if each form, each idea of form, raised a question whose answer required improvement. His style was one of density and concision. Many contemporary sculptors who owe much to him and consider their simplicity of form equal to his have never troubled to discover what really constituted Brancusi's simplicity. It had, sometimes, the appearance of an astonishing technical success, but it was invariably the result of a spiritual process.

The forms of the egg and the bird were used as the bases for an entire series of experiments which were spread over thirty years of Brancusi's life. These began with his second version of *Sleeping Muse* (1909), very different from that of 1906, and the bird, *Maiastra,* done in 1910. The ovoid or Cycladic conception of his *Prometheus,* whose face is almost invisible, dates from 1911. The marble *Bird* of 1912 is even more highly refined than *Maiastra,* while *New Born* (1915) seems a mere variation on *Prometheus,* when one considers both as signs of the same pursuit which finally resulted in the absolute egg of the *Beginning of the World,* in 1924.

The vigor of Brancusi's wood carving, in contrast to the serenity of most of his polished surfaces, recalls the ruggedness of African sculpture. (Serenity and vigor were also characteristic of the man, as one saw him in his studio in Paris.) His work in wood, which developed after 1914, includes *The Prodigal Son,*

Plate 210

Plate XIV

204 Ossip Zadkine. Standing Woman, 1920.
Bronze. Collection of the artist.

205 Ossip Zadkine. Head of a Man, 1914. Stone.
Collection of the artist.

206 Ossip Zadkine. The Accordionist, 1918.
Plaster. Collection Mr. Bay, New York.

205

206

Caryatid, The Witch, The King of Kings, and that *Endless Column,* 90 feet high, later raised in steel in Târqu-Jiu, Rumania, near Pestisani, his birthplace.

Plate 30

Although Brancusi remained attached to the sculpture of earliest antiquity and although he found in the bare forms of Cycladic art a point of departure toward a renewal of form, he also helped to create a style which influenced industrial design. The prefiguration of missile shapes visible in some of his streamlined forms reveals a sense of the future which verges upon prophecy. Brancusi's art thereby constitutes one of the most important links between a past which must be given careful consideration (before being rejected as completely out-of-date), and a contemporary sensibility which cannot be dissociated from its real origins.

Another precursor of contemporary sculptural style was Louis Chauvin, whose work, though figurative at first, assumed a frankly abstract character. Chauvin, who avoided all distracting activity, had little taste for the kind of exhibitions upon which reputations are built. Unfortunately, his work is still little known, even though it constitutes one of the boldest modern explorations of form.

Plates 212, 213

His preoccupation with purity of line and his love of fine materials contributed to the extreme rigor of his work. This is already visible in the "sculptured objects" done in 1913, when he was only twenty-four years old. The word "object" seems, indeed, to suit his work—not that his sculpture was inexpressive, but because of its perfect balance and frequent symmetry, because of the way in which the smooth surfaces invite the eye's caress and the way in which it adapts itself to domestic interiors. For this, smallness of size is partly responsible (the largest do not exceed 30 inches in height), as is the beauty of materials. Chauvin often used exotic woods: teak, May-Doo, cypress wood from Cambodia, Cuba and elsewhere. Although he occasionally becomes too decorative, he expresses with simplicity and unfailing technical power the themes which seem to have been inspired by nature's overflowing force, the call to action and to life. Many of his titles have this kind of resonance: *Flight, Dawn, Genesis, The Rising of the*

Wind, Chrysalis, Burning Seed, to mention a few. Naturally enough, Chauvin's conceptions have a characteristic eroticism in which the phallic theme, though reduced to a synthetic purity, is, nevertheless, clearly suggested.

The development of Chauvin's sculpture is highly representative of the approach to abstraction through the progressive elimination of references to visible reality. Sculpture, now forced to seek justification within itself, abandoned the model. Aesthetically speaking, this was a relatively simple matter; the development of figurative sculpture appears to have been much more complex.

Many sculptors, while treating natural forms with great freedom, had no intention of wholly eliminating them. Some were concerned with something quite different from a synthetic simplification. They wished to substitute, for the sterile style which was still being used at the beginning of the century, a new formal language. They wished to recover, in their own fashion, the basic motives of a sculpture which had been long neglected or disregarded by art historians, the forgotten meanings of an art of the distant past, of distant countries, long considered primitive or barbarous.

African art, between 1910 and 1912, began to influence the sculptors. Together with Henri Gaudier-Brzeska, Picasso was one of the first to derive from it the structure of a new geometry of the human face. It is known that Picasso himself possessed a Wobe mask, its eyes made of two cylinders, its nose a wooden triangle. The eye, in circular relief, also occurs in idols from the Aegean Bronze Age and in certain small statues from Sardinia whose thin, soft forms accentuate their gestures and betray a lack of interest in muscular articulation. These purely linear movements are evident in the sculpture of Picasso, Matisse, and Laurens, who were the first to revive them.

The curiosity awakened by African art spread gradually to all those styles which the ethnologists and archeologists had brought to light, aided by a progress in photography which made accurate reproduction possible. Thus, we find influences of archaic Greek art in the work of Picasso and, later, in that of Braque.

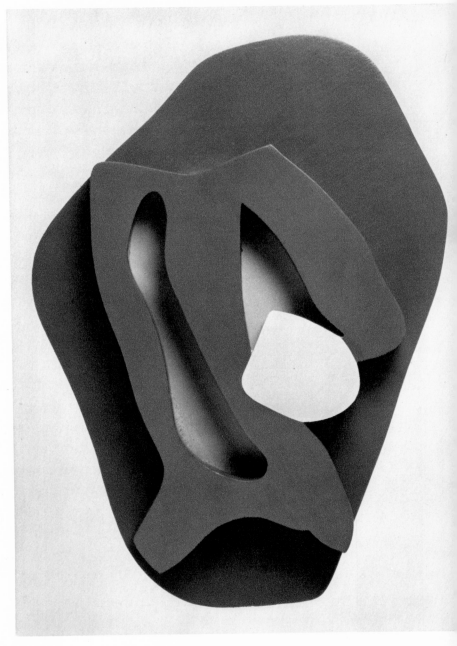

207

208

236

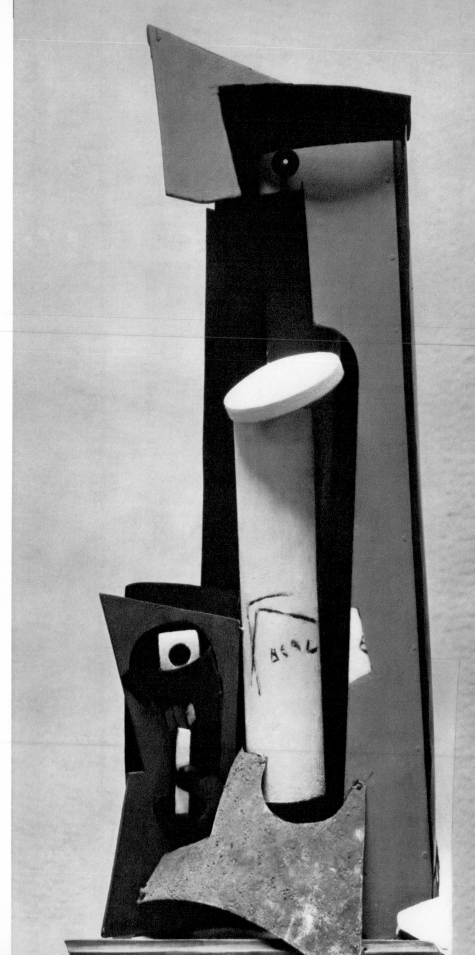

207 Vladimir Tatlin. Construction, 1914.

208 Jean Arp. Earth Forms, called "Tears of Enak,"
1916–17. Painted wood. Collection Arp-
Hagenbach, Meudon.

209 Henri Laurens. The Bottle of Beaune, 1918.
Wood. Collection A. Maremond, Chicago.

Pre-Columbian art, particularly certain pieces of the Mixteca-Puebla period (800 to 1521 A.D.) seem closely related to Duchamp-Villon's *Portrait of Professor Gosset*, while Flannagan's animals recall certain Aztec stone carvings. The Cubist work of Lipchitz and Laurens suggests the reclining *Tlalocs* of ancient Mexico, and the massive heads of Easter Island are echoed in the work of Freundlich. We know that several generations of sculptors, including Brancusi, Arp, Nevelson, Mirko, Stahly and Stackpole, have used the principle of superimposed themes which is embodied in the totem pole.

These artists, stimulated by the beauty of traditions which were basically foreign to Western sculpture, discovered in them new sources of expression. The real importance of this discovery lay, however, not in the forms which were sometimes rather naïvely adopted, but in the renewal of the relation between myth and the human figure, in the revival of a very ancient concept. The sculptor who managed to create a personal style, independent of outside influence, thereby developed an awareness of something which was, as yet, not generally known: namely, that our age possessed its own, impressive mythology.

War and the danger of extinction revived the fear and violence of primitive times, thus creating a new need for exorcism. Sculpture has revived the prehistoric theme of the arrow-pierced enemy, expressing, in contemporary terms, the magical "attraction" of evil to certain human figures, as in the corroded, torn figures of Alberto Giacometti, Germaine Richier, Couturier, Jean Dubuffet, and a dozen other sculptors. This image of man is barely animate, begging for deliverance or death, resigned to bear the burden of death-in-life.

A renewal of sculptural technique which developed at this time facilitated a more general experimentation in materials which had, until then, been neglected. In 1914, Archipenko used glass, painted metal, and oilcloth in some of his "sculpto-paintings." This was of secondary importance for the sculpture in question, but the use of plastics—celluloid and plexiglass—by Naum Gabo in 1915 and, a few years later, by his brother Antoine Pevsner and by Moholy-Nagy, was much more important.

Plates 214-217, XV

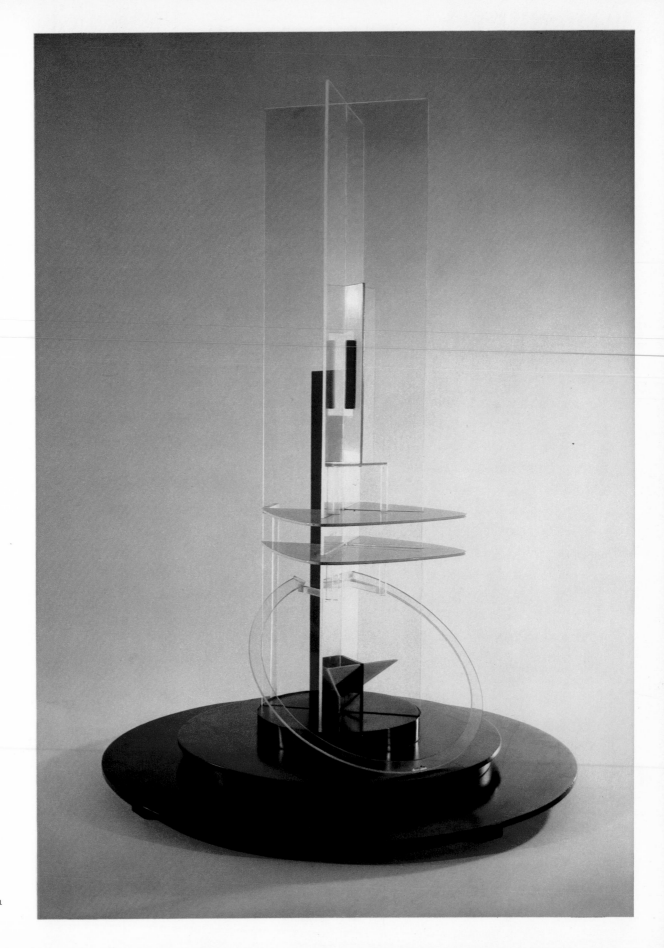

XV Naum Gabo. Column, 1923.
Plastic, wood, metal.
The Solomon R. Guggenheim
Museum, New York.

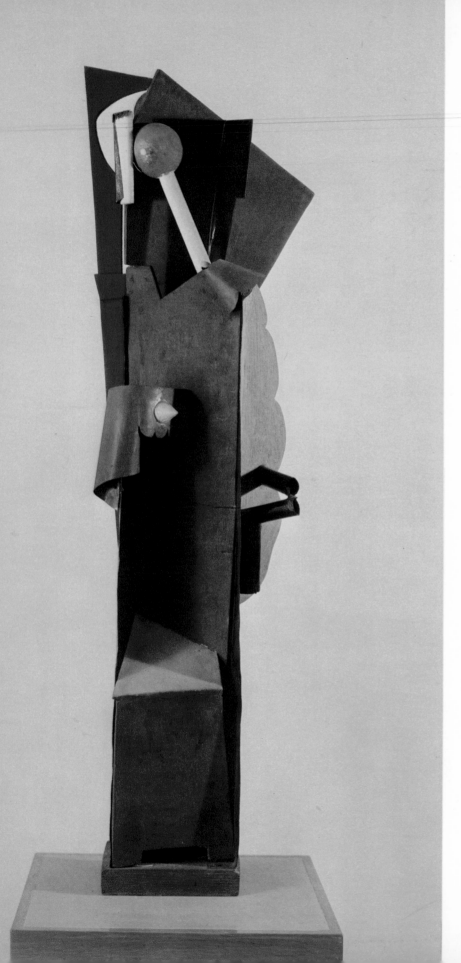

XVI Henri Laurens. Woman, 1918. Painted wood and metal.
Galerie Louise Leiris, Paris.

In the early sculpture of Gabo and Pevsner, transparency becomes the basis of the new Constructivist conception of space. This conception was outlined by Gabo in his *Realist Manifesto* (1920), and continuously developed by both Gabo and Pevsner in a series of pieces which are among the most important of contemporary sculpture. Space thereby acquired a positive presence, indicated by a transparent volume. In similar fashion, Pevsner later suggested time through the use of "developable surfaces" composed of bronze or copper wire combined through soldering.

Sculpture of this kind illustrates one of the aspects of contemporary style in its demonstration that the use of new materials (other sculptors used aluminum, duraluminum, concrete and nylon), or a novel use of classical materials, evolved simultaneously with the discovery of a new expression through the object.

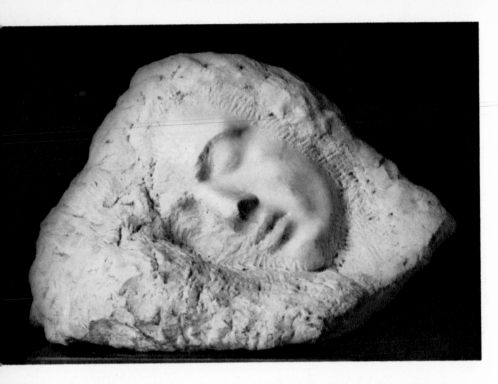

242

212

210 Constantin Brancusi. Sleeping Muse, 1906. Marble. National Gallery, Bucharest.

211 Constantin Brancusi. The Kiss, 1908. Stone. Philadelphia Museum of Art (Arensberg Collection).

212 Louis Chauvin. Motherhood, 1913. Cypress wood. Collection Alex Maguy, Paris.

213 Louis Chauvin. On an Accordion Tune, 1920. Collection Alex Maguy, Paris.

A SUMMING-UP

A final backward glance over the century of successive transformations which marked the slow emergence of sculpture from the lethargy of neoclassicism toward that stylistic pluralism which delights or disconcerts, as the case may be, will enable us to trace a development along two paths of distinctly varying directions and degrees of importance.

One of these paths led sculpture into an impasse. For although neoclassicism began as an attempt to revive or prolong that classical aesthetic which expressed the spirit of an age whose literature and philosophy were inspired by ideals of clarity, balance and logic, it erred in its insistence upon drawing inspiration from ancient sculpture and upon deriving from it, with a confidence which verged upon superstition, supposedly infallible formulas for beauty. In an imitative art of this kind, technique remained so inseparably linked to a certain kind of subject that no artist could envisage abandoning one or the other.

This gave rise to an academicism which was merely a degenerate form of neoclassicism. When artistic creation is no longer determined by a strong, inner, personal impulse, when it involves mere obedience to those general rules which are incompatible with all that makes for individuality, the work of art is impoverished; virtuosity takes the place of inner necessity.

Romantic sculpture was, in its way, a brief reaction against the coldness of classicism. Even at its most literary, it introduced an intensity of movement, a lyricism which was assimilated with varying degrees of success. While Rodin succeeded in turning the example of Rude to his own account, all too many sculptors found in Rude's work merely an encouragement to theatricalize their own academic styles. Naturalism in turn constituted only a pseudo-reaction, for it proposed new subjects, not new techniques. Mythology was replaced by anecdote, but the *midinette* who supplanted the goddess on the pedestal did nothing to advance the art of sculpture. Naturalism simply stimulated a development toward that stylistic dead end of the baroque which disappeared with the passing of Art Nouveau.

Thus ~~we see that~~ the failure of neoclassicism and its direct sculptural derivatives was due partly to the pre-eminence traditionally accorded to the subject and partly to the technical conformity of the sculptors of the period. If classicism managed temporarily to resume its development through the work of Maillol and the handful of "advanced classicists" hitherto referred to, it was only after a technical revolution had stimulated a re-definition of formal problems, thus enabling them to infuse new life into a style which was, nevertheless, doomed to decline.

The sources of this revolution in sculptural technique mark the point of departure for that second path which led toward the conceptions with which we are now familiar. They go back rather far in time, for we find their first traces in the small heads executed in 1832 by Daumier. Daumier's sculpture augured, in a manner which passed almost unnoticed, a new destiny for the medium.

~~We now know that~~ this movement of liberation through which the sculptor gradually became detached from the conventions involving choice of subject and manner of execution, assumed a direction which led from the outside inward: from the modeling of the surface toward the construction of volumes, from the modification of technique toward conceptual changes. The sculptors responsible for this movement—Daumier, Carpeaux in some of his work, Rodin in his bronzes, Rosso, Bourdelle—relate to each other, show a certain continuity of effort; their handling of the surface implied a radical and all-important change in the way of perceiving natural forms.

The reaction against Rodin's style, the reaction against the stormy passion which gave his work that dramatic movement and expressive power which constitute one of the high points in the history of sculpture, was characterized by a sudden return to the use of the smooth surface. In order for this opposition to Rodin to assume a progressive rather than a regressive aspect, the return had to be accompanied by an increased freedom in the interpretation of nature. Sculpture thereby entered the era of schematization.

214

215

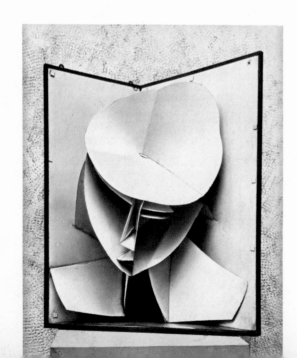

216

214 Naum Gabo. Bust, 1916. Construction in metal and plastic.

215 László Moholy-Nagy. Nickel Construction, 1921. Nickel-plated iron. Museum of Modern Art, New York (Gift of Mrs. Sybil Moholy-Nagy).

216 Naum Gabo. Head of a Woman, ca. 1917–20 (after a work of 1916). Construction in metal and plastic. Museum of Modern Art, New York.

217 Antoine Pevsner. Head of a Woman, 1923. Construction in plastic and wood. Collection André Lefebvre, Paris.

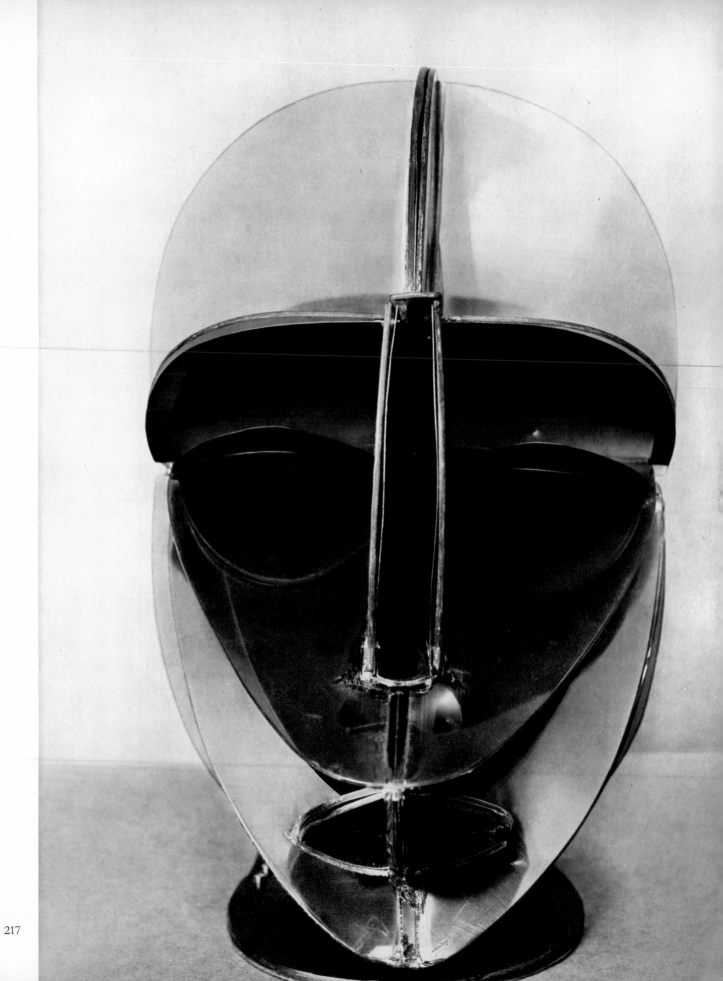

The artists working in this new manner were really aiming at a somewhat calmer movement, a simplification of form, a synthetization accompanied by some degree of geometricization. The subject's importance was consequently sacrificed to that of the personal technique. In the work of some artists who were evolving away from an attachment to nature, the subject was retained only as a pretext for stylistic and technical experiments whose interest and novelty dominated all other considerations. Certain sculptors, while pushing the synthetization process as far as possible, obscuring the link between the work of art and the subject which had inspired it, refused to relinquish this link. Others found it superfluous, and detached the work of art entirely from any representational function, from any reference to reality—even from that of allusion. For these artists, sculpture's justification lay solely in its own invented form. Thus pure sculptural abstraction was born.

Nevertheless, although early abstract sculpture was influenced by the synthetic style from which it was mainly derived—the predominance of simple, largely geometricized forms which expressed the preoccupation with purity which gave natural preference to the polished surface over the modeled one—the somewhat cold simplicity and static quality were gradually abandoned. All the animating techniques of figurative sculpture—the nervousness of Impressionism, the contorted movement of baroque style, etc.—were put to the service of abstraction. Sculpture, in this respect, remains to some degree dependent upon the techniques of the past.

Figurative sculpture, on the other hand, has borrowed from abstraction all the media, forms and techniques which can be used, if not to represent, at least to suggest, a given object. This, I believe, partly explains the difficulty some of us have had in accepting abstraction in sculpture. Figurative sculpture in its most highly developed, least easily identifiable forms, does not differ from abstract sculpture; there is no formal break between them, only a conceptual one, a difference of source and intention. The difference can be revealed only by the artist, through the use or absence of a title; it remains imperceptible to the beholder. Sculpture is really less abstract than it appears to be. For if the new language of sculpture has discredited the traditional notion of the *subject*, this same language has nevertheless proven capable of translating ideas, emotions and feelings formerly subject to the old principle of the allegory and now expressible through the power of form alone.

BIOGRAPHICAL DICTIONARY
OF SCULPTORS

The entries in this Biographical Dictionary are limited to sculptors whose works had achieved a certain importance between the years 1850—1920. It is not meant to be all-inclusive but to supply the reader with useful information supplementary to the text. ASTERISK indicates that the sculptor is given a separate entry in the Bibliography.

ANTONIO, Julio. Spanish. Born 1890 in Tarragona; died 1919. Acquired a considerable reputation in his own country for portraits of Spanish workers, peasants and provincial types. In his realism and sociological bent, Antonio resembles Constantin Meunier, though he lacked the Belgian sculptor's power. *The Race* is the generic title given to his series as a whole. He also designed several monuments, including one commissioned by his native town, in memory of *The Heroes of Spanish Independence.*

*ARCHIPENKO, Alexander. Born 1887 in Kiev, Russia; acquired American citizenship in 1928. In 1902 he entered the School of Fine Arts in Kiev to study painting, then sculpture, from 1902 to 1905. He later went to Moscow and participated in several group shows. In 1908 he moved to Paris, briefly attended classes at the Ecole des Beaux-Arts, but was considerably more impressed by his discovery of Cubism. This influence, however, was soon modified by a personal conception of stylization applied to the use of volume and sculptural space. In 1910 he had his first two one-man shows, both in Germany (at the Folkwang Museum in Hagen and in Berlin). At that time he began the *Medranos,* the experiments with mixed media which eventually developed into "sculpto-paintings," the first of many works in which color was used as an essential element. He opened three schools for sculptors, the first in Paris, another in Berlin and still another in New York. Exhibited in Paris at the Salon des Indépendants, the Salon d'Automne and the Salon de la Section d'Or. His work was ridiculed by the press, but in 1913 and 1914 Apollinaire and André Salmon came to his defense. In 1913 he participated in the Armory Show in New York and joined *Der Sturm* in Berlin, showing at the Herbstsalon at the Herwarth Walden Gallery. He remained in Berlin from 1921 to 1923, then left for the United States. He exhibited frequently in America and his reputation was established there long before he became known in Europe. In 1924 he invented the *Archipentura,* "a machine designed to create the illusion of movement in a painted subject." In 1935 and 1936 he taught at the University of Washington, then joined the New Bauhaus founded in Chicago by Moholy-Nagy. In 1947 he executed his first luminous sculptures, made of plexiglass and lit from within. In 1950 he taught at Kansas City University. He resides at present in Woodstock, New Jersey. He has published an important book on the development of his aesthetics: *Fifty Creative Years, 1908–1958* (Tekhné, New York, 1960). For a discussion of his substantial contribution to the birth of modern sculpture (before 1920), see pages 216 and 219.

*ARP, Jean. French. Born 1887 in Strasbourg. (Although most of his significant work in sculpture was done after the period covered by this book, the following text sums up the principal stages of his career.) Arp was a poet and painter before turning to sculpture. He first published his verse in 1904. During that year he spent some time in Paris. From 1905 to 1907 he studied painting at the Weimar Academy, then returned to Paris in 1908 and attended the Académie Julian. The following year he settled in the Swiss town of Weggis, on the edge of the Vierwaldstaettersee. Here, he first experimented with abstract painting and tried his hand at modeling in clay. In 1912 he took part in the second *Blaue Reiter* show in Munich and met Kandinsky, whose work greatly encouraged him. Arp exhibited in the Berlin Herbstsalon in 1913 and published drawings in *Der Sturm.* His stay in Zurich, where he helped found the Dada movement in 1916, constitutes an important stage of his career. There, he made some collages, his first multicolored reliefs, wrote verse and attended the famous gatherings organized at the Cabaret Voltaire, frequented by Hugo Ball, Janco, Tristan Tzara and Sophie Taeuber, whom he married in 1922. Dada was spreading to Germany; it took Arp, in 1919, to Cologne where he joined Max Ernst. He later spent brief periods in the Tyrol, in Hanover, with Kurt Schwitters, and in Holland, where he worked on the magazine, *De Stijl,* and the Dutch Dadaists' *Mecano.* In 1926 he finally returned to France, settling in Meudon, near Paris. Neither Dada, nor its successor, Surrealism, ever really diverted him from his search for a new language, one from which references to nature were either eliminated or reduced to a bare minimum. Using polished stone, marble or bronze, he developed a new image of the human body, unrelated to realistic anatomy and confined to what he called the "torso." In 1930 he first felt the need to express himself through sculpture in the round. This marks the beginning of a significant body of work which constitutes a visual extension of his poetic imagination in the creation of a universe of simplified forms. The skill and serenity of his work increased steadily as the years passed, and frequent exhibitions on both sides of the Atlantic—in Paris, Berne, Basel, Vienna, Cologne and New York—established his reputation on an international scale. In 1958, the Museum of Modern Art in New York held a large retrospective exhibition of his work. Arp has made several trips to the United States and two to Greece. He executed decorative sculpture in the graduate center at Harvard University. One of his largest pieces, *Cloud Shepherd* (1956), was installed in front of the University residence halls in Caracas.

BAILY, Edward Hodges. English. Born 1788; died 1867. Studied sculpture with John Flaxman, who was celebrated for his imitations of classical statuary. His conservativism earned him official commissions such as the decorations for the facade of Buckingham Palace. He also designed the *Nelson Column* which stands in Trafalgar Square, London.

BALZICO, Alfonso. Italian. Born 1825; died 1901. His work alternated between the most banal neo-classicism illustrated by his *Cleopatra,* and a descriptive realism applied to historical subjects such as the equestrian statue of the *Duke of Genoa.* Surrounded by bas-relief battle-scenes, this piece stands in a public square in Turin. Several of his statues are in the collection of the Galleria Nazionale d'Arte Moderna in Rome.

*BÄNNINGER, Otto Charles. Swiss. Born 1897 in Zurich. After studying sculpture in Zurich during the First World War, Bänninger came to Paris and enrolled in the Académie de la Grande-Chaumière. He later entered Bourdelle's studio and worked with him until his death in 1929. In 1931, he began returning frequently to Zurich, finally settling there permanently in 1939. His work was frequently exhibited in Paris, at the Salon des Tuileries and the Salon d'Automne. In 1941, he was awarded the International First Prize for Sculpture at the Venice Biennale and in 1956, the Grand Prize of the City of Zurich. His work is classical in style, influenced by both Rodin and Maillol. It is animated by a keen sense of observation, especially telling in his remarkable nudes and heads. Bänninger has executed a great many portraits, including those of *Cuno Amiet, C. F. Ramuz* and *Oskar Reinhart,* as well as monumental pieces, such as the *Group of Samaritans* (1931) in Zurich. His most recent major sculptures are a monument for the bridge over the Aar river at Olten, and a pair of bronze doors for the Schaffhausen Cathedral.

*BARLACH, Ernst. German. Born 1870 in Wedel (Holstein); died 1938 in Rostock. First studied at the Hamburg School of Arts and Crafts, from 1888 to 1891, then, until 1895, at the Dresden Academy.

During two periods in Paris he also briefly attended the Académie Julian. From 1898 to 1902 he illustrated the review *Jugend.* Returning to Germany in 1899, he settled for some time in Berlin, then, in 1904, went to teach for two years at the Hör School of Ceramics in the Westerwald. In 1906 he traveled to Russia and, in 1909, spent time in Florence. In 1907 and 1908 he illustrated *Simplicissimus.* In 1910 he settled in Güstow, where he later designed a *War Monument.* In 1919 he was elected to the Academy of Fine Arts in Berlin. His work, which was inspired by medieval sculpture, was typical of German Expressionism. Most of it was done in wood, and his rough-hewn figures are heavily symbolic, frequently half-submerged in the block of wood, animated by a single movement whose unity has a certain rather heavy power. The dramatic, somewhat theatrical quality of *The Vandal* (1910), *The Forsaken* (1913), *The Avenger* (1914) and *Death* (1925) remind us that Barlach also took a writer's interest in the German Expressionist theater. In 1938 he was banned by the Nazis as a "degenerate artist" and 381 of his sculptures were removed from museums and hidden from the public eye. He died that same year.

BARRIAS, Louis Ernest. French. Born 1841 in Paris; died 1905 in Paris. Entered the Ecole des Beaux-Arts in 1858 and won the Grand Prix de Rome in 1861 and in 1865. Began exhibiting at the Salon in 1861. Worked on the decoration of the Opera House and of a townhouse for the celebrated La Païva. He later designed decorations for the Louvre, the Hôtel de Ville and the Sorbonne. His work, which represents the academic style of that period in all its glory, includes: *The Spinner of Megara* (1870), *The Oath of Spartacus* (1872), *The Defense of Paris* at the Rond-Point de Courbevoie (1883) and *Joan of Arc Emprisoned* (1892). Late in life, under the influence of Art Nouveau, his style grew more "modern"; this is illustrated by his statue, *Nature Revealed,* which combines onyx with multicolored marble (1899). Barrias' famous work *First Funeral* is in the Hôtel de Ville (a bronze replica is in the Metropolitan Museum of Art, in New York). He taught at the Beaux-Arts and was elected to the Institute in 1884.

*BARTHOLDI, Frédéric-Auguste. French. Born 1834 in Colmar; died 1904 in Paris. Studied architecture and painting, with Ary Scheffer, before taking up sculpture. He traveled to Greece and the Orient with Gérôme and first exhibited at the Salon of 1857 where he was represented by a large bronze entitled *The Berber Lyre.* He designed many monuments and allegorical statues. The most famous of these is *Liberty Enlightening the World* in New York harbor. The work was originally called *Progress,* and intended for the Suez Canal but refused. His principal sculptures are discussed on page 80. He also designed a *Fountain* in Philadelphia (1875), the *Gambetta Memorial* in Ville d'Avray (1891), *Washington and Lafayette,* erected in 1895 on the Place des

Etats-Unis in Paris. He was elected Vice-President of the Society of French Artists from 1900 to 1903. He died at 82, Rue d'Assas, in the Montparnasse quarter where he had spent much of his life.

BARTHOLOMÉ, Paul-Albert. French. Born 1848; died 1928. A pupil of Léon Gérôme, studied painting with Menns, also. Typifies a lifelong fidelity to academic tradition. He designed a *War Memorial* for the Père-Lachaise Cemetery in 1899.

BARTLETT, Paul Wayland. American. Born 1865 in New Haven; died 1925. Studied at the Ecole des Beaux-Arts and with Frémiet. One of the last exponents of traditional memorial statuary. His *Bohemian Bear Trainer* won the gold medal at the Salon of 1888. The original plaster cast is in the Chicago Art Institute; in bronze it is at the Metropolitan Museum of Art, in New York. Executed the statues of *Michelangelo* and *Christopher Columbus* in the rotunda of the Congressional library in Washington, D. C.

*BARYE, Antoine-Louis. French. Born in Paris, September 24, 1795; died in Paris, June 25, 1875. His life and work are discussed in part on pages 52–53. From 1823 to 1831 he worked for a goldsmith named Fauconnier, decorating pieces with animal patterns. In 1837 a centerpiece, commissioned by the Duke of Orléans and consisting of nine hunting scenes, was refused entrance to the Salon. Barye thereupon gave up the idea of exhibiting under official auspices and decided to become his own dealer. Ten years later this venture ended in bankruptcy. In 1848 he was appointed curator of the Gallery of Plaster Replicas at the Louvre and in 1854 he became a teacher of zoological draftsmanship at the Museum of Natural History. In 1868 he was elected to the Institute. In addition to his sculpture, Barye's work includes a number of paintings and drawings, as well as more than 200 water colors; most of these are animal studies now in the collection of the Louvre, the Petit Palais, the Ecole Nationale des Beaux-Arts and the museums of Rouen, Montpellier and Bayonne. A number of his small statues and bas-reliefs are in the Metropolitan Museum of Art in New York, and over one hundred of his bronzes are in the Corcoran Gallery, Washington, D. C.

BELLVER Y RAMON, Ricardo. Spanish. Born 1845 in Madrid; died 1924. An academic sculptor who designed a number of solemn tombs for Spanish cardinals. These are still to be seen in the churches of Toledo and Seville. Other works include a *Virgin with Rosary,* a *Death of Saint Inez* and a *Fallen Angel* which stands on the Plaza del Retiro in Madrid.

BENLLIURE Y GIL, Don Mariano. Spanish. Born 1862 in Valencia; died 1946. His commemorative statues of *Queen Maria-Christina, Admiral Alvaro de Bazan,* etc. are quite conventional. He also sculpted figures inspired by Goya. His most original works, however, were the studies of bullfighters which earned him the commission for *Joselito's Tomb* in Seville.

*BERNARD, Joseph. French. Born 1866 in Vienne; died 1931 in Boulogne-sur-Seine. His father was a stonecutter. He first studied at the Lyon School of Fine Arts, then at the Beaux-Arts in Paris. His work displays a consistent concern with rhythm, which first found expression in a style of great purity. Later, however, he became excessively infatuated with certain decorative clichés. He spent five years on the *Michel Servet Monument* which stands in his native town. The Museum of Modern Art in Paris and the museums of Grenoble and Lyon have several of his sculptures. See page 160.

BERNSTAMM, Léopold Bernard. Russian. Born 1859 in Riga; died 1910. He began his studies at the Saint Petersburg Academy, continued them in Florence, then in Paris, where he worked with Antonin Mercié. His work often displays the mannered charm typical of the turn of the century. His best-known work includes a *Snake Charmer* and a good many portraits, including one of *Edouard Pailleron,* erected in the Parc Monceau in Paris in 1906.

*BOCCIONI, Umberto. Italian. Born in Reggio, Calabria, October 19, 1882; died in Sorte, Verona, on August 17, 1916. This painter-turned-sculptor studied from 1898 to 1902 with Giacomo Balla in Rome. He traveled to Paris and Saint Petersburg. From 1904 to 1906, he worked in Padua and Venice and, beginning in 1909, in Milan. There he made the acquaintance of F. T. Marinetti with whom he helped organize the Futurist movement. He was one of the group's most ardent theoreticians. See pages 213 and 216. He participated in all the Futurist exhibitions in Paris, London, Berlin and Brussels. After the shock created by an exhibition of his first sculptures in the Galerie La Boëtie in 1913, he showed in Rome at the Galleria Sprovieri and, in 1914, at the Galleria Gonnelli in Florence. He was called up in the army during the First World War and died of injuries suffered during a fall from a horse. In addition to the *Technical Manifesto of Futurist Sculpture* (1912), his writings, all published in Italy, include *Futurist Painting and Sculpture; Plastic Dynamism* (1914). Some of his work in plaster was destroyed in Milan in 1917 by being heaped together after a large posthumous exhibit, 1916–1917, in the Central Art Gallery of the Cova Palace. His bronzes are to be seen in the museums of Rome, Milan, Turin, Basel, Hanover, New York and São Paulo.

BONNARD, Pierre. French. Born 1867 in Fontenay-aux-Roses; died 1947 in Le Cannet. This great painter left only a very few pieces of sculpture, small bronze figures modeled with a freedom and sensitivity that give them an "Impressionist" aspect. They are little known and although certainly done before 1914, cannot be more precisely dated. All are in private collections. The Museum of Modern Art in Paris possesses one bronze centerpiece designed by Bonnard in approximately 1904 or 1905; it depicts a young woman and some children playing with a dog.

BONNASSIEUX, Jean Marie. French. Born 1810; died 1892. An academic sculptor of religious subjects, a fervent Catholic who refused to execute a statue of Voltaire. In 1836 he received the Prix de Rome. He is responsible for the huge *Virgin* which stands overlooking the town of Le Puy (1860), the *Tomb of Monseigneur Darboy* in Notre-Dame de Paris and the statue of *Jeanne Hachette* in the Luxembourg Garden. He was elected to the Institute in 1866.

BOUCHER, Alfred. French. Born 1850; died 1934. A student of Paul Dubois and of Augustin Dumont. Began exhibiting at the Salon in 1874. A superficially attractive sculptor, he modernized the traditions of classical sculpture in an appropriately sentimental fashion. For this he was awarded a Grand Prize for Sculpture at the Universal Exposition of 1900.

*BOURDELLE, Emile Antoine. French. Born 1861 in Montauban; died 1929 in Le Vésinet near Paris. He sculpted a monument, installed at Pointe de Grave, to Americans who died in World War I. Examples of his work may be seen at the Metropolitan and Brooklyn Museums, New York. See pages 134 to 146.

*BRANCUSI, Constantin. Rumanian by birth, he became a French citizen in 1957. Born in Pestisani, near Targu-Jiu (Rumania), February 21, 1876; died in Paris, March 16, 1957. Brancusi's youth was one of hardship; he faced it with the lifelong strength and patience that were expressed in his work. In 1902 he left his country to look for work, making his way on foot to Munich, then to Zurich and Basel. He had just completed four years of study at the School of Fine Arts in Bucharest, to which he had been admitted on a scholarship. In 1904 he arrived in Paris and studied in Antonin Mercié's class at the Ecole des Beaux-Arts. Several sculptures from that period, however, especially the *Head of a Young Boy,* show the stronger influence of Rodin. He sent his first sculpture to the Salon in 1906 and, in the same year, three plaster busts to the Salon d'Automne. The following year, some pieces exhibited at the National Society of Fine Arts attracted the attention of Rodin, who asked him to come to work for him. Brancusi turned down this offer, however, preferring to keep his freedom. He also may have hesitated to submit to the influence of Rodin, although he was soon to free himself of it in any case. During the difficult period that followed he was reduced to taking menial jobs such as that of dishwasher in a restaurant near one of the central railway stations. In a few short years, however, he had laid the foundations of his art, based on a

synthetic stylization of the object. By 1909, his sculpture had developed in a direction which was to make Brancusi one of the founders of a daring aesthetic conception which fostered many of today's trends in abstract sculpture. See page 231. He exhibited at the Salon des Indépendants and took part in the 1913 Armory Show in New York. His first one-man show was also held in New York, in 1914, at Alfred Stieglitz's Gallery 291. In 1920, one of his sculptures, *Princess X,* created a scandal at the Salon des Indépendants. It was judged obscene and had to be removed from the exhibition halls. In 1926, he again exhibited in New York, at the Brummer Gallery. The U.S. Customs officials, still unfamiliar with the new forms of abstract sculpture, refused to regard *Bird in Flight* as a work of art and accused Brancusi of trying to smuggle copper into the United States. In 1937, he went to Rumania, where he designed a number of sculptures for a public park in Targu-Jiu, and to India, where the Maharajah of Indore had asked him to design a small temple. This last project never materialized, however. Brancusi traveled in 1925, 1928 and 1939 to the United States, where he already had many American admirers of long standing. The collector John Quinn, in particular, was one of the first to buy his sculpture; by 1925 he already owned some 30 pieces. Finally, in 1955, a large retrospective show was held in the Guggenheim Museum. The sculptor bequeathed his works to the Museum of Modern Art in Paris, on condition that the Museum duplicate his studio in the Impasse Ronsin.

*BURCKHARDT, Carl. Swiss. Born 1878 in Lindau; died 1923 in Ligornetto. First studied in Basel. Devoted himself to painting while in Munich from 1897 to 1899, then switched to sculpture during various stays in Rome and Capri between 1900 and 1904. One of his first major works was a set of fountains adorned with statues, done in Basel between 1914 and 1921. His *Saint George,* also in Basel, his *Dancer,* and the *Amazon,* executed for a bridge on the Rhine, are his last sculptures. These were done in Ligornetto, in Italian Switzerland, between 1921 and 1923. Following an "archaic" period, Burckhardt adopted a simplified, monumental style which managed to avoid the merely decorative. Two large retrospective exhibitions of his work, one at the Berne Kunsthalle in 1952, and another at the Venice Biennale in 1954, have been organized.

*CARPEAUX, Jean-Baptiste. French. Born 1827 in Valenciennes; died 1875 in Courbevoie. See pages 64 to 76. His chief sculptures are in the Louvre and the Petit Palais in Paris, the Carpeaux Museum in Valenciennes and the Château de Compiègne, north of Paris, also in New York and Washington, D.C.

CARRIER-BELLEUSE, Albert Ernest. French. Born 1824 in Anizy-le-Château; died 1887 in Paris. During an early apprenticeship as engraver and silversmith he acquired a lifelong taste for small-scale work.

His skill was displayed in elegantly mannered pieces inspired by minor eighteenth-century masters. He was admitted to the Ecole des Beaux-Arts in 1840 upon David d'Angers' recommendation. In 1850, he first exhibited in the Salon. From 1851 to 1855 he ran a school of design in England, training decorators for a Staffordshire porcelain factory. Carrier-Belleuse also designed a considerable number of pieces in ceramics. During the Second Empire he became celebrated for his small busts and terra cotta figures. He also executed a few large allegorical statues and monuments: *Masséna* in Nice, *Alexandre Dumas* in Villers-Cotteret, *General San Martino* in Buenos Aires, etc. He also worked on the Palais des Tuileries, the Hôtel de Ville in Paris, the Comédie Française, the Paris Opera House and La Païva's town house. In 1875, he was appointed head of the department of design at the Sèvres porcelain factory.

CHAPU, Henri Michel Antoine. French. Born 1833; died 1891. A pupil of James Pradier and of Francisque Duret, an officially recognized sculptor. His academic conceptions, remotely inspired by the Renaissance, resulted in a highly conventional sculpture, of which the best-known examples are *Mercury Inventing the Caduceus* and *Joan of Arc at Domrémy*.

*CHAUVIN, Louis. French. Born March 30, 1889 at Rochefort-sur-Mer. Came to Paris in 1908. Attended classes at the Ecole des Arts Décoratifs and studied sculpture in Antonin Mercié's studio at the Ecole des Beaux-Arts. Later worked with Joseph Bernard until 1914. Exhibited at the Salon d'Automne and the Salon des Indépendants from 1920 on. First one-man show in 1928 at the Sacre du Printemps Gallery, first inclusive exhibit, in 1949, at the Galerie Maeght, in Paris. Though one of the first to experiment with abstract sculpture, he remained little known until recently, and has participated in major exhibitions organized in Amsterdam, Zurich, Yverdon and Antwerp only during the last ten years. For chief particulars on his work, see pages 234 to 235.

CLARÁ, José. Spanish. Born 1878 in Catalonia. Came to France to study sculpture, first at the Toulouse School of Fine Arts, then in Paris, where he worked for Rodin and was influenced by him. In 1903 he exhibited at the Salon des Artistes Français, in 1905 in London and Italy, and later at the Salon des Tuileries. His sensitively modeled sculpture includes excellent heads, which are restrained and expressive, small figures of dancers and sculptures on literary themes such as *The Enigma, Torment,* etc. Most of these are in the collections of the Madrid and Barcelona museums. A *Goddess* stands on the Plaza de Catalonia in Barcelona.

CLAUDEL, Camille. French. Born 1856 in Fère-en-Tardenois; died 1920. The work executed during the years of her stormy relationship with Rodin, reflects, in its undeniable technical excellence, ex-

pressive power, energy and intellectual content, the spirit of her master. Several of her sculptures, *Abandon* (1888), *Clotho* (1893), and *Maturity* (1899) are in the collection of the Rodin Museum in Paris.

CLÉSINGER, Jean-Baptiste Auguste. French. Born 1814 in Besançon; died 1883. Studied with Thorvaldsen in Rome. Had romantic longings, but an academic sensitivity. Best known for his *Woman Bitten by a Snake,* exhibited in the 1847 Salon; also executed a *Bacchante,* a *Sappho* and many polychrome busts and statues such as *Phryné*. He was George Sand's son-in-law.

COLTON, William Robert. English. Born 1867; died 1921. First studied at Lambeth, then came to Paris, where he exhibited in 1914 at the Salon des Artistes Français. His sensitive, powerful work, including *Ondine* and *The Springtime of Life,* was visibly influenced by Rodin. They may be seen in the Tate Gallery, London.

*COURBET, Gustave. French. Born June 10, 1819 at Ornans; died December 31, 1877 at La Tour-de-Peilz, Switzerland. The leading painter of the French Realist school, he executed only a very few pieces of sculpture toward the end of his life; all are quite classical in style. See pages 30–31 and 171.

*CREEFT, José de. Spanish. Born 1884 in Guadalajara. Began his technical training in a Barcelona foundry, then worked from 1903 to 1904 with an officially recognized sculptor, Don Agustin Querol, in Madrid. In 1905 he went to Paris, settled in Montmartre and, on Rodin's advice, attended the Académie Julian. In 1911 he began carving in stone. This was to become his favorite medium and one in which he excelled. From Cubism he derived his characteristic squat block shapes, sometimes oddly combined with a conception of movement derived from Oriental art. In 1919 he began exhibiting in the various Paris Salons. His work is, however, better known in the United States, where he settled in 1929. He has exhibited frequently in New York since his first exhibition at the Ferargil Gallery in 1932, and most of his major works are now in the collection of the major New York museums (Metropolitan, Modern Art, Whitney). He executed his *Poet* (1950) for the Fairmount Park Association, Philadelphia, and in 1958 his *Alice in Wonderland* was erected in Central Park.

CSAKY, Joseph. Hungarian by birth, became a French citizen in 1922. Born in Szeged in 1888. After briefly attending the School of Decorative Arts in Budapest, he went to Paris in 1908, where, distrusting any form of instruction, he began to work on his own. After a few tentative experiments, he became, in 1911, one of the first sculptors to turn to Cubism. His contributions to the Salon de l'Automne and the Salon des Indépendants aroused the hostility of critics and public alike. After fighting in the French Army during the First World War, he joined the group of Cubist sculptors sponsored by Léonce Rosenberg. In 1920 he began to exhibit, together with Lipchitz, Laurens and Lambert-Rucki, in Rosenberg's gallery on the Rue de La Baume. He was later to break away from Cubism, though not without considerable difficulty and, one suspects, a feeling of regret. Though temporarily drawn to abstraction, he finally turned to a very subdued form of figurative sculpture. The Kröller-Müller Rijksmuseum in Otterlo, Holland possesses an interesting group of Csaky's work, composed of two polychrome reliefs from the 1920's, fourteen pieces of sculpture from his Cubist period and two bronzes done in 1945.

*DALOU, Jules. French. Born 1838 in Paris; died in Paris, 1902. Worked with Carpeaux and, in 1854, entered Duret's class at the Ecole des Beaux-Arts. First exhibited at the Salon in 1867. His political activities forced him to leave France in 1871; he did not return until after the amnesty of 1879. He was one of the instigators of the Salon des Dissidents held on the Champ-de-Mars in 1880. Among his best-known works are *The Triumph of the Republic* (Place de la Nation), the *Eugène Delacroix Memorial* (Luxembourg Gardens), a statue of *Blanqui* (Père-Lachaise Cemetery), *Mirabeau Replying to Monsieur de Dreux-Brézé* (a relief in the French National Assembly) and a statue of *Lavoisier* (in the Sorbonne). See pages 84–85.

DANTAN, Jean-Pierre, called Dantan the younger. French. Born 1800; died 1869. A skillful sculptor known chiefly for his amusing little caricatures of contemporary figures, a form in which Daumier, however, displayed far greater power and originality. Dantan's work is represented in the collection of the Carnavalet Museum in Paris.

*DAUMIER, Honoré. French. Born in Marseilles, February 26, 1808; died in Valmondois, February 11, 1879. See pages 57 to 64. The complete collection of Daumier's 36 small bronze busts and his *Ratapoil*, are in the Museum of Fine Arts in Marseilles. A bronze *Self-Portrait* is in the Print Department of the Bibliothèque Nationale.

*DAVID D'ANGERS, pseudonym for DAVID, Pierre-Jean. Born in Angers, March 12, 1788; died in Paris, January 6, 1856. See pages 48–52.

*DEGAS, Edgar. French. Born 1834 in Paris; died 1917 in Paris. See pages 171–178.

DEJEAN, Louis. French. Born 1872; died 1953 in Paris. While some of this artist's *Bathers* and a *Pilaster* composed of intertwined bodies recall Rodin, with whom he studied; his small terra cotta figures of women in the long-skirted dresses of 1900 are reminiscent of Tanagra figurines. His *Nudes* scarcely

depart from the classical tradition of which he was a belated and rather unexciting disciple.

DERAIN, André. French. Born 1880 in Chatou; died 1954 in Chambourcy. Derain's sculpture constituted a relatively incidental aspect of his career and bore no aesthetic relationship to his painting. In 1906 he first began to carve large stone figures of a rather crude kind which did not seem to reveal any special gift for this medium. Apart from two masks forged from shell-casings during the First World War, Derain did no more sculpture for many years. Between 1939 and the year of his death, he modeled a series of small figures and masks which have since been cast in bronze. Their simplified forms were inspired by various primitive art forms.

*DESPIAU, Charles. French. Born in Mont-de-Marsan, November 4, 1874; died in Paris, October 28, 1946. He arrived in Paris in 1891, entered the School of Decorative Arts and continued at the Beaux-Arts under Barrias. He then went to work for Schnegg and, in 1907, became one of Rodin's best assistants, remaining with him for seven years. He showed in all the main Salons—Artistes Français, Société Nationale des Beaux-Arts, Salon d'Automne —as well as the Salon des Tuileries, of which he was one of the charter members. His quiet, sensitive classicism underwent little change between his first publicly exhibited work—a head of a *Girl from the Landes* (1904)—to the nudes and busts done toward the end of his life. The Museum of Modern Art in Paris has some of his best work—the bust of *Paulette*, several portraits of women, *Eve* (1925) and *Assia* (1937). This bronze nude sums up Despiau's most characteristic qualities: balance, gracefulness, a delicate sensuality and a certain tone of seriousness which prevails in all his work. See pages 157–160.

DRIVIER, Léon Ernest. French. Born 1878 in Grenoble; died 1951 in Paris. The technical strength and poise of his statues attest to a lifelong devotion to the dignity and purity of classicism. Many of Drivier's sculptures, such as his female torsos, *Adolescence*, the busts of *Mademoiselle J.J.* and *Madame X.* in the Museum of Modern Art in Paris, as well as the group known as *The Joy of Living* in the gardens of the Palais de Chaillot, demonstrate that despite Rodin's teachings, he never completely forgot that he had once studied at the Beaux-Arts with the highly academic Barrias.

DUBOIS, Paul. French. Born 1829; died 1905. A perfect example of the officially recognized sculptor, devoid of any personality whatsoever, highly successful and showered with honors. First exhibited at the Salon in 1857. Entered the Ecole des Beaux-Arts in 1858. Studied painting with Henner and acquired a reputation as a portrait painter. In 1859 he traveled to Italy and returned convinced that he could equal the sculptors of the Renaissance. In any case, he acquired his extravagantly high reputation by imitating their work. He received countless commissions for busts and monuments; among the best-known are his statue of *Joan of Arc*, now in the Place Saint-Augustin in Paris, the *Virgin* in Trinity Church in Paris, the General Lamoricière Memorial in Nantes Cathedral, and the tombstone of the *Duke d'Aumale* in Chantilly. He was appointed curator of the Luxembourg Museum in Paris in 1873, was elected to the Institute in 1876, made director of the Ecole des Beaux-Arts in 1878 and awarded the Grand Cordon of the Legion of Honor in 1906.

*DUCHAMP-VILLON, pseudonym for DU-CHAMP, Raymond. French. Born 1876 at Damville; died 1918 in Cannes. After graduating from a Rouen *lycée,* he intended to become a doctor. This ambition was thwarted by illness, however, and he turned to sculpture instead. His first sculptures were a *Reclining Nude*, exhibited at the Société Nationale des Beaux-Arts in 1904, *Woman Reading*, in marble, a group of plaster *Soccer Players*, and a bronze bust of his father shown in 1905 at the Salon d'Automne. Although briefly influenced by Rodin, he soon developed a more synthetic and architectonic style, of which his *Baudelaire* (1911) constituted an early, significant example. He then joined forces to some extent with the Cubists, as did his painter-brothers, Marcel Duchamp and Jacques Villon. In 1912 Duchamp-Villon and André Mare built a large model of a "Cubist house." For an analysis of his principal sculptures—*Maggy, Seated Woman, Horse's Head,* etc.—see pages 219–222. Duchamp-Villon died of blood poisoning at the end of the First World War, leaving only a few works of sculpture. They suffice, nevertheless, to establish his reputation as one of the most original artists of the early part of the century, as one of the most rigorous and intelligent in his approach to the problems of modern sculptural technique.

DUMONT, Augustin Alexandre. French. Born 1801; died 1884. The Dumont family had produced an unbroken line of sculptors since the seventeenth century. His thoroughly traditional and highly academic work would be completely unknown today, except to visitors of the Saumur Museum, where most of it is on display, had he not designed the winged *Spirit of Freedom* which crowns the *July Column* in the Place de la Bastille in Paris.

DUNIKOWSKI, Xavery. Polish. Born 1875 in Cracow. Taught at the Warsaw School of Fine Arts just after the turn of the century. His lyrical, symbolist sculptures express the basic situations of human destiny: suffering, despair, etc. He worked chiefly in wood; volumes and surfaces are greatly simplified, while gestures and attitudes are extremely mannered, theatrically emphasizing the artist's literary intentions, as in *Motherhood* (1900), *The Breath* (1901), and *Fatum* (1901) in the Warsaw National

Museum. He also designed the *Tomb of King Boleslav Smialy* (1916–1917) and several pieces of sculpture for the portal of the Jesuit Church in Cracow.

*DUPRÉ, Giovanni. Italian. Born 1817 in Siena; died 1882. In its diversity, Dupré's sculpture expresses several Italian traditions. Neoclassicism, with its sleek nudes and noble poses, is represented in his *Sappho* (Galleria Nazionale d'Arte Moderna, Rome); academicism, at its most official, is typified by his *Cavour Monument* (in a Turin square). The two prevalent types of "verism"—insipid, as in his *Sant' Antonio,* or melodramatic, as in his *Cain,* are also represented. Both these pieces are in Florence. He also executed a *Mater Dolorosa* and a *Judgment of Savonarola*. His studio in Florence has been converted into a Dupré Museum.

DURET, Francisque Joseph. French. Born 1804; died 1865. The praise heaped upon Duret's contributions to the Salon (especially upon his *Fisherboy Dancing the Tarantella*) brought him numerous government commissions and many students. He executed several allegorical statues and designed the *Saint-Michel Fountain* in Paris.

DU SEIGNEUR, Jean. French. Born 1808; died 1866. One of the last romantic sculptors. Famous in his day for his statue of *Orlando Furioso*. Published several books on the history of sculpture.

EPSTEIN, Sir Jacob. British subject, of Russian-Polish parents. Born 1880 in New York; died 1959 in London. First worked in a foundry, studied at the Art Students League in New York and at the Ecole des Beaux-Arts and the Académie Julian after arriving in Paris in 1902. Settled in London in 1905. His first important work was the execution, in 1908, of 18 statues for the British Medical Association which shocked the extremely conventional English public. In 1911, during another stay in Paris, he received a commission to design the tomb of *Oscar Wilde* in the Père-Lachaise Cemetery. Encounters with Brancusi and with Paris *avant-garde* circles seem to have influenced his sculpture. It was during this period, lasting until 1915, that he executed his most original work, including *The Rock Drill* (1913), a plaster figure mounted on a real drill. This was exhibited in the London Group at the Goupil Gallery in 1915. Although he was, for some years, somewhat tempted by the development of an abstract art, he nevertheless reverted to a more classical style, frequently of a tormented and expressionist kind, often of an archaic character. This is particularly evident in his large-scale pieces, which reveal technical skill rather than creative power. His numerous portraits (of *Einstein, Joseph Conrad, Nehru, George Bernard Shaw,* among others) constitute one of the most interesting aspects of his work. They are powerfully expressive, and their vigorous, highly animated surfaces generate a play of light. Epstein executed sev

257

eral sculptures inspired by religious themes: *The Visitation* (1926), *Madonna and Child,* which was erected in 1951 in the convent of The Holy Child Jesus, in Cavendish Square, a *Christ in Majesty* (1957), etc. One of his last works was executed for the Trade Unions Congress Building in 1958. After a lifetime of violent criticism in England, Epstein was showered with honors; he was knighted in 1954. Several of his works are included in the collection of the Tate Gallery in London and of the Metropolitan Museum of Art in New York.

*ERNST, Max. German, acquired American citizenship in 1948, French citizenship in 1958. Born in Brühl, on the Rhine, 1891. Studied at the University of Bonn. As he himself has observed, his early painting betrayed signs of "the most contradictory influences," ranging from Goya to Van Gogh and from Macke to Kandinsky. Painting was to become his major form of expression, but in 1913 he produced his first work of sculpture, *The Lovers,* carved in wood. That same year he exhibited in the first Herbstsalon in Berlin. His meeting with Arp in 1914 and with the Zurich Dadaists a few years later led him to participate in the founding of the W/3 Dada Central in Cologne in 1919. His work of that period includes lithographs, collages, painted wood-reliefs and a *Dad'art Object* composed in mixed media. He also exhibited in two Dada exhibitions held in Cologne. The second, in 1912, was closed by the police. In 1922, he settled in Paris and became one of the ringleaders of the Surrealist movement. His painting is inspired by a lifelong fidelity to Surrealism; indeed, it constitutes one of the most important achievements of this movement. It was in 1935 that his sculpture began to develop. His solidly balanced, smooth-surfaced plaster and bronze sculptures evoke a universe dominated by a basic ambiguity between man and object, between man and beast. His anthropomorphic figures are animated by a certain humor; more generally, however, they have the disturbing qualities of the idol or the magical object. His horned, round-eyed figures have a power of intense fascination; their bodies are imprisoned in a geometry which seems to dissimulate their inner violence. In 1938, Max Ernst executed a series of large sculptural murals for his home in Saint-Martin-d'Ardèche. He resigned from the Surrealist group. During the war, under pressure from the Gestapo (he had been outlawed by the Nazi party as early as 1933), he left for America where he remained until 1949. In 1947 and 1948, he executed a series of large, decorative cement figures (the *Capricorn* group) for the land surrounding the small pine-wood house he had built for himself at Sedona, in Arizona. Max Ernst is particularly interested in the problem of sculpture designed for an open-air setting, and in 1935 he had already engraved the smooth surfaces of a series of large, ovoid stones, taken from a river bed, for the garden of Alberto Giacometti, in Maloja, Switzerland. Twenty sculptures were included in the large retrospective exhibition organized in 1959 at the Museum of Modern Art in Paris. His chief works in this form were also exhibited in 1961 at the Museum of Modern Art in New York and at the Galerie du Point Cardinal in Paris in 1962. In 1959 he began to design a very fine series of small masks, executed in gold and in silver by the goldsmith, François Hugo. Max Ernst and his wife, Dorothea Tanning, now live in Paris and in Huismes, Touraine.

ETEX, Antoine. French. Born 1808; died 1888. The neoclassical sculptor responsible for the two groups *Peace* and *War* at the sides of the Arch of Triumph, *Hercules Stifling Antaeus, Bacchus and Ino, The Ship-Wreck,* the *Vauban Monument,* and portraits of *Proudhon, The Duke of Orleans, Alfred de Vigny,* etc. See page 41.

FALGUIÈRE, Jean-Alexandre Joseph. French. Born 1831 in Toulouse; died 1900. Son of a mason. In 1854, entered the Ecole des Beaux-Arts where he studied with Jouffroy. First exhibited in the Salon of 1857. Awarded the First Grand Prix de Rome for sculpture in 1859. His academic style, which wavered between a platitudinous severity and a feeble sentimentality was undoubtedly responsible for his huge success. Principal works: *The Winner of the Cockfight, Ophelia, Lamartine, Progress Overcoming Error, Saint Vincent de Paul, Woman with Peacock, Lafayette* (Washington, D.C.), and an extremely insipid *Balzac* which was erected in Paris, on the Avenue de Friedland, without encountering any of the difficulty created by Rodin's masterpiece. His most original—and ephemeral—creation was a colossal statue of *The Resistance* modeled in snow on the ramparts of Paris in December, 1870. For additional details, see page 80.

*FENOSA, Apel'les. Spanish. Born 1899 in Barcelona. Spent a period of apprenticeship in the studio of Casanovas, a Barcelona sculptor, where he executed his first sculptures. His style, which was characterized by an early attachment to a rather placid classicism, rapidly developed an animation and sensitivity which is responsible for the vigor and delicacy of his bronze heads and figures. Fenosa went to live in Paris in 1921, exhibited in 1925 at the Percier Gallery, in 1928 at Zborowsky's and in 1931, 1933 and 1936 at the Maragall Gallery in Barcelona. In 1945, he designed the *Monument for Oradour-sur-Glane.* His portraits (of *Cocteau, Paul Eluard, Colette, Jean Genet,* among others), are rather naturalistic in style, but his female figures are subjected to a poetic metamorphosis; they inhabit a semivegetable kingdom in which the human body is identified with forms of a leaflike character. In 1956, he executed a *Christ* for a church in Friburg. Other exhibitions include those organized in 1960 at the Rosenberg Gallery in New York and in 1961 at the Galerie Jacques Dubourg in Paris.

FERRARI, Ettore. Italian. Born 1849; died 1930. His work contains elements of romanticism, academicism and, on occasion, a certain dramatic realism. Principal sculptures include a *Giordano Bruno* in the Campo dei Fiori in Rome, a statue of *Abraham Lincoln* in the Metropolitan Museum, New York, the group known as *Cum Spartaco Pugnavit* in the Galleria d'Arte Moderna in Rome, and several official monuments.

FORD, Edward Onslow. English. Born 1852; died 1901. A faithful traditionalist, the designer of the *Queen Victoria Monument* in Manchester, statues of *Irving, Gordon, Huxley* and *Shelley's Tomb* in Oxford.

FOYATIER, Denis. French. Born 1793; died 1863. The simple wood figurines carved during his youth, while working as a shepherd, probably had considerably more charm than the ambitious compositions executed after he had completed his training at the Ecole des Beaux-Arts. These include *The Athlete Astydamas Saving Lucilia and her Children from the Destruction of Herculaneum.* The damage wrought by a neoclassical training was also responsible for a *Spartacus* which was honored by admission to the Louvre Museum and the equestrian statue of *Joan of Arc* erected in Orléans.

FRÉMIET, Emmanuel. French. Born 1824 in Paris; died 1910 in Paris. After varied and insecure periods of apprenticeship to a painter of animal subjects, as a retoucher of anatomical pieces for the collection of the Orfila Museum, then as a modeler of commercial religious statuettes, he entered Rude's studio. He became, nonetheless, an officially recognized sculptor, won numerous medals at the Salon, received several decorations and was finally elected to the Academy of Fine Arts. His work includes a *Napoleon,* a *Joan of Arc* (there is a replica of this in Fairmount Park, Philadelphia), a *Grand Condé,* a *Colonel Howard* (Baltimore), various animal figures and the *Pegases* which are mounted on the pylons of the Alexander III Bridge in Paris. In 1875, he succeeded Barye as Professor of Zoological Draftsmanship at the Museum of Natural History.

*FREUNDLICH, Otto. German. Born 1878 in Stolp, Pomerania; died in a concentration camp in Poland, 1943. Studies in art history, begun at the University of Munich and continued while in Florence in 1905, led him to painting and sculpture. He arrived in Paris in 1908 and soon settled in the Bateau Lavoir in Montmartre. "After two years of work," he wrote, "I began, completely on my own, to use colored planes of a sharply defined and purely constructive kind, completely eliminating naturalist or Impressionist elements. I have remained faithful to this technique since 1908. My first abstract canvases date from 1911." Freundlich later applied this purely constructive technique, "eliminating all naturalist elements," to his work in three dimensions, thereby becoming an abstract sculptor. The *Mask of a Man* and *Bust of a Woman,* executed in bronze in 1908, and a plaster *Mask* of 1910, exhibited in the New Secession Group in Berlin and the *Sonderbund* in Cologne, still bear the marks of classicism; they reveal, however, a concern with simplification and an accentuation of certain volumes which later evolved into a style of a very personal kind, of a massive and somewhat "barbarous" aspect, visible in the bronze *Mask* of 1915. In 1918 he executed a large mosaic. His interest in this technique and in that of stained glass was later revived. He exhibited in the *Novembergruppe* in Berlin and, after 1924, in the Salon des Surindepéndants in Paris. He participated, as well, in museum exhibitions organized in Amsterdam, the Hague, Zurich, Basel, at the Guggenheim Gallery in London, the Galerie Jeanne Bucher in Paris and with the *Abstraction-Création* group in Paris. In 1929, his sculpture, which had become completely abstract, began to assume a monumental aspect. The large composition entitled *Elevation,* which was cast in bronze in 1932, is a cluster of stones which spring from an agglomeration of elements that act as a pedestal. In *The New Man,* which figured in the exhibition of "Degenerate Art" organized by the Nazis, and in other sculptures done in 1933 and 1934, there is evidence of an increasingly architectonic concern. Indeed, Freundlich was interested in developing this aspect in the construction of what he termed "Sculpture-Mountains," designed to be placed in the open air, integrated into a country landscape and explored by the beholder. He had opened an art school known as "The Wall" in his studio in the Rue Denfert-Rochereau (now the Rue Henri Barbusse), in Paris. During the German occupation he fled to Saint-Martin-de Fenouillet in the eastern Pyrenees. He was arrested and deported to Poland, never to return.

*GABO, pseudonym for PEVSNER, Naum. Russian. Born 1890 in Briansk. Studied medicine in Munich. Early interests in mathematics and physical sciences. Wölfflin's lectures on art history and the discovery of certain *avant-garde* movements, including *Der Blaue Reiter,* stimulated his interest in art. In 1912, he traveled to Italy and, the following year, to Paris, where his brother, Antoine Pevsner, was studying painting. At the outbreak of the war in 1914, he went to Scandinavia. His first sculptures were done in Oslo, in 1915. These included heads and a torso, an assemblage of several materials: metal, wood, celluloid, etc., done according to a technique which closely resembled that used by Archipenko. Returning to Russia in 1917, he participated in *avant-garde* demonstrations in Moscow, with Malevitch and Tatlin. In 1920, he drew up the *Realist Manifesto,* which proclaimed the necessity of an integration into sculpture of the notion of space, signified by transparency, and a notion of time, expressed by kinetic rhythm. At this time he executed his first "kinetic sculpture," animated by a vibrating movement created by an electric

259

motor. At the same time, he continued to construct reliefs in plastic materials and worked on a project for a bronze and glass monument for the Institute of Physics and Mathematics. He left the U.S.S.R. in 1922 and settled for ten years in Berlin where he took part in the activities of the Constructivist movement and was represented in the *Novembergruppe* exhibitions. He remained faithful to the use of metal and transparent materials, developing the architectonic character of abstract compositions done in an angular geometric style. In 1927, Gabo and Antoine Pevsner did the décor and costumes for Diaghilev's Russian Ballet. In 1930, he showed a group of sculptures at the *Kestnergesellschaft* in Hanover. In Paris, from 1932 to 1935, he joined the *Abstraction-Création* group. He then went to live in England, remaining there until 1946. Preoccupied by the problem of achieving a greater suppleness in his work, he developed a technically ingenious system of curved, overlapping surfaces obtained by a juxtaposition of plastic or metal wires. Gabo settled in the United States in 1946 and now resides in Middlebury, Connecticut. He has continued his experiments in large-scale sculpture and perfected the technique of mixed media. His work is characterized by its boldness, and represents, in its purity and mysterious complexity, one of the most important modern contributions to the exploration of significant sculptural form. Gabo's work is represented in the collection of the Museum of Modern Art in New York, which organized a retrospective exhibition of work by the Pevsner brothers in 1948. In 1949 he designed a monument in plastic and metal for Rockefeller Center. Another large-scale work in steel, executed in 1957, stands in front of the Bijenkorf department store in Rotterdam.

*GARGALLO, Pablo. Spanish. Born 1881 in Maella; died 1934 in Reus. For biographical and other details, see pages 206–209. Four retrospective exhibitions of this artist's work have been organized: in 1935, at the Museum of Modern Art in Madrid and at the Salon d'Automne in Paris; in 1947, at the Museum of the Petit Palais in Paris; in 1955, at the Venice Biennale. Sculptures by Gargallo are to be seen in the collections of the following museums: The Museum of Modern Art and the Metropolitan Museum in New York; the Museum of France Art Institute in Philadelphia; the Museum of Modern Art in Baltimore; the Museums of Modern Art in Paris, Madrid, Barcelona and Brussels.

*GAUDIER-BRZESKA, pseudonym for GAUDIER, Henri. French. Born 1891 in Saint-Jean-de Braye; killed in the First World War at Neuville-Saint-Vaast, 1915. Son of a cabinet-maker and wood-carver. Upon completion of his studies in Orléans, he obtained a scholarship for study in England. In 1908 he spent some time in London and Bristol. He traveled to Germany in 1909, then to Paris, where, in 1910, he began to work at sculpture. His relationship with Sophie Brzeska, whose

name he added to his own, dates from this time. The following year he left for London. He took part in the Vorticist and London Group exhibitions at the Goupil Gallery. It was chiefly in England (where he spent the last years of his life before leaving for the French front, where he was killed) that Gaudier-Brzeska left the imprint of an *oeuvre* which, though limited, contributed to the renewal of sculptural form. The style and technique of his early sculpture were classical, but developed, in 1913 and 1914, after a period of somewhat hesitant experimentation, toward the creation of small, schematic figures which constitute a transition toward the condensation of Cubism and the simplicity of abstraction. A commemorative exhibition was held in London, at the Leicester Galleries, in 1918. The Museum of Fine Arts in Orléans organized a retrospective exhibition of his work in 1956. His sculpture is represented in the Tate Gallery in London and the Museum of Modern Art in New York.

*GAUGUIN, Paul. French. Born 1848 in Paris; died at Atuana, in the Marquesas, 1903. For a discussion of his sculpture, see pages 181–185.

GAUL, August. German. Born 1869 in Gross-Auheim. Died 1921 in Berlin. Son of a stonecutter. After serving a period of apprenticeship to a goldsmith and studying at the Academy of Design in Hanau, he was admitted in 1893 to the Academy of Fine Arts in Berlin; there he studied with Reinhold Begas until 1898. He was awarded the Prix de Rome and exhibited at the Berlin Secession. It was at this point that he established his lifelong reputation as an animal sculptor. The calm realism of his work is far removed from Barye's romanticism; it is equally dissimilar to the somewhat Impressionist sensitivity of Renée Sintenis, another German sculptor of animal subjects. His restraint is well suited to the monumental style of the fountains designed for Krefeld, Charlottenburg and Königsberg. The museums of Berlin, Bremen and Hamburg possess several of his sculptures.

GEEFS, Guillaume. Belgian. Born 1806 in Antwerp; died 1883 in Brussels. Studied at the Academy of Fine Arts in Antwerp, where he was awarded the Grand Prize for Sculpture in 1828. He later became a member of the faculty. He designed monuments, typical of the prevailingly academic and conventional style of the period, for the public squares of several Belgian towns, and for the museums of Antwerp, Liège and Douai. These include *Genevieve of Brabant, Rubens, Leopold I,* the *Count of Mérode* and *General Béliard.*

*GEISER, Karl. Swiss. Born 1898 in Berne; died 1957 in Zurich. Entirely self-taught. In 1920, after a period of residence in Berlin, he settled in Zurich, where he remained for the rest of his life. His work shows occasional traces of a classicism characterized by a mixture of grace and heaviness which recalls that of Maillol. Certain *Nudes, Female Figures* and *Young Girls* are remarkable for the sensitivity of their facial expressions and postures and for the sensitive modeling of their surfaces. He traveled to Rome in 1932. In 1937, he completed a *Group of Three Young Girls* and in 1938, the *Group of Three Boys* designed for the Berne *Gymnasium*. A large one-man show of his work was held in Winterthur in 1941. At the time of his death in his Zurich studio, he left a number of large, incompleted pieces: a *David*, which had been commissioned by the town of Soleure, the *Memorial of the Bombardment of Schaffhausen* and a *Labor Monument*. Exhibitions devoted to the work of Geiser were organized in Antwerp in 1957, in Arnhem in 1958. That same year a complete retrospective exhibition was held in Basel.

*GEMITO, Vincenzo. Italian. Born 1852 in Naples; died 1929. Studied with Stanislas Lista. His sculpture, a real synthesis of all the stylistic tendencies which succeeded Italian neoclassicism, is dominated by a turn-of-the-century naturalism (see page 88). Between 1879 and 1900 he exhibited frequently in Paris, and achieved considerable fame in his own country. His principal works are to be seen in the museums of Rome, Florence, Milan and Turin.

GÉRÔME, Jean-Léon. French. Born 1824 in Vesoul; died 1904 in Paris. Studied with Paul Delaroche at the Ecole des Beaux-Arts from 1842 to 1844. First exhibited as a painter in the 1847 Salon. Exhibited his first work of sculpture at a rather late date in his career: in 1878. He had, in the meantime, been appointed to a professorship at the Ecole des Beaux-Arts and been elected to the Institute. His academic manner began, at about 1900, to adjust with ease to the style of Art Nouveau. He attempted to revive the ancient technique of chryselephantine sculpture by combining the use of bronze with that of ivory and by coloring his marbles with wax, as in his statues of *Bellone* and *Tanagra* and his bust of *Sarah Bernhardt*. His work includes an equestrian statue of the *Duke of Aumale*, erected in Chantilly in 1899, a *Washington*, exhibited in the Salon of 1901, and a *Dying Eagle* erected in 1904 on the Waterloo battlefield.

GIBSON, John. English. Born 1790 in Gyffin; died 1866 in Rome. Son of a landscape-gardener from Liverpool. Was apprenticed at the age of fourteen to a cabinet-maker, then to a wood-carver and finally, to a marble-mason. His first major work, *Psyche*, was exhibited in Liverpool. Faithful to a neoclassical tradition, he became a student of Canova in Rome. He studied also with Bertel Thorvaldsen. His work abounded in the inevitable *Cupids, Venuses* and *Proserpines*. He received several commissions from the Duke of Devonshire and executed an immense statue of *The Queen of England* (1851), a bust of *The Prince of Wales* (1854), a *Polychrome Venus* and *Love Disguised as a Shepherd*. Gibson's sculpture is represented in the Tate Gallery in London and in the Liverpool and Manchester museums.

GILBERT, Sir Alfred. English. Born 1854; died 1934. Painter and sculptor, the designer of officially commissioned works which eventually won him membership in the Royal Academy. A member of the Society of British Sculptors, he began exhibiting in 1882. A *Monument to Queen Victoria*, in Winchester, another *Monument to the Duke of Clarence* in Windsor, the statue of *Watts* in the National Gallery, are among his principal works.

*GONZALEZ, Julio. Spanish. Born 1876 in Barcelona; died 1942 at Arcueil. For a discussion of his life and work, see pages 209 and 212. Posthumously organized retrospective exhibitions of his work were held in Paris at the Museum of Modern Art in 1952, at the Stedelijk Museum in Amsterdam and the Palais des Beaux-Arts in Brussels, at the Kunsthalle in Berne in 1955, at the Museum of Modern Art in New York and in Philadelphia in 1956.

GRIS, Juan, pseudonym of GONZALEZ, José Victoriano. Spanish. Born 1887 in Madrid; died 1927 in Boulogne-sur-Seine. Primarily a painter, Gris took only a passing interest in sculpture. Among his very few experiments in this medium are a series of small plaster figures, including a *Harlequin* (1917); these illustrate certain aspects of the rigorous Cubism of his painting.

GUILLAUME, Jean-Baptiste Claude Eugène, known as Eugène. French. Born 1822; died 1905. First studied drawing in Dijon, entered the Ecole des Beaux-Arts in Paris in 1841, where he studied with Pradier. Obtained the Prix de Rome in 1845, lived in Italy from 1846 to 1850. His style was partly realistic, but predominantly neoclassical. He designed decorations for the Louvre, the Opera and Saint Clotilda's Church and statues of *Colbert, Ingres, Claude Bernard*. He was elected to the Institute in 1862, became director of the Ecole des Beaux-Arts in 1864, and in 1891, became director of the Beaux-Arts in Rome.

*HALLER, Hermann. Swiss. Born 1880 in Berne; died 1950 in Zurich. First studied architecture and painting in Munich and Stuttgart. In 1901, while traveling in Italy, he made the acquaintance of Paul Klee. He began to work at sculpture while in Rome, in 1905. Settled in Paris in 1907, remaining there until 1914. The development of his work shows a gradual humanizing of a rather cold classicism through a close observation of nature. A certain grace and expressiveness began to be apparent in his portraits and statues of adolescent girls. In 1934, the Florence Academy awarded him a gold medal at the Venice Biennale. In 1949 he was awarded the Grand Prize of the City of Zurich. His *Wadman Monument* was erected in that city. In 1950, he was elected an honorary member of the Munich Academy.

HANAK, Anton. Austrian. Born 1875 in Brünn; died 1934 in Vienna. After learning the technique of wood carving from a cabinet-maker, he studied sculpture at the Vienna Academy. He joined the Viennese Secession Group in 1911 and, in 1914, exhibited a number of large-scale works including *The Creator* and *Transfiguration,* in which literary themes are treated with a characteristic, overemphatic use of gesture which is also visible in both the *Grande Douleur* of 1917 and in the *Elevation* of 1928. His courses at the Vienna Academy were very popular. Sculpture by Hanak is owned by the museums of Vienna and Munich.

*HILDEBRAND, Adolf von. German. Born 1847 in Marburg; died 1921 in Munich. See page 85.

KAFKA, Bohumil. Czechoslovakian. Born 1878 in Nová Paka; died 1942 in Prague. A student of Myslbek, he continued his studies in London and spent some time in Vienna, Berlin and Rome before settling in Prague. In 1902 he exhibited at the Salon de la Société Nationale des Beaux-Arts in Paris. His work evolved from classicism toward a naturalism which occasionally attained considerable expressive power. Among his principal works are the *Madonna of the Shepherds* (1912), the *Borovsky Monument* and a bust of *Masaryk* (1925).

KISSLING, Richard. Swiss. Born 1848 in Wolfwil; died 1919 in Zurich. Studied sculpture in Rome from 1870 to 1883, then settled in Zurich. His conventional sensitivity predestined him to the execution of the austere commemorative monument: *Monument to Alfred Escher* (1889), the bust of *Gottfried Keller* in Zurich, the *Monument to William Tell* (1895) in Altdorf, the *Fontana Monument* in Coire. *The Runner* is in the collection of the Basel Museum.

*KLINGER, Max. German. Born 1857; died 1920. See page 150.

*KOLBE, Georg. German. Born 1877 in Waldheim; died 1947 in Berlin. He first studied painting in Leipzig and Munich. After some time spent in Paris, where he met Rodin, and a journey to Italy he decided to become a sculptor. He went to live in Berlin in 1903, returned to Italy in 1905, traveled to Egypt in 1913. In 1931 he visited Greece. His *Young Girl Standing* was placed in Goethe's house in Frankfort-on-Main. He was awarded the Goethe Prize in 1936. Some of his best-known sculptures include *Awakening* (1911), *The Slave* (1917), *The Annunciation* (1924). Kolbe's sculpture, which had been influenced at first by Rodin, remained predominantly classical in style; it was occasionally somewhat affected, as in his *Groups of Children.* Towards 1933, as he tried to conform to Hitler's "heroic" ideal, his sculpture developed the weaknesses inherent in the monu-

mentality then popular in his country. This is particularly apparent in works such as *Zarathustra* and the *Discobolus.* His best work, however—his nudes and female figures—reveal sensitivity, restraint and a very personal kind of grace. See page 150.

*KOLLWITZ, Käthe. German. Born 1867 in Königsberg; died 1945 in Moritzburg. In 1891 she married a humanitarian doctor and settled in the poor quarter of Berlin. After completing studies in Berlin, Berne and Munich, she studied in Paris, in 1904, at the Académie Julian. Spent the year 1907 in Italy, then settled in Berlin. First interested in painting, she was influenced for some time by the sculpture of Rodin. Her work, like that of Constantin Meunier, is strongly influenced in its choice of subjects by a powerful but rather heavy social realism. Her dramatically expressionist style recalls that of Barlach. Human suffering and misery provided the main themes for her graphic work as well. She was expelled by the Nazis from the Berlin Academy where she had been teaching graphic techniques, but she remained in Germany. Her more characteristic work includes *The War Memorial* in the Essen Cemetery (1932), designed in memory of her son who had been killed in the First World War, the *Tower of the Mothers* (1937), and a *Pietà* (1938).

KURSAWA, Antoine. Polish. Born 1843 in Podhale; died 1898. His sculpture, which shows occasional traces of realism, is actually of a traditionally neo-classical kind. Representative works include *Christ and the Magdalen* (1864), a bust of *Wielogowsky* (1865), *The Kiss of Judas* (1887). The Cracow Museum owns his *Mickiewicz Monument.*

*LACHAISE, Gaston. French. Born 1882 in Paris; died 1935 in New York. Son of a Parisian cabinet-maker. First studied drawing at the Bernard Palissy School, then entered the Ecole des Beaux-Arts. Departed in 1906 for the United States where he remained for the rest of his life. There, he acquired a fame which was never equalled in his native land. After arriving in America, he worked as assistant to two academic sculptors in Boston and New York. He settled in New York in 1912. His first exhibition was held in 1920 at the Bourgeois Gallery. He participated in a show organized by Alfred Stieglitz in 1927 at the Intimate Gallery. A retrospective exhibition was held in 1928 at the Brummer Gallery. His best-known and most characteristic work of sculpture is his athletic *Standing Woman* (1932). Although the impression of intense life and excessive power obtained by a systematic exaggeration of the female form does not, perhaps, express a vision of great refinement, it did, however, stimulate the reaction of young sculptors against the decadent and static aspect of academic sculpture. Lachaise also produced an *Acrobat,* a great many portrait-busts, including those of *Cummings* and *John Marin,* bas-reliefs for Rockefeller Center and the New York Telephone

Building and several *Floating and Flying Figures,* etc. See pages 164 and 165.

LACOMBE, Georges. French. Born 1868 in Versailles; died 1916 in Saint-Nicolas-des-Bois. Studied painting at the Académie Julian. His meeting with Paul Sérusier and other of Gauguin's associates stimulated the development of a rather symbolist style which resulted in sculpture clearly related to the Nabis. Like Gauguin, he worked mainly in wood, and some of his figures and reliefs are polychrome.

*LA FRESNAYE, Roger de. French. Born 1885; died 1925. La Fresnaye, who was primarily a painter, produced only a few works of sculpture; they occupy an important place, however, in the period of transition from Cézanne to Cubism. He attended the Académie Julian in 1903, the Académie de la Grande-Chaumière and, in 1908, the Académie Ranson, where Maillol was then teaching. La Fresnaye's work, including his very first piece of sculpture, an *Eve,* modeled in plaster in 1910 (formerly in the collection of Paul Vera and now in the Museum of Decorative Arts) was briefly influenced by Maillol. Between 1910 and 1912 he executed 10 small figures which constitute all that is known of his sculptural *oeuvre.* A few of these were exhibited in 1910 and 1911 in the Salon des Indépendants and the Salon d'Automne. The *Young Girl Dressing* (1911), reveals a simplification which was accentuated in work of the following year, done in a style which anticipated Cubism. La Fresnaye suffered from a severe case of tuberculosis contracted during a First World War gas-raid and died at the age of forty after a long hospital stay.

LAMBEAUX, Joseph Marie Thomas or Jef. Belgian. Born 1852 in Antwerp; died 1908 in Brussels. Attended the Academy of Fine Arts in Antwerp, worked under Jean Geefs. The realism which was fashionable at the turn of the century is exploited with a characteristically Flemish enthusiasm in a sculpture which celebrates the full-blown sort of female inspired by the painting of Jordaens. Sculpture by Jef Lambeaux is represented in most of the principal Belgian cities: *The Kiss* in Antwerp, *The Wrestlers* in Brussels, etc. The Jubilee Park (or *Parc du Cinquantenaire*) also contains his bas-relief, *Human Passions.*

LAMBERT-RUCKI, Jean. Born 1888 in Poland, acquired French citizenship. After attending the Academy of Fine Arts in Cracow, at that time the cultural center of Poland, he traveled throughout Europe and settled in France. He joined the group known as the *Section d'Or* and exhibited during the 1920's with Léonce Rosenberg, at the Galerie de l'Effort Moderne, together with the Cubist sculptors. He continued in agreement with their ideas for some time, but his sculpture later developed in the direction of a style which retained only a mild geometricization which was applied to compositions of a rather decorative sort. His predilection for subjects of a religious kind procured him several commissions for the decoration of churches in France, Belgium and America. In 1954 he exhibited in the Levitt Gallery, New York.

*LAURENS, Henri. French. Born February 18, 1885 in Paris; died May 8, 1954 in Paris. After a period of apprenticeship to a decorative carver, he worked as a sculptor in construction enterprises. Without any formal instruction, he began to work on his own in clay. He was at first influenced by Rodin but began, in 1911, to work toward a more synthetic style; he remained for the moment uninfluenced by Cubism, despite his meeting with Braque and his group. His work in 1912 was an attempt to achieve a hieratic quality inspired by medieval sculpture. The following year he exhibited at the Salon des Indépendants. Gradually, however, his work began to develop in the direction of Cubism, and in 1915 he executed compositions in sheet metal, plaster and polychrome wood. During his Cubist period, he frequently used color in his stone *Still Lives (Bottle and Glass,* 1919, *Guitar and Clarinet,* 1920*)* and in his work in terra cotta. In 1918, he signed a contract with Léonce Rosenberg and exhibited in his gallery. In 1921, Laurens' Cubism was somewhat modified by the introduction of curved forms (wavy hair, etc.) which prefigured an important change in his style and gave his work a decorative aspect. He seems to have had difficulty in breaking away from Cubism and in finding a new approach to replace the rigor of his own. In contrast to the hardness characteristic of Cubist style, he then began to use excessively relaxed forms which became rather soft and heavy in the stone and marble pieces, the *Reclining Figures* and *Crouching Nudes,* done between 1925 and 1930. His later bronzes are more vigorous; the interplay of contorted forms sometimes results in a highly deformed vision of the female figure, but the curved line remains predominant. Laurens took part in the exhibition of "Cubism and Abstract Art" in New York in 1936, exhibited at the Brummer Gallery 1937, the Art Club in Chicago in 1941 and at the Palais des Beaux-Arts in Brussels in 1949. The Museum of Modern Art in Paris organized a large exhibition of his sculpture in 1951. His decorative motifs in cast iron (1927) are in San Francisco.

*LEHMBRUCK, Wilhelm. German. Born 1881 in Meiderich; died 1919 in Berlin. Son of a miner, worked as a young man in a foundry. From 1895 to 1907, studied at the School of Decorative Arts and the Academy of Fine Arts in Dusseldorf. Traveled to Paris in 1908, and returned to settle there between 1910 and 1914. Exhibited at the Levesque Gallery and at the Salon d'Automne. He traveled to Italy, returned to Berlin, lived for a while in Switzerland, where he exhibited at the Kunsthaus in Zurich. Be-

263

came a member of the Berlin Academy in 1919, committed suicide that same year after working as a nurse in a military hospital in Berlin. See page 161. His sculpture is represented in the Duisberg Museum of Art and the Kunsthalle in Mannheim, Germany, in the Kröller-Müller Rijksmuseum in Otterlo, and at the Museum of Modern Art in New York.

*LIPCHITZ, Jacques. Born 1891 in Druskieniki, Lithuania, acquired French citizenship in 1925. Studied at the School of Business in Bialystok from 1902, and in 1909, completed his studies in Vilna. Went to Paris in October, 1909, and studied at the Ecole des Beaux-Arts where he learned the technique of stone carving. Subsequently studied at the Julian and Colarossi academies. Lived in Belgium in 1911. Went to Russia in 1912 for his military service, then returned to Paris and settled in the Montparnasse quarter. By 1913 his sculpture had acquired a very personal style, still quite removed from that of Cubism, but involving a simplification of forms and the use of sharply defined planes. He exhibited for the first time at the Salon d'Automne *(Woman with Gazelles)*. He had been exempted from military service in his own country and in 1914, he left for Majorca, then spent some time in Madrid. Upon his return to Paris, he executed his first Cubist sculpture and, in 1916, signed a contract with Léonce Rosenberg. His first one-man show was held at Rosenberg's Gallery in 1920. In 1922, he was commissioned to do five reliefs for the Barnes Foundation in Merion, Pennsylvania. His sculpture evolved, nevertheless, toward a somewhat less rigid conception of movement, thereby departing from Cubism. In 1925, his style began to undergo a complete change; his forms became more flexible, he began to pierce his volumes in application of his theory of "transparent" sculpture, and he attempted constructions that were almost purely linear (as in *Man with Guitar,* 1926) but in which the subject remained highly stylized. In 1935, a large exhibition of his work was held at the Brummer Gallery in New York. Although at one time his sculpture seemed, in part, at least, to tend toward abstraction, his large, twisted, rather baroque compositions developed in the direction of a figuration which, though not very realistic, was increasingly emphatic. His *Prometheus Overcoming the Vulture* illustrates this particular development. His studio, which had been installed in New York in 1941, was destroyed by fire in 1950; he then moved to Hastings-on-Hudson, where he still resides. Several exhibitions of Lipchitz's sculpture were held in the Bucholz Gallery, and he received a number of commissions in the United States, including one for a large bas-relief, *The Birth of the Muses,* executed at the request of Mrs. John D. Rockefeller III. Since 1950, a number of American and European museums have exhibited his sculpture, and two large retrospectives were organized at the Museum of Modern Art in New York, in 1954, and at the Museum of Modern Art in Paris, in 1959.

MAGNELLI, Alberto. Italian. Born 1888 in Florence. For a discussion of the sculpture of this painter, whose abstract canvases date from 1915, see pages 199–202. He now lives in Bellevue, near Paris.

*MAILLOL, Aristide. French. Born December 8, 1861 and died September 27, 1944 in Banyuls-sur-Mer. For an account of his life and work, see pages 153 to 157. In 1961, the Museum of Modern Art in Paris, which possesses several of his sculptures, organized a large retrospective exhibition in celebration of the centennial of his birth.

MAINDRON, Hippolyte. French. Born 1801; died 1884. A student of David d'Angers. His highly academic romanticism brought him great success in the mid-nineteenth-century Salons. His work includes a *Shepherd-Boy Stung by a Snake*. He also executed busts of historical figures. The Pantheon in Paris, the Angers and Versailles museums own several of his sculptures.

*MALFRAY, Charles. French. Born 1887 in Orléans; died 1940 in Dijon. See pages 146–147. Several of his sculptures are in the collection of the Museum of Modern Art in Paris. These include *Silence* (1918), *Truth* (1932) and *The Torrent's Source* (1938).

*MANOLO, Manuel, pseudonym for HUGUÉ, Manuel Martinez. Spanish. Born 1876 in Barcelona; died 1945 in Catalonia. See page 168.

MARCKS, Gerhard. German. Born 1889 in Berlin. Studied sculpture with Gaul and Kolbe. His style is largely Expressionist, but more delicate than that of Barlach and imbued with a nostalgia for medieval sculpture. He taught at the Berlin School of Arts and Crafts in 1918, at the Bauhaus in Weimar, from 1920 to 1925, and, finally, in another school on the outskirts of Halle, from which he was expelled in 1933 by the Nazis. He was then forbidden to exhibit his work. It was not until after the war, in 1946, that he was again offered a teaching post, in the Central School of Fine Arts in Hamburg. He executed a series of large-scale figures for Saint Catherine's Church in Lübeck, an *Orpheus* for the theater in Lünen and several monuments in Hamburg, Cologne, Mannheim, etc. Exhibitions of his work were held in several German cities in 1949, and, in 1951, at the Curt Valentin Gallery in New York.

*MAROCHETTI, Baron Carlo. Italian. Born 1805 in Turin; died 1867 in London. He lived for many years in France and in England. Designed a number of historical monuments of imposing size and conventional style. In Paris, where he studied with Bosio, he executed one of the bas-reliefs *(Jemmapes)* for the Arch of Triumph on the Place de l'Etoile and the *Apotheosis of Mary Magdalen* for the church known as "The Madeleine." Sculptures by Marochetti are in the collection of the Galleria d'Arte

Moderna in Turin, and two of his equestrian monuments, designed in commemoration of *Emanuele Filiberto* and *Carlo Alberto,* stand in public squares in that city. In the Metropolitan Museum of Art in New York there is a model of his equestrian *Washington* (made for the Crystal Palace in New York but destroyed).

MARQUESTE, Laurent-Honoré. French. Born 1850 in Toulouse; died 1920. A rather dull academic sculptor who worked in a style of insipid naturalism, with an occasional burst of lyricism. His statue of *Etienne Marcel* at the Paris Hôtel de Ville, his *Perseus and the Gorgon* (exhibited at the 1876 Salon), and his *Monument to Waldeck-Rousseau,* erected in the Tuileries Garden (1909), illustrate the chief aspects of his style.

*MARTINI, Arturo. Italian. Born 1889 in Treviso; died 1947 in Milan. Was apprenticed to a jeweler at the age of twelve, then worked in a ceramics factory. Began in 1905 to devote himself completely to sculpture. In 1909, after having studied with several sculptors in Treviso and Venice, he went to Munich —probably in order to study with Hildebrand. (A number of facts concerning Martini's life are still uncertain.) He made one or two trips to Paris and exhibited there in the Salon d'Automne of 1911. His apprenticeship to a ceramist had given him a lifelong attachment to the medium of terra cotta. His first one-man show was held in Milan in 1920. In 1921, he joined the *Valori Plastici* movement in Rome. In 1928, he executed his large monument to the *Italian Pioneers in America,* erected in Worcester, Massachusetts. In 1931 he was awarded the First Prize for Sculpture in the First Roman Quadrennial Exhibition. Several posthumous retrospective exhibitions were organized in Italy—in Treviso, Venice, Rome and elsewhere. The variety, unevenness and abundance of Martini's sculpture render analysis of his style somewhat difficult. He was opposed to the idea of the "school," but derived frequent inspiration from the archaic style and the simple forms of ancient Roman clay figures. The freedom—from the point of view of composition if not of technique—with which he treated his subjects, gave him the aspect of a revolutionary, and he is considered to have exercised an immense influence over an entire generation of Italian sculptors. In 1945 he published a book with the curious title, *Sculpture as a Dead Language;* the title referred, however, to the sculpture of his contemporaries. Martini's work is represented in the museums of Rome, Milan, Turin, Venice, Vienna, Antwerp, etc.

*MATISSE, Henri. French. Born 1869 at Cateau; died 1954 in Nice. For a discussion of his sculpture, see pages 189–192.

MATVEEVITCH, Mardoukh Matysovitch Antokolski, called Mark. Russian. Born 1843; died 1902. Executed statues in a traditional style, in commemoration of the exploits of national heroes and martyrs. *Ivan the Terrible, Ermak the Cossack, Peter the Great, Socrates Drinking the Hemlock, Christ in Judgment,* etc.

MELIDA Y ALINARI, Arturo. Spanish. Born 1848 in Madrid; died 1902. Architect, painter and sculptor. Designed public monuments and the *Tomb of Christopher Columbus* in Seville Cathedral.

MERCIÉ, Marius Jean Antonin. French. Born 1845 in Toulouse; died 1916 in Paris. Studied with Jouffroy and Falguière at the Ecole des Beaux-Arts where, in 1868, he won the Second Grand Prize for Sculpture with a *Theseus Defeating the Minotaur.* First exhibited at the Salon that same year. With Paul Dubois, he formed a group of sculptors whose Renaissance-inspired, academic style earned them the title of "Florentines." He executed a *David* (1872), a *Gloria Victis* (1874), a *Spirit of the Arts* (1877), the tombstones of *Michelet,* and *Thiers* at the Père-Lachaise Cemetery, a *Gounod* for the Monceau Park in Paris (1902), a *William Tell* in Lausanne and a *La Fayette* in New York. Was elected to the Institute in 1891, appointed to teach at the Ecole des Beaux-Arts in 1900, became President of the French Artists' Society in 1913.

MEŠTROVIĆ, Ivan. Yugoslavian. Born 1883 in Dalmatia. As a boy was a shepherd. After serving apprenticeship to a stone-carver in Split, he traveled to Vienna, where he studied at the Fine Arts Academy, until 1905. He had one-man shows in Belgrade (1904) and Zagreb (1905). In Paris, where he lived from 1907 to 1909, he met Rodin, whose work greatly encouraged him, though it did not exert any real influence on his own development. He exhibited in the Salon d'Automne and later returned to his own country, where his work met with great success. He spent the period of the First World War in France, Switzerland, England and Italy. He then settled in Zagreb where his studio was converted into a museum devoted to his work. Meštrović's sculpture, which is in part a celebration of the heroic legends of his native land and partly devoted to religious subjects, reveals more sensitivity in its simple treatment of the female figure than in its more monumental aspects. His work is frequently spoiled by an excessive affectation and literary sentimentality. He designed the monument to the Croatian poet, *Botic,* which stands in Split (1905), a statue of *Bishop Strossmayer* in Zagreb (1926), a bas-relief of the *Annunciation* (1929), another entitled *Waiting* (1929) and a *Pietà* (1932). The Brooklyn Museum in New York acquired *The Archangel Gabriel* in 1947. Meštrović retired to the United States and lives in the state of Indiana.

*MEUNIER, Constantin. Belgian. Born 1831 in Brussels; died 1905 in Brussels. See page 88.

*MILLES, Vilhelm Carl Emil, known as Carl. Original surname, Anderson. Swedish-born, acquired American citizenship in 1930. Born 1875 in Lagga; died 1955 in Lidingö, near Stockholm. Worked for a carpenter in Stockholm, then studied for three years at a technical training school. He studied at the Colarossi Academy in Paris from 1897 to 1904, exhibited in the Salon, in 1899. He spent some time in Munich in 1904, then returned to Sweden. Exhibited in Malmö in 1913, at the Tate Gallery, London, in 1920. Emigrated to the United States in 1930 and settled in Cranbrook, where he soon began to receive numerous commissions, including the *Peace Monument* for the City Hall in Saint Paul, Minnesota, *Man and Nature* for the Time and Life Building in New York. After spending several years in America, he returned to Sweden. His *Aganippe* fountain was set up in the Metropolitan Museum, in New York, shortly after his death. His house, with its surrounding gardens and terraces in Lidingö, has been converted into a museum containing his sculpture (Millesgården). See page 160.

MILLET, Aimé. French. Born 1819 in Paris; died 1891 in Paris. Was taught drawing by his father, a painter of miniatures, then studied with Viollet-le-Duc. His studies at the Ecole des Beaux-Arts in Paris with David d'Angers gave him the technical training of an academic sculptor. He began to exhibit in the Salon in 1840. His *Ariadne* (1857) was very well received. He also executed a *Mercury* (1859), a statue of *Chateaubriand* (1875), a bust of *George Sand* (1878) and a *Phidias* (1887). In 1870 he was appointed to a teaching post at the School of Decorative Arts in Paris.

*MINNE, Georges. Belgian. Born 1866 in Ghent; died 1941 in Laethem-Saint-Martin. See page 147.

*MODIGLIANI, Amedeo. Italian. Born 1884 in Livorno; died 1920 in Paris. Studied painting successively at the Schools of Fine Arts in Livorno, Florence and Venice between 1898 and 1903. Suffering from tuberculosis, he arrived in Paris in 1906. He seems to have begun to work in wood and plaster at that time. It was, however, in 1910, as a result of his meeting with Brancusi, that he became intensely interested in sculpture, a form which he considered extremely important, although he worked mostly as a painter. In 1911, he exhibited a few sculptures, some *Heads* and *Caryatids* in the Parisian studio of Amedeo de Souza Cardoso. In 1912, he exhibited seven *Heads* in the Salon d'Automne; they were designed to form a "decorative ensemble." His last works of sculpture were done in 1915. The highly stylized forms of these heads reveal a curious mingling of the influences of medieval and primitive sculpture, dominated, however, by a personal style and an extreme technical purity. The elongated heads and forms of the eyes recall the style and grave expression of his painted portraits; they take on a new grandeur in stone. Modigliani's sculpture is represented in the collections of the Museum of Modern Art in New York, the Museum of Modern Art in Paris and the Tate Gallery in London.

*MOHOLY-NAGY, László. Hungarian. Born 1895 in Bacsbarsod; died 1946 in Chicago. Studied law at the Budapest University until 1915. Began to paint in 1917 and joined the *Magrupp*. Began to develop an interest in sculpture in Berlin in 1920. His meeting with Lissitsky had drawn him toward abstraction; his encounter with Malevitch and Constructivist theory influenced his assemblages of wood and metal. To these he later added the use of glass and plexiglass. The style and technique of his abstract compositions occasionally recall those of Gabo; like Gabo, he produced kinetic sculptures. His exhibit at Der Sturm Gallery in 1922 elicited an invitation from Walter Gropius to teach at the Bauhaus in Weimar. In 1928, after leaving the Bauhaus, he went to live in Berlin. During periods spent in Paris between 1932 and 1936, he exhibited with the *Abstraction-Création* group. He traveled extensively in Europe (to Italy, Greece, Scandinavia), and lived in London from 1935 to 1937, where he designed the sets for the motion picture, *The Shape of Things To Come.* There, he constructed his *Space Modulators* with interchangeable elements. He went to the United States in 1938 and settled in Chicago where he organized the New Bauhaus. The wide range of Moholy-Nagy's activities included work in architecture, photography, films and theatrical design. Moholy-Nagy was also the author of several published volumes. (See Bibliography.) Several works of sculpture are in the collection of the Museum of Modern Art in New York.

MOLIN, Johann Peter. Swedish. Born 1814 in Göteborg; died 1873 in Ekudden. Painter and sculptor. Studied in Copenhagen, Paris and Rome. Designed a number of public monuments. Exhibited his *Wrestlers* in the 1857 Salon in Paris, where he lived for several years. The National Museum in Stockholm owns his statue of *Oscar I,* a bust of *Queen Louise,* and a *Sleeping Bacchante.* Other sculptures are owned by the Göteborg Museum.

*MOREAU, Gustave. French. Born 1826 in Paris; died 1898. For a discussion of this painter's sculpture, see pages 178 and 181.

MORICE, Léopold. French. Born 1846 in Nîmes; died 1920 in Paris. Studied with Jouffroy, exhibited in the Salon in 1868. An academic sculptor, designer of public monuments and religious statues. His work includes a bust of *General Championnet* (in the Valence Museum), a *Virgin and Child* (Aimargues Church), a bas-relief of *Christ Adored by Angels* (Saint Stephen's Church in Tours), *The Republic* (Place de la République, Paris).

MYSLBEK, Joseph Václav. Czechoslovakian. Born 1848 in Prague; died 1922 in Prague. His romanticism strongly influenced the younger Czech sculptors, many of whom were trained by him. Designed the equestrian statue of *Saint Wenceslas* and the *Tomb of Cardinal Schwarzenberg*. His work is represented in the collection of the Prague Museum.

*NADELMAN, Elie. Born 1885 in Warsaw; died 1946. While studying classical Greek sculpture in Munich, he became intensely interested in folk art and made a collection for the Bavarian Museum. He was later to collect American folk art. During the early years of the century, he studied at the Colarossi Academy in Paris. He attempted to establish in his drawings the interplay of curves which he later used in sculpture. He exhibited at the Galerie Druet in 1909, and was represented in the Armory Show, New York, 1913. He went to New York in 1917 and exhibited at Alfred Stieglitz's Gallery 291. He remained in the United States until his death. Several of his sculptures are owned by the Museum of Modern Art in New York. See page 164.

NIEDERHAÜSERN, Auguste de (known as Niederhaüsern-Rodo). Swiss. Born 1863 in Vevey; died 1913 in Munich. After early studies in Geneva, he went to Paris and worked under Falguière at the Ecole des Beaux-Arts. He then worked for eight years as assistant to Rodin. He exhibited in the Paris Salon in 1885. Among his symbolic and allegorical statues are *The Initiates, The Transit of Venus* and the *Torrent*. His work is represented in the principal Swiss museums (*Psyche* and *Bitterness* in Geneva, a bust of *Hodler* in Berne, etc.). He was a friend of Paul Verlaine and designed the *Monument to Verlaine* in the Luxembourg Garden.

*NIELSEN, Kai. Danish. Born 1882 in Svenborg; died 1924. Studied at the School of Fine Arts in Copenhagen. The study of classical sculpture and the discovery of Rodin were responsible for an attachment to classical form modified by a somewhat more personal, tormented style and sensitivity. His first mature work was a *Young Girl,* done in marble in 1909. In 1914 he completed work on a gigantic statue of *Rasmussen*. In 1916, he began work on a group in granite for a public square in Copenhagen. He also did several *Ledas*. His sculpture is to be seen in the State Museum and the Glyptotek in Copenhagen and in the Faaborg Museum.

OBRIST, Hermann. Swiss. Born 1863 in Kilchberg; died 1927 in Munich. Studied medicine in Weimar, then entered the School of Arts and Crafts in Karlsruhe. Always interested in experimentation, he studied pottery-making at Thuringen, began working in clay in 1892, went to Paris in 1889, opened an embroidery factory in Florence in 1892, settled in Munich in 1894. In 1901, he published a book on *New Possibilities in the Plastics Arts* in Leipzig. In 1901 he opened a school of applied arts in Munich. He exhibited at the Cologne Werkbund in 1914. Obrist's sculpture, fountains and designs for public monuments occupy a curious place between the ornamental, baroque style of Art Nouveau and the abstract art toward which he naturally inclined. In this respect he may be considered a precursor.

O'CONNOR, Jr., Andrew. American. Born 1874 in Worcester, Mass. Studied sculpture in New York, then in London. In 1898 he executed the bronze doors of St. Bartholomew's Church in New York. Was stimulated by the influence of Rodin while living in Paris in 1905. Designed the monuments to *Lincoln* (Springfield, 1916), *Joan Barry* (Washington), *Johnson* (Saint Paul), *Roosevelt* (Glen View) and an equestrian statue of *La Fayette* (Baltimore, 1922). His work can be seen at the Baltimore and Brooklyn (New York) Museums.

*ORLOFF, Chana. Born 1888 in the Ukraine; acquired French citizenship in 1925. Lived in Palestine from 1905 to 1910, then settled in Paris. Studied at the School of Decorative Arts. On the advice of Joseph Bernard, she began to study sculpture at the Académie Russe. (See page 165.) After a Cubist-influenced period she continued to use stylized forms, but worked with greater freedom and flexibility. Her studio was raided by the Germans in 1942. She then went to live in Switzerland, returning to Paris in 1945. Exhibitions of her work have been held in Paris, New York, Haifa and Oslo. In 1950 and 1953 she executed two monuments in Israel. The Museum of Modern Art in Paris owns her bust of *Lucien Vogel* (1922), *The Painter, Widhopff* (1923), and *Crouching Woman* (1924). At present she lives in Paris.

OTTIN, Auguste Louis Marie. French. Born 1811 in Paris; died 1890 in Paris. Studied at the Ecole des Beaux-Arts with David d'Angers. First exhibited in the Salon in 1841. An academic sculptor, he received many government commissions, worked for the Louvre, the Opéra, the Hôtel de Ville, the churches of Saint Eustace, Saint Augustine and Saint Clotilda. Ottin did a *Polyphemus* for the *Medici Fountain* in Paris, a *Napoleon III* (1861) and a gigantic *Henri IV* (1868) in Fontainebleau.

*PICASSO, Pablo Ruiz y. Spanish. Born 1881 in Malaga. See pages 193 and 196.

POMEROY, Frederick William. English. Born 1857; died 1924. Studied with Dalou at the time of his exile in England, at the Lambeth School and with Mercié in Paris. Pomeroy, a conventional sculptor and clever portraitist, executed statues of *Burns* and *Gladstone*. The Tate Gallery in London owns his *Bacchus and Nymphs*.

*POMPON, François. French. Born 1855 in Saulieu; died 1933 in Paris. See page 165. A large collection of his sculpture is owned by the Museum of Fine Arts in Dijon. A small Pompon Museum has been installed in his native town of Saulieu. The local church contains a thirteenth-century capital representing two boars which, according to the artist, influenced his decision to become an animal sculptor. Some of Pompon's sculpture is to be seen in Paris, at the Museum of Natural History and at the Museum of Modern Art, which possesses 20 pieces, including the *Polar Bear,* exhibited in the Salon d'Automne of 1922, which established the sculptor's reputation.

*POUGNY, Jean. Born 1892 in Finland; died 1956 in Paris. Of Russian-Italian descent. Acquired French citizenship in 1946. For a discussion of his constructions in relief see page 202.

POUPELET, Jane. French. Born 1878 at Saint-Paul-Lizonne; died 1932 in Paris. Studied with Schnegg, whose work considerably influenced her own, then with Rodin. Exhibited at the Salon of the Société Nationale des Beaux-Arts and at the Salon d'Automne. Her work, which expresses a delicate vision of femininity is quietly classical, as in her *Bather, Woman at Her Toilette, Woman Admiring Herself in the Water,* etc. She also produced a great many animal sculptures; a dozen of these, done between 1902 and 1930, are in the collection of the Museum of Modern Art in Paris. Several American museums, including those in New York, Chicago, Detroit and Buffalo, own examples of her work.

*PRADIER, Jean-Jacques, known as James. Swiss. Born 1792 in Geneva; died 1852 in Bougival. See page 37.

PRÉAULT, Antoine-Augustin, known as Auguste. French. Born 1809; died 1879. After a period of apprenticeship to an ornamenter, he studied briefly with David d'Angers. A romantic sculptor, he executed *Carnage* (1833), statues of *Marceau* (1851), *Mickiewicz* (1868), *Jacques Coeur* (1875), an *Ophelia* (1876). Several sculptures by Préault are owned by the Chartres Museum.

QUEROL, Agustin. Spanish. Born 1863 in Tortosa; died 1909 in Madrid. As an officially recognized sculptor, he was the obvious person to design a statue entitled *Tradition.* He also executed a portrait of *Quevedo,* of *Tulia,* of *Saint Francis Nursing the Lepers,* the *Tomb of Canovas del Castillo,* and the pediment of the National Library in Madrid.

*RAEDECKER, Johan Anton, known as John. Dutch. Born 1885 in Amsterdam; died 1955 in Amsterdam. Studied at the Academy of Fine Arts in Amsterdam and at the Academy of Antwerp. Lived in Paris from 1912 to 1914. His first wood carvings, done at that time, betray the influence of Cubism. He later worked in a somewhat impersonally classical style which brought him a considerable reputation in his native country. His work is uneven, frequently rather heavy, but his female figures and busts are treated with restraint and a delicate sensuality. His work is represented in the principal museums in Holland. The Kröller-Müller Rijksmuseum in Otterlo possesses 40 sculptures done between 1911 and 1937; these include a *Selfportrait* (1912), *Head of a Child* (1919), *Monnik* (1924), *Madonna* (1928) and *Venus Anadyomene* (1936).

RAUCH, Christian-Daniel. German. Born 1777 in Arolsen; died 1857. A protégé of the king of Prussia, he executed a great many commemorative monuments in a pompous style suited to the dignity of his models: statues of *Blücher, Queen Louise,* in Charlottenburg, an equestrian statue of *Friedrich II* in Berlin (1851), among others. He was associated with Thorvaldsen in Rome, 1804–1810.

*RENOIR, Pierre-Auguste. French. Born 1841 in Limoges; died 1919 in Cagnes. For a discussion of this painter's sculpture, see pages 185 and 188.

*RIETSCHEL, Ernst Friedrich August. German. Born 1804 in Pulsnitz; died 1861. Studied at the Dresden Academy, then with Rauch, from whom he acquired the taste for the historical monument. His work includes statues of *King Friedrich-August, Luther,* etc.

RODCHENKO, Aleksandr. Russian. Born 1891 in Saint Petersburg. Painter and sculptor. Studied in Kazan. Began working in an abstract vein in 1914. Joined the Constructivist group in Moscow in 1915. His *Play of Spheres in Space* (1921) is an attempt at a new sculptural expression of movement.

*RODIN, François Auguste René. French. Born November 12, 1840 in Paris; died November 17, 1917 in Meudon. For a discussion of his life and work see pages 93 to 117. Apart from the Rodin Museum (in the Hôtel Biron in the Rue de Varenne, Paris), where most of his work is assembled, many of his sculptures—and particularly his plaster models—are to be seen at his home in Meudon which has been transformed into a museum. Many are in the Metropolitan Museum in New York, including *Adam* (from the *Gate of Hell*) and the marble groups *Cupid and Psyche, Orpheus and Eurydice* and *Hand of God.* He is buried in the garden in Meudon, next to Rose Beuret, his life-long companion whom he married shortly before her death. A Rodin Museum has also been founded in Philadelphia.

*ROSSO, Medardo. Italian. Born 1858 in Turin; died 1928 in Milan. For an account of his life and work, see pages 117 to 125. Rosso's major works are to be seen in Italy at the Galleria Nazionale d'Arte Moderna in Rome, at the Rosso Museum in Barzio, and in the museums of Florence, Turin, Milan and Venice. His sculpture is also represented in the Museums of Dresden and Essen, at the Museum of Modern Art in Paris and the Petit Palais Museum in Paris.

*RUDE, François. French. Born January 4, 1784 in Dijon; died November 3, 1855 in Paris. For an account of his life and work, see pages 45 and 48. A Rude Museum has been installed at the Museum of Fine Arts in Dijon, in the Palais des Etats de Bourgogne, where a large centennial exhibition was held in 1955.

*SAINT-GAUDENS, Augustus. American. Born in Dublin in 1848; died 1907. Worked in New York and Cornish, N. H. His equestrian statues *General Sherman* and *General Logan* are in New York (Central Park) and Chicago, respectively. His works also include *Lincoln* (Chicago), *Farragut* (New York), *Deacon Chapin* or *The Puritan* (Springfield, Mass.), *Amor Caritas* (in the Luxembourg, Paris). See page 81.

SCHILLING, Johann. German. Born 1828; died 1910. Studied at the Fine Arts Academy in Berlin, but learned to design historical monuments in the studio of Rietschel, a specialist in this form. His work includes an impressive *Germania*, the *Demiani Monument* in Gorlitz (1862) and many portraits of illustrious Germans.

SCHNEGG, Lucien. French. Born 1864 in Bordeaux; died 1909 in Paris. Studied in Bordeaux, then in Paris with Falguière. His work was, however, influenced by that of Rodin. Began to exhibit at the Salon in 1887. He showed at the Salon des Indépendants in 1905. His *Aphrodite, Young Boy*, his portraits of children and his busts are the work of an intelligent but somewhat dull technician; they show real sensitivity, expressed with a somewhat excessive restraint. He trained a great many young sculptors, and his teaching was highly esteemed.

SCHWITTERS, Kurt. German. Born 1887 in Hanover; died 1948 in Ambleside, England. Studied painting in Munich in 1913. His first reliefs, done in 1919, were composed of elements in various materials, then painted. He participated in the Dada movement, in *Der Sturm*, and founded the review entitled *Merz*. He set up a studio in Hanover in 1926, went to Paris in 1930 and joined the *Abstraction-Création* group. He settled in England, and there executed a series of works entitled *Construction*.

*SINTENIS, Renée. German. Born 1888 in Glatz. Studied at the School of Fine Arts in Stuttgart; in 1908, entered the School of Arts and Crafts in Berlin. Was chiefly an animal sculptor, but executed a series of interesting portraits. Her impressionist treatment of movement was achieved by the use of a highly animated surface. Elected to the Prussian

Academy of Fine Arts in 1929, from which she was later expelled by the Nazis. She was, however, appointed to a teaching post, which she has held since, at the Berlin School of Fine Arts after the war.

SOLÁ, Antonio. Spanish. Born 1787 in Barcelona; died 1861. His neoclassical sensibility was stimulated by a long period spent in Rome. Designed a *Cervantes Monument* and a *Roman Charity*. His work is represented in the collection of the Madrid Museum.

STEVENS, Alfred George. English. Born 1817; died 1875. Studied with Thorvaldsen in Rome, became a fashionable sculptor and taught in London. His work includes the *Caryatids* at Dorchester House and the *Wellington Monument* in Saint Paul's.

ŠTURSA, Jan. Czechoslovakian. Born 1880; died 1925. Studied with Myslbek at the Prague Academy. His sculpture is representative of the work of a generation whose only possibility of escape from academic tradition was the influence of Rodin. His work includes several *Eves*, a *Wounded Soldier*, and many busts. The Prague and Munich museums possess sculpture by this artist.

*TAEUBER-ARP, Sophie. Swiss. Born 1889 in Davos; died 1943 in Zurich. Studied applied art in Saint-Gall and in Munich, then went to Zurich, where, in 1915, she met Jean Arp. They collaborated on work in embroidery, tapestry and collage. With Arp, the following year, she began to take an active part in the founding of the Dada movement. She did a number of sculptures in wood: heads of a Dadaist humor. She married Arp in 1922 and, in 1928, the couple went to live in Meudon, France. With Arp and Theo van Doesburg, she worked on the decoration of *l'Aubette* in Strasbourg. Her sculptural work consists chiefly of wood reliefs characterized by extreme formal purity and a stylization which tends toward abstraction.

TATARKIEWICZ, Jacob. Polish. Born 1798 in Warsaw; died 1854. After attending Warsaw University, he studied sculpture and, encouraged by Thorvaldsen whose acquaintance he made while traveling in Italy, adopted a neoclassical style. He then traveled to Paris. He eventually became a celebrated sculptor of portraits in his native country. His work includes a *Napoleon*, a *Mickiewicz* and a *Chopin* which are preserved in the National Museum in Warsaw. He also executed the *Tomb of Woyczechowsky* for the Jesuit church in Warsaw.

TATLIN, Vladimir Yevgrafovich. Russian. Born 1885 in Moscow; died 1956. Studied painting in Moscow. Did not begin to make reliefs until 1913, following a brief stay in Paris, where his meeting with Picasso seems to have determined his Constructivist orientation. See pages 223 and 226.

THORNYCROFT, Sir William Hamo. English. Born 1850 in London; died 1925 in Oxford. Studied with Dalou. Began to exhibit at the Royal Academy in 1872. He was elected a member of the Academy in 1888. Executed an *Artemis* (at Eaton Hall) and a number of austere and traditionally conceived statues, including a *General Gordon, Bishop Goodwin* and *Bishop Creighton* (at Lambeth Palace). His work is represented in the collection of the Tate Gallery, also in Cambridge, Copenhagen and Chicago.

TENERANI, Pietro. Italian. Born 1789; died 1869. A student of Thorvaldsen and Canova. His neo-classical technique was put to the service of a rather naturalistic vision. The Galleria d'Arte Moderna in Rome possesses his statue of *Pellegrino Rossi* and his *Sleeping Psyche.* He also designed the *Tomb of Pius VIII* and that of *Lady Northampton* at Ashby and a monument, *Bolívar,* for Colombia.

TROUBETZKOY, Prince Paul. Russian. Born 1864 in Italy; died 1936 in Charlottesville, Va. He lived for long periods in Italy and in France, where he studied sculpture. His work was influenced by that of Rodin. He was inclined to a somewhat excessively mannered elegance (as in his portrait of *Marquise Casati,* portrayed with her dog), but his work was frequently vigorous and full of character, as in his busts, including that of *Rietti,* now in the Trieste Museum. One of his best sculptures is a *Tolstoy on Horseback.* He had designed an equestrian statue of *Alexander III* for Russia which was, curiously enough, left intact by the revolution. The pretext given was that it constituted an object lesson in "decadent art."

TUAILLON, Louis. German, of French descent. Born 1862 in Berlin; died 1919. Studied at the Berlin Academy of Fine Arts from 1879 to 1883, lived in Rome from 1885 to 1892. His style, which derives from classicism, is frequently powerful and expressive. His work includes an *Amazon* and several monuments erected in German towns, including that of *Emperor Friedrich Wilhelm III* in Bremen. His work is represented in the museums of Berlin, Cologne, Essen, Leipzig, and others. His *Amazon,* in the form of a bronze statuette, is in the Metropolitan Museum in New York.

*VALLOTTON, Félix. Swiss. Born 1865 in Lausanne; died 1925 in Paris. Went to Paris in 1882, worked at the Académie Julian and exhibited his first painting at the Salon in 1885. Vallotton, who was primarily a painter and printmaker, later joined the Nabi group; his style differed considerably from theirs in its realism and intensity of color. He worked only briefly in sculpture—in 1903 and 1904. Only six small pieces remain: *Reclining Nude, Faun with Cymbals, Woman with Jug, Youth, Young Mother* and *Woman with Shirt.* These last four were reproduced in bronze through a lost-wax process by Hébrard. The figures are of the same physical types, and are portrayed in the attitudes of the nudes painted during the same period.

*VANTONGERLOO, Georges. Belgian. Born 1886 in Antwerp. Studied painting, sculpture and architecture at the Academy of Fine Arts in Antwerp. Wounded during the First World War. Joined the De Stijl group in the Hague and executed his first abstract sculptures in 1917. He lived in Menton between 1919 and 1927, and there executed a series of strictly geometrical sculptures. He later settled in Paris, where he still lives. In 1931, he was one of the chief organizers of the *Abstraction-Création* group. He later changed his style, introduced curves into his compositions and, in 1945, began to use wire in an attempt at linear composition. Still later he began to work in plexiglass. In 1924, he published a volume entitled *l'Art et son Avenir.*

*VELA, Vincenzo. Swiss. Born 1820 in Ligornetto; died 1891 in Milan. His monuments and his statues —both austere and light—are in the tradition of naturalism. His dramatic style was rather theatrical, his lighter vein somewhat mannered. In Italy, where he spent the greater part of his life, he achieved a reputation with work such as *Spartacus* (1847), *Desolation* (1850), *Spring* (1857), *Giotto, Dante* (1866), *Prayer* (1882). His work is represented in the museums of Padua and Rome, and in the Vela Museum in Ligornetto. His *Napoleon Dying* is in the Versailles Museum.

VIGELAND, Adolf Gustav. Norwegian. Born 1869 in Mandal; died 1943. Studied sculpture in Oslo and Copenhagen, went to Paris in 1892 and worked for a few months with Rodin. See pages 160–161.

VOLMAR, Joseph. Swiss. Born 1796 in Berne; died 1865. Painter and sculptor. Was taught by his father, Georg Volmar, a well-known animal sculptor, then studied painting with Horace Vernet and Géricault while in Paris, in 1814, before entering the studio of David d'Angers. Was appointed to teach drawing at Berne University in 1836. His academic work includes the equestrian statue of *Rudolph von Erlach,* erected on the cathedral square in Berne (1849), the *Monument to Father Girard* in Friburg (1860), statues of *Fatio, Waldmann* and *Zwingli.*

WARD, John Quincy Adams. American. Born 1830; died 1910. Son of an Ohio farmer. Worked for a potter, then entered the studio of Henry Kirke Brown. Although his work indicates an attempt at a vigorous realism, it remains, nevertheless, quite traditional in style. His work includes a statue of *General Thomas* in Washington (1878), *The Puritan* in Central Park, New York (1885) and several other public monuments.

WATTS, George Frederick. English. Born 1817;

died 1904. A neoclassical sculptor whose style, which derived from Greek statuary, was somewhat modernized by an increasingly free treatment of surface. His work includes a *Daphne*, a *Clytia*, the equestrian statue of *Hugh Lupus* (in Eaton Hall), and is represented, as well, in the Tate Gallery, London.

WELOŇSKY, Pius. Polish. Born 1849; died 1931. Painter and sculptor. Studied in Warsaw, Saint Petersburg and Rome, lived in Germany and France. An academic sculptor whose work is preserved in the museums of Warsaw and Cracow. He won a gold medal in Berlin in 1891. He became chief curator of the Warsaw Museum in 1906. His work includes a *Gladiator with Trident*, *Prometheus*, *The Slave*, *The Tomb of Cardinal Radziwill*, etc.

*WITTIG, Edouard. Polish. Born 1879 in Warsaw; died 1941. Went to Paris, worked with Rodin and Schnegg; both these sculptors exercised an influence upon his work. Wittig became one of the most interesting of the Polish sculptors. His restrained and expressive style was applied to large-scale sculpture, including *The Monument to the Aviators Killed in the War*, in Warsaw. Many of Wittig's monuments, including this one, were destroyed during the Second World War. Some of his sculpture is to be seen in the National Museum in Warsaw.

WOLFF, Albert. German. Born 1814; died 1892 in Berlin. Studied with Rauch. Entered the Berlin Academy of Fine Arts in 1836, later spent the year of 1844–1845 studying in Italy. His work illustrates all the conventions of academic, commemorative sculpture. He executed a statue of *Countess Potocka* in Posen, a bust of *Schadow*, in the Dusseldorf Museum, a *Flora* in the Sans-Souci Gardens, a *Dionysos and Eros* in the Berlin Museum, and an equestrian statue of *Friedrich Wilhelm III*, which was placed in the Lustgarten in Berlin in 1868 and destroyed during the last war. His *Dying Lioness* is in Fairmount Park, Philadelphia. He was appointed to a chair at the Berlin Academy in 1866.

WOOLNER, Thomas. English. Born 1825; died 1892. Originally a neoclassical sculptor, he later developed a pre-Raphaelite-influenced style. Executed an *Eros and Euphrosyne*, *The Death of Boadicea*, a monumental *Moses* in Manchester, busts of *Gladstone*, *Richard Cobden*, etc.

*WOUTERS, Rik. Belgian. Born 1882 in Malines; died 1916 in Amsterdam. Painter and sculptor. Studied at the Academies of Fine Arts in Malines and Brussels. Had his first one-man show at the Galerie Giroux in Paris in 1914. See page 146. His major works are in the collection of the Museum of Fine Arts in Antwerp.

*ZADKINE, Ossip. Russian-born, acquired French citizenship. Born in Smolensk, 1890. Was sent by his father to complete his studies in England, began to study sculpture in London, continuing his training in Paris upon his arrival there in 1909. Was quickly drawn to the more advanced forms of expression and was particularly attracted by Cubism. He was one of the first to apply the principles of Cubism to sculpture and to use them as the basis for a sculptural *oeuvre* of considerable range. He joined the French army in 1914, and it was not until 1919 that he was able to hold his first one-man show in Brussels. He had by then completely mastered a style of his own which gradually dissociated itself from the geometricism of the massive simplifications of Cubism. See page 222f. His sculptures done between 1930 and 1937 show a more powerful expression of movement (*Diane*, 1936). He later achieved a still greater freedom through the use of interstices in his sculptured forms; these forms again became rather highly geometricized (*The Acrobats*, 1942, *The Elves, Human Forest*, 1948, *Germination*, 1952). A large exhibition composed of 73 sculptures was held at the Museum of Modern Art in Paris in 1949. This Museum also possesses several of Zadkine's major works, including *Orpheus, The Maenads, Homo Sapiens, The Composer*, etc. He spent the years of the Second World War in the United States and in 1943 he exhibited at the Curt Valentin Gallery in New York. Other major exhibitions of his sculpture have been held in Brussels and Amsterdam in 1948, Rotterdam in 1949, in London in 1952, and in Tokyo in 1954. Zadkine lives in Paris and teaches in his studio on the Rue d'Assas and at the Académie de la Grande-Chaumière.

ZORN, Anders Leonhard. Swedish. Born 1860 in Mora; died 1920. A painter, who studied at the Academy of Fine Arts in Stockholm from 1875 to 1881, he began to sculpt at the age of thirty. He had already traveled extensively in the Mediterranean, lived in England and in Paris, where he had met Rodin, and exhibited at the Salon. In 1893 he went to the United States and exhibited at the Chicago World's Fair. He returned on several occasions to America and traveled throughout Europe before settling in Mora, where his house was converted into a Zorn Museum after his death. His work as a sculptor was less extensive than his painting; he produced, however, in addition to a number of conventional statues, a series of busts which are more highly expressive and testify to a much subtler sensitivity. He had organized a school in Mora and created a system of scholarships to aid scientific exchange between Sweden and the United States.

LIST OF PLATES

1. ALEXANDER FALGUIÈRE. *Woman with Peacock,* 1890. Marble. Museum, Toulouse. Photo Giraudon.

2. JACQUES LIPCHITZ. *Seated Bather,* 1917. Stone. Otto Gerson Gallery, New York. Photo Adolph Studly.

3. JULES FRANCESCHI. *Fortune,* 1886. Plaster. Paris. Photo Roger-Viollet.

4. RAOUL LARCHE. *Monument to Corot,* 1904. Marble. Paris. Photo Bulloz.

5. LÉOPOLD MORICE. *Diana and Endymion,* ca. 1900. Plaster. Paris.

6. ALBERTO GIACOMETTI. *Slim Bust,* 1955. Bronze. Galerie Maeght, Paris. Photo Paul Facchetti.

7. VOLTI. *Sleeping Nude,* 1960. Bronze. Galerie Chardin, Paris. Photo Jean Weber.

8. HENRY MOORE. *Reclining Figure,* 1939. Lead. Collection Sir Kenneth Clark, London.

9. EMILE GILIOLI. *The Sleeper,* 1946–61. Marble. Collection Carozzi, Pisa.

10. APEL'LES FENOSA. *Hair,* 1960. Bronze. Private Collection, Paris. Photo Etienne Weill.

11. ROBERT COUTURIER. *Hollow Woman,* 1954. Bronze. French Institute, Milan. Photo Marc Vaux.

12. GERMAINE RICHIER. *The Wasp,* 1953. Bronze. Galerie Creuzevault, Paris. Photo Hervochon.

13. JAMES ROSATI. *Hermes Trismegistus,* 1958. Stone. Owned by the artist.

14. CLAUDE VISEUX. *Petrified Crowd,* 1959. Bronze. Collection D.B.C., Paris. Photo Jean Biaugeaud.

15. MORICE LIPSI. *Lava,* 1960. Volcanic stone. Galerie Denise René, Paris.

16. FRANÇOIS STAHLY. *Combat of Birds,* 1960. Wood. Park in Louveciennes (Seine-et-Oise). Photo P. Willi.

17. JEAN ARP. *Extreme of an Outer Mythology,* 1952. Stone. The Art Institute of Chicago. Photo Etienne Weill.

18. ROBERT MÜLLER. *The Pyre,* 1959. Iron. Collection Myriam Prévot, Paris. Photo Joubert.

19. HENRI-GEORGES ADAM. *St. Matthew,* 1960. Bronze. Editions La Hune, Paris. Photo Muller.

20. LOUISE NEVELSON. *Royal Tide V.* 1958–60. Gilded wood. Photo Rudolph Burckhardt.

21. ANTOINE PEVSNER. *Kinetic Construction,* 1953. Metal pipes. Photo Adolph Studly.

22. BERTO LARDERA. *Love of the Stars II,* 1959–60. Steel and iron. Collection of the artist, Paris.

23. DAVID SMITH. *Agricola V,* 1952. Steel. Otto Gerson Gallery, New York.

24. JEAN TINGUELY. *Metamechanical Sculpture,* 1953. Steel wire. Collection Kramer. Photo Shunk-Kender.

25. PIETRO CONSAGRA. *Chorus,* 1958. Burnt wood. Galerie de France, Paris.

26. ALEXANDER CALDER. *Red Pyramid,* 1945. Mobile. Galerie Louis Carré, Paris.

27. *Venus of Lespugne,* Paleolithic Age. Ivory. National Museum of Antiquities, Saint-Germain-en-Laye. Photo Archives Photographiques.

28. *Poseidon,* Early 5th Century B.C. Bronze. National Museum, Athens. Photo Alindri-Giraudon.

29. *Anthropomorphic Statuette from Ossyeba* (Gabon, Africa). Copper. Museum of Man, Paris. Photo Giraudon.

30. *Head of a Cycladic Idol,* ca. 2500–2000 B.C. Marble. Louvre, Paris. Photo Giraudon.

31. *Crucifix,* 12th Century. Painted wood. Louvre, Paris. Photo Bulloz.

32. *Cretan Idol,* ca. 2500–2000 B.C. Marble. Louvre, Paris. Photo Giraudon.

33. *Cypriot Idol,* ca. 2000 B.C. Terra cotta. Louvre, Paris. Photo Archives Photographiques.

34. *Funerary Figure from Bakota* (Gabon, Africa). Wood and copper. Private Collection. Photo Giraudon.

35. *Spanish-Peruvian Christ*, Late Colonial Period. Agate covered with painted plaster. Museum, Cuzco (Peru). Photo Giraudon.

36. BERTEL THORVALDSEN. *Cupid and the Three Graces*, 1817–19. Marble. Thorvaldsen Museum, Copenhagen.

37. ANTONIO CANOVA. *Cupid and Psyche*, Late 18th Century. Marble. Louvre, Paris. Photo Bulloz.

38. GIOVANNI DUPRÉ. *Sappho*, 1857. Marble. National Gallery of Modern Art, Rome.

39. VINCENZO VELA. *Spring*, 1857. Marble. Civic Museum, Padua.

40. JAMES PRADIER. *Atlanta at Her Toilet*, 1830. Marble. Louvre, Paris. Photo Bulloz.

41. ALBERT WOLFF. *Monument to Friedrich Wilhelm III*, 1868. Bronze. Berlin (destroyed). Photo Roger-Viollet.

42 ALFONSO BALZICO. *Monument to the Duke of Genoa*, 1860–70. Bronze. Turin.

43. ALBERT CARRIER-BELLEUSE. *Sleeping Hebe*, 1869. Marble. Louvre, Paris. Photo Roger-Viollet.

44. AIMÉ MILLET. *Ariadne*, 1857. Marble. Hôtel des Invalides, Paris. Photo Roger-Viollet.

45. FRANÇOIS RUDE. *Mercury Fastening His Heel-Wings*, 1834. Bronze. Louvre, Paris.

46. FRANÇOIS RUDE. *The Prophet Jeremiah*, ca. 1850–55. Terra-cotta sketch. Museum, Dijon. Photo Remy.

47. FRANÇOIS RUDE. *The Departure of the Volunteers*, 1836. Stone. Arch of Triumph, Paris. Photo Bulloz.

48. DAVID D'ANGERS. *Bust of Paganini*, 1830. Bronze. Museum, Angers. Photo J. Evers.

49. DAVID D'ANGERS. *Bust of Lamennais*, 1839. Marble. Museum, Rennes. Photo Bulloz.

50. DAVID D'ANGERS. *Napoleon I*, 1833. Bronze. Museum, Angers. Photo Jean Roubier.

51. ANTOINE-LOUIS BARYE. *Study for a Monument to Napoleon I*, ca. 1863. Bronze. Petit Palais, Paris. Photo Bulloz.

52. ANTOINE-LOUIS BARYE. *Lion Vanquishing an Ibex*. Bronze. Museum, Marseilles. Photo Bulloz.

53. ANTOINE-LOUIS BARYE. *Thesus Fighting the Centaur Bienor*, 1850. Bronze. Museum, Le Puy. Photo Bulloz.

54. HONORÉ DAUMIER. *Bust of Jean Fulchiron*, 1830–32. Bronze. Museum, Marseilles. Photo Giraudon.

55. HONORÉ DAUMIER. *Bust of an Unknown Man*, 1830–32. Bronze. Museum, Marseilles. Photo Giraudon.

56. HONORÉ DAUMIER. *The Burden*, ca. 1850. Terra cotta. The Walters Art Gallery, Baltimore.

57. HONORÉ DAUMIER. *The Emigrants* (First Version). Plaster. Louvre, Paris. Photo Larousse.

58. HONORÉ DAUMIER. *Self-Portrait*, 1855–58. Bronze. National Library, Paris. Photo Larousse.

59. JEAN-BAPTISTE CARPEAUX. *Temperance*, 1863. Wax. Massena Museum, Nice. Photo Bulloz.

60. JEAN-BAPTISTE CARPEAUX. *Study for Ugolin*, ca. 1859. Terra cotta. Louvre, Paris. Photo Archives Photographiques.

61. JEAN-BAPTISTE CARPEAUX. *Study for Watteau*, ca. 1860–62. Plaster. Petit Palais, Paris. Photo Archives Photographiques.

62. JEAN-BAPTISTE CARPEAUX. *The Three Graces*, 1874. Terra cotta. Petit Palais, Paris. Photo Bulloz.

63. JEAN-BAPTISTE CARPEAUX. *The Betrothed*, 1869. Plaster. Louvre, Paris. Photo Archives Photographiques.

64. JEAN-BAPTISTE CARPEAUX. *Bust of Eugénie Fiocre*, 1869. Plaster. Petit Palais, Paris. Photo Bulloz.

65. JEAN-BAPTISTE CARPEAUX. *The Dance*, 1865–69. Stone. Opera House, Paris. Photo Jean Roubier.

66. ALFRED BOUCHER. *Thought*, ca. 1900. Marble. Prayssas (Lot-et-Garonne). Photo Roger-Viollet.

67. LÉON GÉRÔME. *Tanagra*, 1890. Marble. Louvre, Paris. Photo Roger-Viollet.

68. LAURENT-HONORÉ MARQUESTE. *Per-*

seus and the Gorgon, 1876. Marble. Villeurbanne (Rhône). Photo Roger-Viollet.

69. AUGUSTUS SAINT-GAUDENS. *Victory*, 1903. Bronze. Metropolitan Museum of Art, New York.

70. LOUIS BARRIAS. *Nature Unveiling Herself*, 1899. Marble and onyx. Conservatory of Arts and Crafts, Paris. Photo Roger-Viollet.

71. JULES DALOU. *Woman Sewing*, ca. 1870–80. Terra cotta. Petit Palais, Paris. Photo Bulloz.

72. JULES DALOU. *Woman Reading*, ca. 1880. Plaster. Petit Palais, Paris. Photo Giraudon.

73. JULES DALOU. *Woman Taking Off Her Stockings*, ca. 1870–80. Terra cotta. Petit Palais, Paris. Photo Giraudon.

74. ADOLF VON HILDEBRAND. *The Net Carrier*, 1874–75. Stone. New Picture Gallery, Munich. Photo Bayerisches Staatsgemäldesammlungen.

75. CONSTANTIN MEUNIER. *The Reaper*. Bronze. Photo Giraudon.

76. CONSTANTIN MEUNIER. *The Soil*. Bronze. Photo Giraudon.

77. MEDARDO ROSSO. *Child in the Sun*, 1892. Wax. Kröller-Müller Rijksmuseum, Otterlo (Holland).

78. AUGUSTE RODIN. *Study for Balzac* (Detail), 1893. Bronze. Rodin Museum, Paris. Photo René-Jacques.

79. AUGUSTE RODIN. *The Man with the Broken Nose*, 1864. Bronze. Rodin Museum, Paris. Photo Adelys.

80. AUGUSTE RODIN. *Bust of Falguière*, 1897. Bronze. Rodin Museum, Paris. Photo Bulloz.

81. AUGUSTE RODIN. *Bust of Dalou*, 1883. Bronze. Rodin Museum, Paris. Photo René-Jacques.

82. AUGUSTE RODIN. *Drawing*. Collection Madame Dufet-Bourdelle, Paris. Photo Bulloz.

83. AUGUSTE RODIN. *Head of Sorrow*, 1892. Bronze. Rodin Museum, Paris. Photo René-Jacques.

84. AUGUSTE RODIN. *The Martyr*, 1885. Bronze. Rodin Museum, Paris. Photo Foucault.

85. AUGUSTE RODIN. *Head of Jacques de Wiessant*, 1884–86. Bronze. Rodin Museum, Paris. Photo Foucault.

86. AUGUSTE RODIN. *The Thinker* (Detail), 1880. Bronze. Rodin Museum, Paris. Photo René-Jacques.

87. AUGUSTE RODIN. *The Bronze Age* (Detail), 1876. Bronze. Rodin Museum, Paris. Photo René-Jacques.

88. AUGUSTE RODIN. *The Burghers of Calais*, 1884–86. Bronze. Rodin Museum, Paris. Photo René Jacques.

89. AUGUSTE RODIN. *Paolo Malatesta and Francesca da Rimini in the Clouds*, 1905. Marble. Rodin Museum, Paris. Photo René-Jacques.

90. AUGUSTE RODIN. *Large Head of Iris*, 1891. Bronze. Rodin Museum, Paris. Photo Foucault.

91. AUGUSTE RODIN. *Torso of Adele*, 1882. Plaster. Rodin Museum, Paris. Photo Foucault.

92. AUGUSTE RODIN. *Man Walking*, 1888. Bronze. Rodin Museum, Paris. Photo Joubert.

93. AUGUSTE RODIN. *Detail of Tympanum of the Gates of Hell*, 1880–1917. Bronze. Rodin Museum, Paris. Photo René-Jacques.

94. AUGUSTE RODIN. *The Cathedral*, 1908. Stone. Rodin Museum, Paris. Photo René-Jacques.

95. AUGUSTE RODIN. *The Kiss*, 1886. Marble. Rodin Museum, Paris. Photo Bulloz.

96. AUGUSTE RODIN. *Bust of Clemenceau*, 1911. Bronze. Rodin Museum, Paris. Photo René-Jacques.

97. MEDARDO ROSSO. *Bust of Yvette*, 1895. Wax. National Gallery of Modern Art, Rome.

98. MEDARDO ROSSO. *Laughing Woman*, 1890. National Gallery of Modern Art, Rome.

99. MEDARDO ROSSO. *Woman with Veil*, 1893. National Gallery of Modern Art, Venice.

100. MEDARDO ROSSO. *Portrait of Henri Rouart*, 1890. Bronze. National Gallery of Modern Art, Rome.

101. MEDARDO ROSSO. *Portrait of Madame Noblet*, 1896. Plaster. National Gallery of Modern Art, Rome.

102. MEDARDO ROSSO. *Sick Child*, 1892. Bronze. National Gallery of Modern Art, Rome.

103. MEDARDO ROSSO. *Conversation in a Gar-*

274

den, 1893. Bronze. National Gallery of Modern Art, Rome.

104. ANTOINE BOURDELLE. *Love in Agony,* 1886. Plaster. Bourdelle Museum, Paris.

105. ANTOINE BOURDELLE. *Study for Monument on Mount Montauban,* 1893–94. Plaster. Bourdelle Museum, Paris. Photo Marc Lavrillier.

106. ANTOINE BOURDELLE. *Pallas with Drapery,* ca. 1889. Bronze. Bourdelle Museum, Paris. Photo Bulloz.

107. ANTOINE BOURDELLE. *Head of Eloquence, Study for Alvear Monument,* 1917. Bronze. Bourdelle Museum, Paris. Photo Marc Lavrillier.

108. ANTOINE BOURDELLE. *Tragic Mask of Beethoven,* 1901. Bronze. Bourdelle Museum, Paris. Photo Marc Lavrillier.

109. ANTOINE BOURDELLE. *Head of Apollo,* 1900. Bronze. Bourdelle Museum, Paris. Photo Bulloz.

110. ANTOINE BOURDELLE. *Head of Beethoven,* 1902. Plaster. Bourdelle Museum, Paris.

111. ANTOINE BOURDELLE. *Study for Monument to Mickiewicz,* 1909. Plaster. Bourdelle Museum, Paris. Photo Marc Lavrillier.

112. ANTOINE BOURDELLE. *Tolstoi,* ca. 1906. Bronze. Bourdelle Museum, Paris. Photo Marc Lavrillier.

113. GEORG KOLBE. *Young Girl Standing,* 1915. Bronze. Art Gallery, Mannheim.

114. LUCIEN SCHNEGG. *Bust of Jane Poupelet,* 1897. Bronze. Municipal Museum of Modern Art, Paris. Photo Bulloz.

115. RIK WOUTERS. *Nel with a Chignon,* 1909. Bronze. Collection Madame de Carnière-Wouters, Overijse (Belgium).

116. MAX KLINGER. *Bust of Wilhelm Wundt,* 1908. Bronze. Art Gallery, Mannheim.

117. GEORGES MINNE. *The Relic Bearer.* Bronze.

118. CHARLES MALFRAY. *Torso of a Swimmer.* Bronze. Collection Dina Vierny, Paris. Photo Maywald.

119. FRANÇOIS STAHLY. *Serpent of Fire,* 1956. Bronze. Galerie Jeanne Bucher, Paris. Photo Joubert.

120. CHARLES MALFRAY. *Two Swimmers,* 1940. Bronze. Collection Dina Vierny, Paris. Photo Maywald.

121. AUGUSTE RODIN. *Fugit Amor,* 1882. Bronze. Rodin Museum, Paris. Photo Bulloz.

122. ARISTIDE MAILLOL. *Woman with a Dove,* 1905. Bronze. Private Collection, Paris. Photo Maywald.

123. ARISTIDE MAILLOL. *Bather with Drapery,* 1905. Bronze. Collection Dina Vierny, Paris. Photo Maywald.

124. ARISTIDE MAILLOL. *Pomona,* 1910. Bronze. Private Collection, Paris. Photo Maywald.

125. ARISTIDE MAILLOL. *Young Girl Sitting,* 1900. Terra cotta. Collection Dina Vierny, Paris. Photo Maywald.

126. ARISTIDE MAILLOL. *Study for Monument to Cézanne,* 1912. Bronze. Collection Dina Vierny, Paris. Photo Maywald.

127. CHARLES DESPIAU. *Paulette,* 1907. Marble. Museum of Modern Art, Paris. Photo Bulloz.

128. WILHELM LEHMBRUCK. *Young Man Seated,* 1918. Bronze. Art Museum, Duisberg.

129. CARL MILLES. *Bust of Ferdinand Boberg,* 1906. Bronze. Millesgården, Lidingö. Photo Sundahl.

130. JOSEPH BERNARD. *Girl with a Jug,* 1910. Bronze. Museum of Modern Art, Paris. Photo Archives Photographiques.

131. WILHELM LEHMBRUCK. *Bather,* 1914. Stone. Art Gallery, Mannheim.

132. GUSTAV VIGELAND. *The Monolith.* Stone. Frogner Park, Oslo.

133. CARL MILLES. *Study for Monument of the Resurrection* (Detail). Bronze. Millesgården, Lidingö. Photo Sundahl.

134. ELIE NADELMAN. *Man in the Open Air,* ca. 1915. Bronze. Museum of Modern Art, New York. Photo Soichi Sunami.

135. GUSTAVE MOREAU. *Hercules,* ca. 1875–80. Wax. Gustave Moreau Museum, Paris. Photo Paul Facchetti.

136. GUSTAVE MOREAU. *Lucretia,* ca. 1875–80. Wax. Gustave Moreau Museum, Paris. Photo Paul Facchetti.

137. GUSTAVE COURBET. *Bust of Madame Max Buchon,* ca. 1864. Plaster. Collection Alfred Daber, Paris.

138. EDGAR DEGAS. *Trotting Horse,* ca. 1879–81. Bronze. Collection Jacques Dubourg, Paris.

139. EDGAR DEGAS. *Dancer Looking at the Sole of Right Foot,* ca. 1896–1911. Bronze. Collection Jacques Dubourg, Paris.

140. EDGAR DEGAS. *Grand Arabesque, Second Time,* ca. 1882–95. Bronze. Collection Jacques Dubourg, Paris.

141. GASTON LACHAISE. *Equestrian Woman,* 1918. Bronze. Museum of Modern Art, New York.

142. MANOLO. *Crouching Woman,* 1914. Bronze. Galerie Louise Leiris, Paris.

143. FRANÇOIS POMPON. *Little Owl with Sunken Eyes,* 1918. Bronze. Museum of Modern Art, Paris. Photo Bulloz.

144. ELIE NADELMAN. *Wounded Bull,* 1915. Bronze. Museum of Modern Art, New York. Photo Soichi Sunami.

145. FRANÇOIS POMPON. *Brown Bear,* 1918. Bronze. Private Collection. Photo B. Larenceau.

146. PAUL GAUGUIN. *Bust of Madame Gauguin,* 1877. Marble. Courtauld Institute, London.

147. PAUL GAUGUIN. *Bust of Madame Emile Schuffenecker,* ca. 1889. Plaster. Louvre, Paris. Photo Giraudon.

148. PAUL GAUGUIN. *Adam and Eve,* 1891–93. Wood. Photo Giraudon.

149. PAUL GAUGUIN. *Head of Tehura,* 1891–93. Wood. Otto Gerson Gallery, New York. Photo Rudolph Burckhardt.

150. AUGUSTE RENOIR. *Bust of Coco,* 1908. Bronze.

151. AUGUSTE RENOIR. *Mother and Child,* 1916. Bronze.

152. AUGUSTE RENOIR. *The Washerwoman,* 1916. Plaster. Collection Renou, Paris. Photo Bonhotal.

153. HENRI MATISSE. *The Slave,* ca. 1900–03. Bronze. The Art Institute of Chicago.

154. HENRI MATISSE. *Seated Nude with Arms Behind Head,* 1904. Bronze.

155. HENRI MATISSE. *Head of Jeannette III,* 1910–13. Bronze.

156. FÉLIX VALLOTTON. *Young Mother,* 1904. Bronze. Collection Paul Vallotton, Lausanne.

157. ROGER DE LA FRESNAYE. *Young Girl Removing Her Dress,* 1912. Bronze. Galerie Maeght, Paris.

158. ROGER DE LA FRESNAYE. *The Italian Girl,* 1912. Bronze. Galerie Maeght, Paris.

159. PIERRE BONNARD. *Standing Nude.* Bronze. Private Collection, Paris. Photo L. Czigany.

160. PIERRE BONNARD. *Sitting Nude.* Bronze. Private Collection, Paris. Photo L. Czigany.

161. PABLO PICASSO. *Crouching Woman,* 1906. Bronze. Galerie Berggruen, Paris. Photo Cauvin.

162. PABLO PICASSO. *Head of a Beggar,* 1903. Bronze. Galerie Berggruen, Paris. Photo Cauvin.

163. PABLO PICASSO. *Bust of Fernande Olivier,* 1905. Bronze. Petit Palais, Paris. Photo Bulloz.

164. *Etruscan God,* Hellenistic Period. Bronze. Louvre, Paris. Photo Archives Photographiques.

165. ANTOINE BOURDELLE. *Madeleine Charnaux,* 1917. Bronze. Bourdelle Museum, Paris. Photo Marc Lavrillier.

166. PABLO PICASSO. *Figure,* 1931. Bronze. Collection Mrs. Meric Callery, Paris.

167. ALBERTO GIACOMETTI. *Large Figure,* 1958. Painted plaster. Galerie Maeght, Paris.

168. AMEDEO MODIGLIANI. *Head of a Woman,* 1919. Stone. Museum of Modern Art, Paris. Photo Bulloz.

169. ANDRÉ DERAIN. *Nude Woman Standing,* 1906. Stone. Collection Mouradian and Vallotton, Paris. Photo L. R. Adrion.

170. ALBERTO MAGNELLI. *Rhythms,* 1914. Plaster and copper. Collection of the artist.

171. JUAN GRIS. *Harlequin,* 1917. Plaster. Galerie Louise Leiris, Paris.

172. ALBERTO MAGNELLI. *Still Life,* 1914. Plaster, glass, stone. Collection of the artist. Photo Hervochon.

173. MAX ERNST. *Fruit of Long Experience,*

1919. Painted wood and metal. Collection Roland Penrose, London. Photo Brompton.

174. JEAN POUGNY. *Relief,* 1915. Colored cardboard.

175. JACOB EPSTEIN. *The Rock Drill,* 1913. Bronze. Collection of the artist. Photo John R. Freeman.

176. JACOB EPSTEIN. *Bust of Admiral Lord Fisher,* 1915. Bronze. Imperial War Museum, London.

177. PABLO GARGALLO. *Faunesse,* 1908. Copper. Collection Anguera, Paris. Photo Delattre.

178. PABLO GARGALLO. *Head,* 1903. Terra cotta. Collection Anguera, Paris. Photo Delattre.

179. PABLO GARGALLO. *Small Mask,* 1911. Copper. Collection Anguera, Paris. Photo Delattre.

180. PABLO GARGALLO. *Portrait of Monsieur de Soto,* 1920. Lead. Collection Anguera, Arcueil.

181. JULIO GONZALEZ. *Tia Lola,* ca. 1912–14. Bronze. Collection Madame Roberta Gonzalez, Arcueil. Photo Henri Guilband.

182. JULIO GONZALEZ. *Mask, Called Meditative,* ca. 1912–14. Bronze. Collection Madame Roberta Gonzalez, Arcueil.

183. JULIO GONZALEZ. *Inclined Antique Head,* 1910. Bronze. Collection Madame Roberta Gonzalez. Paris. Photo Maywald.

184. OTTO FREUNDLICH. *Mask,* 1911. Plaster. Collection Madame Freundlich, Paris.

185. OTTO FREUNDLICH. *Mask,* 1915. Bronze. Private Collection, Paris.

186. JOSEPH CSAKY. *Head,* 1914. Bronze. Museum, St-Etienne. Photo J. Josué.

187. UMBERTO BOCCIONI. *The Mother,* 1911. Bronze. National Gallery of Modern Art, Rome.

188. UMBERTO BOCCIONI. *Development of a Bottle in Space,* 1912. Bronze. Museum of Modern Art, New York (Aristide Maillol Fund).

189. UMBERTO BOCCIONI. *Synthesis of a Human Dynamism,* 1912. Plaster.

190. ALEXANDER ARCHIPENKO. *Silhouette,* 1910. Chromium-plated bronze. Hessian Museum, Darmstadt.

191. HENRI GAUDIER-BRZESKA. *The Red Stone Dancer,* ca. 1913. Waxed stone. Tate Gallery, London. Photo Roland Federn.

192. HENRI GAUDIER-BRZESKA. *Birds Erect,* 1914. Stone. Museum of Modern Art, New York (Gift of Mrs. W. Murray Crane). Photo Soichi Sunami.

193. ALEXANDER ARCHIPENKO. *Médrano,* 1914. Painted tin, glass, wood, oil cloth. The Solomon R. Guggenheim Museum, New York.

194. ALEXANDER ARCHIPENKO. *Torso of a Woman,* 1922. Marble. Art Gallery, Mannheim.

195. ALEXANDER ARCHIPENKO. *Struggle,* 1914. Painted plaster. The Solomon R. Guggenheim Museum, New York.

196. RAYMOND DUCHAMP-VILLON. *Head of a Horse,* 1914. Bronze. Galerie Louis Carré, Paris.

197. RAYMOND DUCHAMP-VILLON. *Seated Woman,* 1914. Bronze. Galerie Louis Carré, Paris.

198. RAYMOND DUCHAMP-VILLON. *Horse and Rider* (First State), 1914. Bronze. Galerie Louis Carré, Paris.

199. HENRI LAURENS. *Portrait of Marthe Girieud,* 1912. Stone. Galerie Louise Leiris, Paris.

200. OSSIP ZADKINE. *Portrait of Georges Annenkof,* 1912. Plaster. Collection of the artist.

201. JACQUES LIPCHITZ. *Dancer,* 1913. Bronze. Museum of Modern Art, Paris.

202. HENRI LAURENS. *Woman with a Guitar,* 1919. Stone. Galerie Louise Leiris, Paris.

203. JACQUES LIPCHITZ. *Acrobat on a Horse,* 1914. Bronze. Private Collection.

204. OSSIP ZADKINE. *Standing Woman,* 1920. Bronze. Collection of the artist. Photo Marc Vaux.

205. OSSIP ZADKINE. *Head of a Man,* 1914. Stone. Collection of the artist. Photo Marc Vaux.

206. OSSIP ZADKINE. *The Accordionist,* 1918. Plaster. Collection Mr. Bay, New York. Photo Marc Vaux.

207. VLADIMIR TATLIN. *Construction,* 1914.

208. JEAN ARP. *Earth Forms, Called "Tears of Enak,"* 1916–17. Painted wood. Collection Arp-Hagenbach, Meudon. Photo D. Widmer.

209. HENRI LAURENS. *The Bottle of Beaune,* 1918. Wood. Collection A. Maremond, Chicago.

210. CONSTANTIN BRANCUSI. *Sleeping Muse,* 1906. Marble. National Gallery, Bucharest.

211. CONSTANTIN BRANCUSI. *The Kiss,* 1908. Stone. Philadelphia Museum of Art (Arensberg Collection).

212. LOUIS CHAUVIN. *Motherhood,* 1913. Cypress wood. Collection Alex Maguy, Paris. Photo Etienne Weill.

213. LOUIS CHAUVIN. *On an Accordion Tune,* 1920. Collection Alex Maguy, Paris. Photo Etienne Weill.

214. NAUM GABO. *Bust,* 1916. Construction in metal and plastic.

215. LÁSZLÓ MOHOLY-NAGY. *Nickel Construction,* 1921. Nickel-plated iron. Museum of Modern Art, New York (Gift of Mrs. Sybil Moholy-Nagy). Photo Soichi Sunami.

216. NAUM GABO. *Head of a Woman,* ca. 1917–20 (after a work of 1916). Construction in metal and plastic. Museum of Modern Art, New York. Photo Soichi Sunami.

217. ANTOINE PEVSNER. *Head of a Woman,* 1923. Construction in plastic and wood. Collection André Lefebvre, Paris.

COLOR PLATES

I. HONORÉ DAUMIER. *Bust of Benjamin Delessert,* ca. 1830–32. Bronze. The Joseph H. Hirshhorn Collection, New York. Photo Michael Katz.

II. JEAN-BAPTISTE CARPEAUX. *The Violinist,* 1870. Plaster. Petit Palais, Paris. Photo Joubert.

III. AUGUSTE RODIN. *Balzac,* 1898. Bronze. Rodin Museum, Paris. Photo Joubert.

IV. AUGUSTE RODIN. *Danaid,* 1885. Marble. Rodin Museum, Paris. Photo Joubert.

V. MEDARDO ROSSO. *The Golden Age,* 1886. Wax. The Joseph H. Hirshhorn Collection, New York. Photo Michael Katz.

VI. ANTOINE BOURDELLE. *Study for Monument of Beethoven on a Rock,* 1903. Plaster. Bourdelle Museum, Paris. Photo Joubert.

VII. ARISTIDE MAILLOL. *Night,* 1905. Terra cotta. Collection Dina Vierny, Paris. Photo Joubert.

VIII. HENRI MATISSE. *Decorative Figure,* 1903. The Joseph H. Hirshhorn Collection, New York. Photo Michael Katz.

IX. PABLO PICASSO. *The Absinthe Glass,* 1914. Painted bronze. Galerie Berggruen, Paris. Photo Joubert.

X. PABLO PICASSO. *Head of a Woman,* 1909–10. Bronze. Galerie Berggruen, Paris. Photo Joubert.

XI. UMBERTO BOCCIONI. *Unique Forms of Continuity in Space,* 1913. Bronze. Museum of Modern Art, New York.

XII. ALEXANDER ARCHIPENKO. *Carrousel Pierrot,* 1913. Painted plaster. The Solomon R. Guggenheim Museum, New York. Photo Michael Katz.

XIII. RAYMOND DUCHAMP-VILLON. *Maggy,* 1912. Bronze. Galerie Louis Carré, Paris. Photo Joubert.

XIV. CONSTANTIN BRANCUSI. *The New Born,* 1920 (after a marble of 1915). Bronze. Museum of Modern Art, New York.

XV. NAUM GABO. *Column,* 1923. Plastic, wood, metal. The Solomon R. Guggenheim Museum, New York. Photo Michael Katz.

XVI. HENRI LAURENS. *Woman,* 1918. Painted wood and metal. Galerie Louise Leiris, Paris. Photo Joubert.

BIBLIOGRAPHY

GENERAL WORKS

1865 POGGI E. *Della scultura e della pittura in Italia da Canova ai nostri giorni*. Florence.

1869 LÜBKE W. *Die moderne berliner Plastik*. Stuttgart.
HÜBNER J. *Schadow und seine Schule*. Bonn.

1878 JOUIN Henry. *La sculpture en Europe*. Plon. Paris.

1885 BELLIER DE LA CHAVIGNERIE and AURAY Louis. *Dictionnaire général des Artistes de l'Ecole Française*. Librairie Renouard. Paris.

1888 PFAU L. *Kunst und Kritik. Plastische Bildwerke*. Stuttgart.

1893 *Sculpteurs contemporains*. Librairie de l'Art. Paris.

1898 JOUIN Henry. *La Sculpture dans les cimetières de Paris*. Nouvelles Archives de l'Art français. Mâcon.

1901 BÉNÉDITE Léonce. *Les Sculpteurs français contemporains*. Paris.

1902 CLARIS Edmond. *De l'Impressionnisme en Sculpture*. Editions de la Nouvelle Revue. Paris.

1903 HEILMEYER Alex. *Die moderne Plastik in Deutschland*. Bielefeld. Freiburg.
TAFT Lorado. *History of American Sculpture*. Macmillan. New York.

1904 SCHEFFLER Karl. *Die moderne Malerei und Plastik*. Cassirer. Berlin.

1905 OSBORN Max. *Plastik moderne*. Berlin.

1907 HEILMEYER Alex. *Die Plastik des 19. Jahrhundert*. Leipzig.

1912 RADENBERG Wilhelm. *Modern Plastik. Einige deutsche und ausländische Bildhauer und Medailleure unserer Zeit*. Leipzig.

1913 CAFFIN Charles. *American Masters of Sculpture*. New York.
EATON D. CADY. *A Handbook of Modern French Sculpture*. New York.
WUNDERER Carl. *Einführung in die antike Kunst mit besonderer Berücksichtigung der modernen Plastik*. Erlangen.

1914 COQUIOT Gustave. *Cubistes, Futuristes, Passéistes*. Paris.
LAMI Stanislas. *Dictionnaire des Sculpteurs de l'Ecole Française au XIXe siècle*. Champion. 4 vols. 1914–1921. Paris.

1915 BURGER Fritz. *Die Malerei und Plastik des 19. und 20. Jahrhunderts*. Berlin.

1918 *An exhibition of American Sculpture*. The Metropolitan Museum of Art. New York.

1920 UMANSKIJ Konstantin. *Neue Kunst in Russland, 1914–1919*. Potsdam—Munich.

1921 KUHN Alfred. *Die neuere Plastik von 1800 bis zur Gegenwart*. Delphin Verlag. Munich.
TAFT Lorado. *Modern Tendencies in Sculpture*. University of Chicago Press. Chicago.

1923 *Contemporary American Sculpture*. Catalogue of the Exhibitions of National Sculpture Society, New York.
McSPADEN Walker J. *Famous Sculptors of America*. New York.

1925 SAUERLANDT Max. *Deutsche Bildhauer um 1900*. Königstein.

1926 FIELDING Mantle. *Dictionary of American Painters, Sculptors and Engravers*. Philadelphia.

1927 *Catalogue des collections du Palais des Beaux-Arts de la Ville de Paris*. (Petit Palais.) Paris.
SCHEFFLER Karl. *Geschichte der europäischen Plastik im neunzehnten und zwanzigsten Jahrhunderts*. Cassirer. Berlin.

1928 BARR Alfred. *German Painting and Sculpture*. The Museum of Modern Art. New York.
BASLER Adolphe. *La Sculpture moderne en France*. Crès. Paris.

1931 HEILMEYER Alex. *Die Plastik des 19. Jahrhundert in München*. Munich.

1932 CAHILL Holger. *American Painting and Sculpture, 1862–1932*. The Museum of Modern Art. New York.
VIGEZZI S. *La Scultura italiana dell'ottocento*. Florence.

1933 FIERENS Paul. *Sculpteurs d'aujourd'hui*. (Brancusi, Despiau, Epstein, Gargallo, Lachaise, Laurens, Lipchitz, Maillol, Martini, Zadkine, etc.) Editions des Chroniques du Jour. Paris.

1934 RAVE Paul Ortwin. *Deutsche Bildwerkkunst von Schadow bis zur Gegenwart*. Ein Führer zu den Bildwerken der National-Galerie. Berlin.
VITRY Paul. *La Sculpture française classique de Jean Goujon à Rodin*. Paris.

1935 WILENSKI R. H. *The Meaning of Modern Sculpture*. Stokes. New York.

1936 BARR Alfred. *Cubism and Abstract Art*. Museum of Modern Art. New York.
TARCHIANI N. *La Scultura italiana dell'ottocento*. Florence.

1940 COSTANTINI V. *La Scultura e la pittura italiana contemporanea, 1880–1926*. Hoepli. Milan.

1942 ROTHSCHILD Lincoln. *Sculpture through the Ages*. McGraw-Hill. New York.

1945 GISCHIA Léon and VEDRÈS Nicole. *La Sculpture en France depuis Rodin*. Editions du Seuil. Paris.

1947 BARR Alfred. *Fantastic Art (Dada) Surrealism*. Museum of Modern Art. New York.

1948 BARR Alfred. *Painting and Sculpture in the Museum of Modern Art*. New York.
BRUMMÉ C. Ludwig. *Contemporary American Sculpture*. Crown. New York.
FIERENS Paul. *Laethem-Saint-Martin, colonie d'artistes en Flandre, 1890-1940*. (Foreword by Jean Cassou.) Editions de la Connaisance. Brussels.

1949 RAMSDEN E. H. *Twentieth Century Sculpture*. Pleiades. London.
SEUPHOR Michel. *L'Art abstrait, ses origines, ses premiers maîtres*. Maeght. Paris.
SEYMOUR Chas. Jr. *Tradition and Experiment in Modern Sculpture*. American University Press. Washington, D. C.
SOBY J. T. and BARR Alfred. *Twentieth Century Italian Art*. Museum of Modern Art. New York.

1950 CARRIERI R. *Pittura e scultura d'avanguardia in Italia, 1890–1950*. Conchiglia. Milan.
THIEME Ulrich und BECKER Felix. *Allgemeines Lexikon der Bildenden Künstler von der Antike bis zur Gegenwart*. Leipzig. 1907–1950.
"Un demi-siècle d'art italien." *Cahiers d'Art*. Paris.

1952 Catalogue to the exhibition *L'Oeuvre du XXe siècle*. Musée National d'Art Moderne. Paris.
RITCHIE Andrew Carnduff. *Sculpture of the Twentieth Century*. Museum of Modern Art. New York.

1953 GUNNIS Rupert. *Dictionary of British Sculptors*. Odhams Press. London.

1954 *Catalogue du Musée National d'Art Moderne*. Editions des Musées Nationaux. Paris.
FIERENS Paul. *Sculptures de peintres*. Brussels.
Les Sculpteurs célèbres. Editions d'Art Lucien Mazenod. Paris.
MERLINO Adriàn. *Diccionario de artistas plàsticos de la Argentina, XVIIIe–XXe s.* Buenos-Aires.
PAMPLONA Fernando de. *Dicionàrio de pintores e escultores portugueses*. Oficina gràfica. Lisbon.
ROCHÉ H. P. and SEUPHOR Michel. *Sept pionniers de la sculpture moderne*. Yverdon. Switzerland.
TRIER Eduard. *Moderne Plastik von Auguste Rodin bis Marino Marini*. Berlin.

1955 BÉNÉZIT Emmanuel. *Dictionnaire critique et documentaire des peintres, sculpteurs, dessinateurs et graveurs de tous les temps et de tous les pays*. 8 vols. Gründ. Paris. 1948–1955.
Catalogue to the exhibition *50 ans d'art aux Etats-Unis*. (Collection of the Museum of Modern Art, New York.) Musée National d'Art Moderne. Paris.

JORAY Marcel. *La Sculpture moderne en Suisse*. Editions du Griffon. Neuchâtel.

1956 CASTELFRANCO G. and VALSECCHI M. *Pittura e scultura italiana dal 1910 al 1930*. De Luca. Rome.

1957 *German Art of the Twentieth Century*. Edited by A. C. Ritchie. Museum of Modern Art. New York.
MARCHIORI G. "Scultura italiana tra due tempi: 1914, 1945, 1956."
Quadrum, No. 3. Brussels.
Sculpture 1880–1957. Fine Arts Associates. New York.
Scultura italiana del XXo secolo. Editalia. Rome.
Verzeichnis der Skulpturensammlung. Kunsthalle. Mannheim.

1958 *Katalog der Gemälde und Plastiken*. Kunstmuseum. Winterthur.

1960 Catalogue to the exhibition *Les Sources du XXe siècle*. (Les Arts en Europe de 1884 à 1914.) Musée National d'Art Moderne. Paris.
Catalogue to the exhibition *Cent Sculpteurs de Daumier à nos jours*. Musée d'Art et d'Industrie. Saint-Etienne.
Dictionnaire de la Sculpture moderne. Hazan. Paris.
GIEDION-WELCKER Carola. *Contemporary Sculpture*. Wittenborn. New York.
MARCHIORI G. *Scultura italiana dell'ottocento*. Mondadori. Milan.
NOVOTNY Fritz. *Painting and Sculpture in Europe, 1780–1880*. The Pelican History of Art. Penguin Books. London.
SEUPHOR Michel. *Sculpture of This Century*. Braziller. New York.

1962 *Modern Sculpture from the Joseph H. Hirshhorn Collection*. Exhibition Catalogue. Text by H. H. Arnason. Guggenheim Museum. New York.
TRIER Edward. *Form and Space*. Praeger. New York.

MONOGRAPHS, CATALOGUES, AND INDIVIDUAL REFERENCES, BY ARTIST

ARCHIPENKO Alexander.

1921 GOLL Ivan and DÄUBLER Theodor and CENDRARS Blaise. *Archipenko Album*. Gustav Kiepenheuer Verlag. Potsdam.

1922 HOLUBETZ Nicola. *Archipenko*. Ukrainske Mistetsvo. Lwów.

1923 HILDEBRANDT Prof. Hans. *Alexander Archipenko*. Ukrainske Slowo. Berlin.
HILDEBRANDT Prof. Hans. *Alejandro Archipenko*. Editora Internacional. Buenos Aires.
RAYNAL Maurice. *A. Archipenko*. Ed. "Valori Plastici." Rome.
SCHACHT Dr. Roland. *Alexander Archi-*

penko. Sturm Bilderbuch II. Der Sturm Verlag. Berlin.
1960 ARCHIPENKO Alexander. *Fifty creative years, 1908–1958*. Tekhné. New York.

ARP Jean.
1925 ARP and LISSITZKY. *Les ismes de l'art*. Rentsch. Zurich.
1952 BUFFET-PICABIA. *Jean Arp*. Presses Littéraires de France. Paris.
1953 "Arp, poète et sculpteur." *Cahiers d'Art*, pp. 76–81. Paris.
1957 GIEDION-WELCKER Carola. *Jean Arp*. Abrams. New York.
     SEUPHOR Michel. *Arp*. Prisme. Paris.
1958 SOBY, James Thrall, ed. *Arp*. The Museum of Modern Art. New York.
1959 CATHELIN Jean. *Arp*. Musée de Poche. Paris.
1962 Catalogue to the exhibition *Arp*. Musée National d'Art Moderne. Paris.

BÄNNINGER Otto-Charles.
1949 CINGRIA Charles-Albert. *Otto-Charles Bänninger*. Zurich.

BARLACH Ernst.
1928 BARLACH Ernst. *Ein Selbsterzähltes Leben*. Berlin.
1929 WALTER Reinhold. *Ernst Barlach*. Berlin.
1951 CARLS. *Ernst Barlach*. Berlin.
1959 SCHULDT F. *Ernst Barlach, das plastische Werk*. Hamburg.
1961 WERNER Alfred. "Universal Humanism of Ernst Barlach." *American Artist,* Vol. 25, March, pp. 22–27. New York.

BARTHOLDI Frédéric-Auguste.
1881 LEFEBVRE Charles. *L'oeuvre de Bartholdi*. Paris.
1954 BETZ Jacques. *Bartholdi*. Editions de Minuit. Paris.

BARYE Antoine-Louis.
1851 PLANCHE Gustave. "Barye." *Revue des Deux Mondes,* July 1, 1851. Paris.
1855 *Catalogue des bronzes de Barye*. Exposition Universelle de 1855. Paris.
1876 *Catalogue des oeuvres de feu Barye*. Sale at the Hôtel Drouot February 7 and 12, 1876. Paris.
1884 *Catalogue des bronzes de Barye*. Sale at the Hôtel Drouot April 24, 1884. Paris.
1886 *Catalogue des bronzes de Barye*. Collection Auguste Sichel. Sale at the Hôtel Drouot February 27, 1886. Paris.
1889 ALEXANDRE Arsène. *A.-L. Barye*. (Collection "Les Artistes Célèbres.") Paris.
     Catalogue des oeuvres de Barye exposées à l'Ecole des Beaux-Arts. Paris.

KAY Charles de. *Life and Works of A.-L. Barye*. New York.
1890 BALLU Roger. *L'Oeuvre de Barye*. Quantin. Paris.
1910 DELTEIL Loys. *Barye*. "Le Peintre graveur illustré." Vol. VI. Paris.
1925 SAUNIER Charles. *Barye*. Rieder. Paris.
1956 *Catalogue de l'Exposition Barye au Musée du Louvre*. Text by Pierre Pradel. Editions des Musées Nationaux. Paris.

BERNARD Joseph.
1924 KLINGSOR Tristan. *Joseph Bernard*. (Collection "Les Sculpteurs français nouveaux," No. 2.) N.R.F. Paris.
1932 Catalogue to the retrospective exhibition *Joseph Bernard*. Musée de l'Orangerie. Paris.
1948 FUMET Stanislas. *Joseph Bernard*. (24 photographs.) Les Albums d'Art Druet, XV. Paris.

BOCCIONI Umberto.
1914 BOCCIONI Umberto. *Pittura, scultura futurista; dinamismo plastico*. Edizioni di Poesia. Milan.
     BOCCIONI Umberto. "La Scultura futurista." *Lacerba*, No. 13, pp. 139–140. July. Florence.
1927 MARINETTI F. T. *Boccioni, opera completa*. Foligno. Italy.
1953 ARGAN G. C. *Umberto Boccioni*. Rome.
1961 TAYLOR Joshua C. *Futurism*. Museum of Modern Art. New York.
1962 BALLO Guido. *Umberto Boccioni*. Mondadori. Milan.

BOURDELLE Antoine.
1928 FOSCA François. *Bourdelle*. N.R.F. Paris.
     MONOD François. *L'Oeuvre d'Antoine Bourdelle*. Brussels.
1929 *L'Oeuvre d'Antoine Bourdelle*. Catalogue of the Exhibition at the Palais des Beaux-Arts. Brussels.
1930 Catalogue of the Exhibition *Antoine Bourdelle*. Text by André Suarès and Michel Dufet. Galerie Vignon. Paris.
     FONTAINAS André. *Bourdelle*. Rieder. Paris.
     LÉGER Charles. *Antoine Bourdelle*. (38 reproductions in héliogravure.) Paris.
1933 Catalogue of the Exhibition *Antoine Bourdelle*. Palais des Beaux-Arts (Petit Palais). Paris.
1937 VARENNE Gaston. *Bourdelle par lui-même*. Fasquelle. Paris.
1951 GAUTHIER Maximilien. *Bourdelle*. Les Gémeaux. Paris.
1952 BOURDELLE Antoine. *La matière et l'esprit dans l'art*. Presses littéraires de France. Paris.
1954 DESCARGUES Pierre. *Bourdelle*. Musée Bourdelle. Paris.

1955 AURICOSTE Emmanuel. *Bourdelle*. Braun. Paris.

BOURDELLE Antoine. *Ecrits sur l'art et la vie*. Plon. Paris.

1960 FÖRSTER Otto H. *Antoine Bourdelle*. Herausgegeben von Wallraf-Richartz-Kuratorium. Cologne.

1961 Charles E. Slatkin Galleries Catalogue. *Antoine Bourdelle*. Philip Rhys Adams, Jean Cassou, and Jean Charbonneaux. New York.

BRANCUSI Constantin.

1921 POUND Ezra. "Brancusi." *The Little Review*, Autumn, pp. 3–7. New York.

1926 Catalogue of Brancusi Exhibition. Brummer Gallery. (Introduction by Paul Morand.) New York.

ZORACH William. "The Sculpture of Constantin Brancusi." *The Arts*, Vol. 9, March, pp. 143–150. New York.

1948 PALEOLOG V.G.C. *Brancusi*. Bucharest.

1957 LEWIS David. *Brancusi*. Wittenborn. New York.

ROCHÉ H.P. "Souvenirs sur Brancusi." *L'Oeil*, No. 29. Paris.

ZERVOS Christian. "Constantin Brancusi." *Cahiers d'Art*. Paris.

1960 GIEDION-WELCKER Carola. *Constantin Brancusi*. Braziller. New York.

BURCKHARDT Carl.

1936 BARTH Wilhelm. *Carl Burckhardt, der Bildhauer und Maler*. Zurich-Leipzig.

1937 BURCKHARDT Carl J. *Rodin und das plastische Problem*. Schwabe. Basel.

CARPEAUX Jean-Baptiste.

1869 SALELLES C. A. de. *Le Groupe de la Danse de M. Carpeaux jugé du point de vue de la morale*. Dentu. Paris.

1875 CLARETIE Jules. *J.-B. Carpeaux*. Librairie illustrée. Paris.

1880 CHESNEAU Ernest. *Jean-Baptiste Carpeaux, sa vie et son oeuvre*. Quantin. Paris.

1882 CLARETIE Jules. *Carpeaux*. Librairie des Bibliophiles. Paris.

1906 RIOTOR Léon. *Carpeaux*. (Collection "Les Grands Artistes.") Laurens. Paris.

1910 DELTEIL Loys. *Carpeaux*. "Le Peintre graveur illustré," Vol. VI. Paris.

1912 VITRY Paul. *Carpeaux*. (Collection "L'Art de notre temps.") Librairie Centrale des Beaux-Arts. Paris.

1913 PARMENTIER Florian. *Carpeaux*. Michaud. Paris.

1921 MABILLE DE PONCHEVILLE André. *Carpeaux inconnu ou la Tradition recueillie*. van Oest. Paris and Brussels.

1927 SARRADIN Edouard. *Carpeaux*. (Collection "Maîtres de l'Art Moderne.") Rieder. Paris.

1929 Catalogue to the exhibition *J.-B. Carpeaux*.

(Preface by A. Lefrancq.) Palais des Beaux-Arts. Brussels.

1935 CLÉMENT-CARPEAUX Louise. *La vérité sur l'oeuvre et la vie de J.-B. Carpeaux*. 2 vols. Paris and Nemours.

1955 Catalogue to the Exhibition *J.-B. Carpeaux*. Musée du Petit Palais. Paris.

CHAUVIN Louis.

1949 FUMET Stanislas. "Chauvin." *Derrière le miroir*, No. 18, March. Paris.

ZERVOS Christian. "Note sur les sculptures de Chauvin." *Cahiers d'Art*, Vol. 24, pp. 105–107. Paris.

1960 ZERVOS Christian. "Chauvin." *Cahiers d'Art*, Vol. 25. Paris.

COURBET Gustave.

1929 LÉGER Charles. *Courbet*. Crès. Paris.

CREEFT José de.

1945 CAMPOS Jules. *José de Creeft*. Hermann. New York.

1960 DEVREE Charlotte. *José de Creeft*. American Federation of the Arts. New York.

DALOU Jules.

1935 CAILLAUX Henriette. *Aimé-Jules Dalou*. Delagrave. Paris.

DAUMIER Honoré.

1905 GEFFROY Gustave. *Daumier sculpteur*. "L'Art et les artistes," Vol. I. Paris.

1932 BOUVY Eugène. *Trente-six bustes de Honoré Daumier*. Le Garrec. Paris.

1936 SCHEIWILLER Giovanni. *Honoré Daumier*. Hoepli. Milan.

1952 GOBIN Maurice. *Daumier sculpteur*. Cailler. Geneva.

1954 ADHÉMAR Jean. *Honoré Daumier*. Tisné. Paris.

1958 Catalogue to the exhibition *Daumier*. Bibliothèque Nationale. Paris.

1959 BECHSTEIN Hanns. *Honoré Daumier. Das Parlament der Juli-Monarchie*. (36 Bronzes.) Insel Verlag. Wiesbaden.

DAVID D'ANGERS Pierre-Jean.

1878 JOUIN Henry. *David d'Angers. Sa vie, son oeuvre, ses écrits et ses contemporains*. 2 vols. Plon. Paris.

1910 DAVID D'ANGERS. *Un grand statuaire, David d'Angers. Sa vie, ses oeuvres, par son fils*. Société d'Edition et de Publications. Paris.

1931 CLASSENS H. "David d'Angers." *L'Art et les artistes*, Vol. XXIII. Paris.

1932 VALOTAIRE M. *David d'Angers, étude critique*. Laurens. Paris.

1934 CHESNEAU G. and METZGER Dr. H.

Catalogue des oeuvres de David d'Angers au Musée des Beaux-Arts d'Angers. Angers.

1956 MORANT Henry de. *David d'Angers et son temps.* Siraudeau. Angers.

DEGAS Edgar.

1921 FOSCA François. "Degas sculpteur." *L'Art et les artistes,* June. Paris.
VITRY Paul. Introduction to the *Catalogue de l'Exposition des Sculptures de Degas.* Galerie A. Hebrard. Paris.

1943 REWALD John. *Edgar Degas.* Braun. Paris.

1944 REWALD John. *Degas. Works in Sculpture, a Complete Catalogue.* Pantheon. New York.

1949 BOREL Pierre. *Les Sculptures méditées de Degas.* Cailler. Geneva.

1957 REWALD John. *Complete Degas Sculpture.* Abrams. New York.

DESPIAU Charles.

1927 *Despiau.* (Text by Adolphe Basler. 24 photographs.) Albums d'Art Druet, IX. Paris.

1930 DESHAIRS Léon. *C. Despiau.* Crès. Paris.

1947 GEORGE Waldemar. *Despiau vivant. L'Homme et l'oeuvre.* Dupont. Paris.

1949 GAUTHIER Maximilien. *Despiau.* (Collection "Les Gémeaux," No. 3.) Paris.

1954 GEORGE Waldemar. *Despiau.* Kiepenheuer and Witsch. Cologne.

DUCHAMP-VILLON Raymond.

1924 PACH Walter. *Raymond Duchamp-Villon, sculpteur.* Paris.
POVOLOVZKY. *Raymond Duchamp-Villon, sculpteur.* Paris.

1931 SALMON André. *Sculptures de Duchamp-Villon.* Exhibition catalogue. Galerie Pierre. Paris.

DUPRÉ Giovanni.

1880 DUPRÉ Giovanni. *Pensieri sull'arte e ricordi autobiografici.* Florence.

EPSTEIN Jacob.

1931 HASKELL A. *Epstein. The Sculptor Speaks.* London.

1932 EPSTEIN Jacob. *The Sculptor Speaks.* Doubleday Doran. New York.
POWELL L. B. *Epstein.* London.

1942 BLACK Robert. *The Art of Jacob Epstein.* World Publishing. Cleveland, Ohio.

1955 EPSTEIN Jacob. *Autobiography.* London

ERNST Max.

1937 "Max Ernst. Oeuvres de 1919–1936." (Texts by Max Ernst, André Breton, Paul Eluard, Benjamin Péret, Joë Bousquet, René Crevel, etc.) *Cahiers d'Art.* Paris.

1942 "Max Ernst." *View Magazine,* Vol. 2, No. 1, April, special number. New York.

1959 Catalogue to the exhibition *Max Ernst.* Musée National d'Art Moderne. Paris.

1961 Catalogue to the exhibition *L'Oeuvre sculpté de Max Ernst.* Galerie du Point Cardinal. Paris.

FENOSA Apel'les.

1958 CIRICI-PELLICER Alexandre. *Apel'les Fenosa.* Barcelona.

1961 Catalogue to the exhibition *Fenosa.* (Text by Francis Ponge.) Galerie Jacques Dubourg. Paris.

DE LA FRESNAYE Roger.

1935 NEBELTHAU E. *Roger de La Fresnaye.* Montaignac. Paris.

1950 COGNIAT R. and GEORGE W. *Oeuvre Complet de Roger de La Fresnaye.* Paris.

FREUNDLICH Otto.

1952 GINDERTAEL R.V. "Freundlich." *Art d'Aujourd'hui,* October, 1952. Paris.

GABO Naum.

1920 GABO Naum and PEVSNER Antoine. *The Constructivist Manifesto.* Moscow.

1948 CHANIN A. and OLSEN R. *Gabo—Pevsner.* The Museum of Modern Art. New York.

1953 "Gabo Makes a Construction." *Art News,* November 1953. New York.

1957 "An Interview with Naum Gabo." *The World of Abstract Art.* New York.
READ and MARTINS. *Gabo.* Humphries. London.

1962 GABO Naum. *Of Divers Arts.* Pantheon. New York.

GARGALLO Pablo.

1927 "Gargallo." *Cahiers d'Art,* Nos. 7 and 8. Paris.

1937 COURTHION Pierre. *Gargallo.* Skira. Paris.

1947 Catalogue to the retrospective exhibition of the Musée du Petit Palais. Text by Jean Cassou.) Paris.

GAUDIER-BRZESKA Henri.

1916 POUND Ezra. *Gaudier-Brzeska.* Lane. New York.

1930 EDE H.S. *Gaudier-Brzeska.* London.

GAUGUIN Paul.

1936 REWALD John. *Post-Impressionism from Van Gogh to Gauguin.* Museum of Modern Art. New York.

1938 REWALD John. *Gauguin.* Paris—London—Toronto.

1953 LINDBERG-HANSEN J.C. "Discovering Paul Gauguin, the Wood-Carver." *College Art Journal,* Vol. 12, No. 2, pp. 117–120. New York.

1956 *Gauguin og hans venner*. Catalogue. Winkel and Magnussen. Copenhagen.

1957 GOLDWATER Robert. *Gauguin*. Abrams. New York.

1959 *Gauguin. Paintings, Drawing, Prints, Sculpture*. The Art Institute of Chicago. Chicago.

1960 Catalogue to the exhibition *"Cent oeuvres de Gauguin."* Galerie Charpentier. Paris.

GEISER Karl.

1932 GEORGE Waldemar. *Karl Geiser*. Editions des Quatre Chemins. Paris.

1957 NAEF H. "Karl Geiser." *Du*, No. 10. Zurich.

GEMITO Vincenzo.

1905 GIACOMO S. di. *Vincenzo Gemito: la vita e l'opera*. Naples.

GONZALEZ Julio.

1934 ALFONSECA Ricardo Perez. *Julio Gonzalez*. Cartillas. Madrid.

1952 Catalogue to the retrospective exhibition *Gonzalez*. Palais des Beaux-Arts. Brussels and Stedelijk Museum, Amsterdam.

1956 RITCHIE Andrew Carnduff. *Julio Gonzalez*. The Museum of Modern Art. New York.

1959 Catalogue to the exhibition *Julio Gonzalez*. Galerie de France. Paris.

HALLER Hermann.

1927 KUHN Alfred. *Der Bildhauer Hermann Haller*. Zurich.

HILDEBRAND Adolf von.

1893 HILDEBRAND Adolf von. *Problem der Form*. Strasbourg.

KLINGER Max.

1904 KLINGER Max. *Die Hauptwerke der Malerei und Plastik des Künstlers näbst einer Einführung in seine Kunst*. Leipzig.

1906 SCHMID Max. *Max Klinger*. Leipzig.

1907 KÜHN P. *Max Klinger*. Leipzig.

KOLBE Georg.

1913 *Georg Kolbe. Bildwerke*. Berlin.

1922 VALENTINER Wilhelm R. *Georg Kolbe. Plastik und Zeichnung*. Munich.

KOLLWITZ Käthe.

1929 HEILBORN Adolph. *Käthe Kollwitz*. Rembrandt. Berlin-Zehlendorf.

1946 ZIGROSSER Carl. *Käthe Kollwitz*. Bittner. New York.

1947 *Käthe Kollwitz*. Boymans Museum. Rotterdam.

1952 KOLLWITZ Hans. *Käthe Kollwitz*. Berlin.

LACHAISE Gaston.

1935 KIRSTEIN Lincoln. *Gaston Lachaise*. Retrospective Exhibition. Museum of Modern Art. New York.

LAURENS Henri.

1920 RAYNAL Maurice. "Laurens." *L'Esprit Nouveau*, No. 1. Paris.

1926 FIERENS Paul. "Henri Laurens." *Cahiers d'Art*. Paris.

1927 TÉRIADE E. "Henri Laurens." *Cahiers d'Art*. Paris.

1930 ZERVOS Christian. "Les constructions de Laurens." *Cahiers d'Art*, No. 4. Paris.

1932 GUÉGUEN P. "La conjonction de la réalité sensuelle et de l'abstraction dans l'oeuvre de Henri Laurens." *Cahiers d'Art*, Nos. 1–2. Paris.

1945 GIACOMETTI Alberto. "Henri Laurens. Un sculpteur vu par un autre sculpteur." *Labyrinthe*, No. 4. Geneva.

1946 "Henri Laurens." *Le Point*. Lanzac.

1949 KAHNWEILER D.H. *Preface to the Laurens Exhibition*. Palais des Beaux-Arts. Editions de la Connaissance. Brussels.

1951 Catalogue to the exhibition *Laurens*. Musée National d'Art Moderne. Paris.

1953 GUÉGUEN P. "Les débuts cubistes de Laurens." *Art d'Aujourd'hui*, Nos. 3–4. Paris.

1955 LAURENS Marthe. *Henri Laurens, sculpteur*. (1915–1924.) Berès. Paris.

1956 GOLDSCHEIDER C. *Laurens*. Collection "Europäische Bildhauer." Kiepenheuer und Witsch. Cologne—Berlin.

1960 Catalogue to the exhibition *Laurens*. Galerie Claude Bernard. Paris.

LEHMBRUCK Wilhelm.

1922 WESTHEIM Paul. *Wilhelm Lehmbruck*. Potsdam.

1930 ABBOTT Jere. *Wilhelm Lehmbruck and Aristide Maillol*. The Museum of Modern Art. New York.

1936 HOFF A. *Wilhelm Lehmbruck, seine Sendung und sein Werk*. Berlin.

1949 *Wilhelm Lehmbruck*. Exhibition Catalogue. Städtische Kunsthalle. Mannheim.

1957 HOFFMANN W. *Wilhelm Lehmbruck*. Amsterdam.

1958 HOFFMANN W. *Wilhelm Lehmbruck*. London.

LIPCHITZ Jacques.

1920 DERMÉE Paul. "Lipchitz." *L'Esprit Nouveau*, No. 2. Paris.

1926 SALMON André. "Jacques Lipchitz." *Cahiers d'Art*. Paris.

1929 VITRAC Roger. *Jacques Lipchitz*. (Collection "Les Sculpteurs nouveaux," No. 7.) N.R.F. Paris.

1947 RAYNAL Maurice. *Jacques Lipchitz*. Editions Jeanne Bucher. Paris.

1950 FROST. "Lipchitz Makes a Sculpture." *Art News*, April 1950. New York.
RITCHIE Andrew Carduff. *Jacques Lipchitz, An Exhibition of His Sculpture and Drawings 1914–1950*. Portland Art Museum.

1954 GOLDWATER. *Jacques Lipchitz*. Amsterdam.
HOPE Henry R. *The Sculpture of Jacques Lipchitz*. Museum of Modern Art. New York.

1959 Catalogue of the exhibition *Lipchitz*. Musée National d'Art Moderne. Paris.

MAILLOL Aristide.

1902 FAGUS Félicien. "Maillol." *Revue Blanche*, August, 1902. Paris.

1921 MIRBEAU Octave. *Aristide Maillol*. Crès. Paris.

1924 FISCHER Adam. *Maillol*. Kunstbladet. Copenhagen.

1925 DENIS Maurice. *Aristide Maillol*. Crès. Paris.
KUHN Alfred. *Aristide Maillol*. Seeman. Leipzig.
LAFARGUE Marc. *Aristide Maillol, sculpteur et lithographe*. Frapier. Paris.

1926 CAMO Pierre. *Aristide Maillol*. (Collection "Les Sculpteurs français nouveaux," No. 5.) N.R.F. Paris.

1930 ABBOTT Jere. *Wilhelm Lehmbruck and Aristide Maillol*. The Museum of Modern Art. New York.

1936 SENTENAC Paul. *Aristide Maillol*. Peyre. Paris.

1937 CLADEL Judith. *Aristide Maillol, sa vie, son oeuvre, ses idées*. Grasset. Paris.
CLADEL Judith. "Maillol devant le modèle." *Verve*, No. I. December. Paris.

1939 REWALD John. *Maillol*. Hyperion. London—Paris—New York.

1940 APPEL Heinrich. *Das Meisterwerk Maillol*. Basel.

1942 PAYRO Julio. *Aristide Maillol*. Editorial Poseidon. Buenos-Aires.

1943 REWALD John. *The Woodcuts of Aristide Maillol*. A complete catalogue. Pantheon Books. New York.

1947 ROY Claude. *Maillol vivant*. (Photographs by Karquel.) Cailler. Geneva.

1950 CAMO Pierre. *Maillol, mon ami*. Kaeser. Lausanne.
REWALD John. *Aristide Maillol*. Braun. Paris.

1958 Catalogue of *Maillol Exhibition* for 10 museums across the United States. Paul Rosenberg and Company. New York.

1961 Catalogue of the exhibition *Maillol*. Musée National d'Art Moderne. Paris.

MALFRAY Charles.

1947 Catalogue of the exhibition *Charles Malfray*.

(Text by André Chamson.) Musée du Petit Palais. Paris.

MANOLO.

1930 PIA Pascal. *Manolo*. (Collection "Les Sculpteurs nouveaux," No. 9.) N.R.F. Paris.

1961 Catalogue of the exhibition *Manolo*. Galerie Louise Leiris. Paris.

MAROCHETTI Baron Carlo.

1928 CALDERINI M. *Carlo Marochetti*. Turin.

MARTINI Arturo.

1948 MARTINI Arturo. *La Scultura lingua morta*. Mandersteig. Verona.

1956 ARGAN. *Martini*. De Lange. Amsterdam.

1958 PEROCCO Guido. *Arturo Martini a Cá Pesaro*. Bulletin of the Musei Civici Veneziani, No. I. Venice.

MATISSE Henri.

1938 GUÉGUEN Pierre. "The Sculpture of a Great Painter: Henri Matisse." *Twentieth Century*, No. 4, pp. 3–13. December.

1951 BARR Alfred. *Matisse*. Museum of Modern Art. New York.

1953 SYLVESTER David. "The Sculpture of Matisse." *The Listener*, Vol. 49, No. 1248, January 29. London.

1960 Catalogue of *Forty-nine Bronzes by Matisse*. Collection of Mr. and Mrs. Theodor Ahrenberg of Stockholm. Sotheby and Co. London.

MEUNIER Constantin.

1896 *L'Oeuvre de Constantin Meunier, peintre et sculpteur*. (Review by Camille Lemonnier.) Becker-Holemans. Brussels.

1915 BAZALGETTE. *Constantin Meunier et son oeuvre*. La Plume. Paris.

1947 CHRISTOPHE Lucien. *Constantin Meunier*. (Monographies de l'Art Belge.) De Sikkel. Antwerp.

MILLES Carl.

1940 ROGERS Meyric R. *Carl Milles*. Yale University Press.

MINNE Georges.

1930 PUYVELDE Léo van. *Georges Minne*. Brussels.

1947 RIDDER André de. *Georges Minne*. (Monographies de l'Art Belge.) De Sikkel. Antwerp.

MODIGLIANI Amedeo.

1929 PFANNSTIEL A. *Modigliani*. Paris.

1931 BASLER Adolphe. *Modigliani*. Crès. Paris.

1946 FRANCHI. *Modigliani*. Florence.

1951 SOBY James Thrall. *Modigliani: Paintings, Drawings, Sculpture*. Museum of Modern Art. New York.

1953 LIPCHITZ Jacques. *Amedeo Modigliani.* New York.

1956 SALMON André. *Modigliani, sa vie, son oeuvre.* Editions des Quatre Chemins. Paris.

1958 MODIGLIANI Jeanne. *Modigliani senza leggenda.* Florence.

1959 *Amedeo Modigliani. Paintings, Sculpture and Drawings.* Cincinnati Art Museum. Cincinnati.

1963 WERNER Alfred. *Modigliani as Sculptor.* Arts. New York. (In preparation.)

MOHOLY-NAGY László.

1929 MOHOLY-NAGY László. *Von Material zu Architektur.* Bauhausbücher. Munich.

1947 MOHOLY-NAGY László. *Vision in Motion.* Theobald. Chicago.

1949 MOHOLY-NAGY László. *The New Vision.* Wittenborn. New York.

1950 MOHOLY-NAGY Sibyl. *Moholy-Nagy, Experiment in Totality.* Harper. New York.

MOREAU Gustave.

1960 HOLTEN Ragnar von. *L'Art fantastique de Gustave Moreau.* Pauvert. Paris.

1961 Catalogue of the exhibition *Gustave Moreau.* Musée du Louvre. Editions des Musées Nationaux. Paris.

1961 *Redon, Moreau and Bresdin.* Exhibition Catalogue. (Moreau text by Dore Ashton.) Museum of Modern Art. New York.

NADELMAN Elie.

1920 Catalogue of the exhibition *Nadelman.* Galerie Bernheim-Jeune. Paris.

1948 KIRSTEIN Lincoln. *The Sculpture of Elie Nadelman.* Museum of Modern Art. New York.

NIELSEN Kai.

1925 SWANE S. *Kai Nielsen.* Copenhagen.

ORLOFF Chana.

1927 DES COURIÈRES E. *Chana Orloff.* (Collection "Les Sculpteurs nouveaux," No. 6.) N.R.F. Paris.

PICASSO Pablo.

1943 PRAMPOLINI. *Picasso scultore.* Rome.

1946 BARR Alfred. *Picasso, Fifty Years of His Art.* Museum of Modern Art. New York.

1949 KAHNWEILER D.-H. *Les Sculptures de Picasso.* (Photographs by Brassaï.) Editions du Chêne. Paris.

1953 ARGAN. *Scultura di Picasso.* Venice.

1957 KAHNWEILER D.-H. *Picasso. Sculpture.* New York.

1962 *Picasso, An American Tribute.* Exhibition catalogue edited by John Richardson for nine New York galleries. Sculpture exhibition at Otto Gerson Gallery.

POMPON François.

1926 DES COURIÈRES E. *François Pompon.* (Collection "Les Sculpteurs nouveaux," No. 4.) N.R.F. Paris.

1928 REY Robert. *François Pompon.* Paris.

1934 *Catalogue des oeuvres de François Pompon.* (Preface by René Demeurisse.) Société des Amis du Musée. Paris.

POUGNY Jean.

1957 GINDERTAEL R.V. *Pougny.* Cailler. Geneva.

1962 Catalogue of the exhibition *Pougny.* Galerie Charpentier. Paris.

PRADIER James.

1853 ROCHETTE Raoul. *Notice historique sur la vie et les ouvrages de M. Pradier.* Institut de France. Paris.

1859 ETEX Antoine. *James Pradier. Etude sur sa vie et ses ouvrages.* Paris.

RAEDECKER John.

1926 BREMMER. *John Raedecker.* Amsterdam.

1940 HAMMACHER. *John Raedecker.* Amsterdam.

RENOIR Auguste.

1947 HAESAERTS Paul. *Renoir sculptor.* Reynal and Hitchcock. New York.

1962 TILLIM Sidney. "Renoir Sculpture." *Arts,* Vol. 36, No. 7, April, p. 49. New York.

RIETSCHEL Ernst.

1873 OPPERMANN Andreas. *Ernst Rietschel.* Leipzig.

RODIN Auguste.

1893 GEFFROY Gustave. *Auguste Rodin.* La Vie artistique. Dentu. Paris.

1898 ROD Edouard. "L'atelier de Rodin." *Gazette des Beaux-Arts,* May 1, 1898.

1900 BERTHELOT René. "Auguste Rodin." *Grande Encyclopédie.* Paris.
Catalogue of the exhibition *Rodin.* Texts by Arsène Alexandre, Albert Besnard, Eugène Carrière, Jean-Paul Laurens, and Claude Monnet. Société d'Edition artistique. Paris.
CLADEL Judith. *Auguste Rodin pris sur le vif.* "La Plume." Paris.
MORICE Charles. *Rodin.* Floury. Paris.

1905 CLEMEN Paul. "Auguste Rodin." *Kunst für alle.* Berlin.

1906 KAHN Gustave. "Auguste Rodin." *L'Art et le Beau.* Paris.
LAWTON Frederic. *The Life and Work of Rodin.* London.

1907 ROGER-MARX. *Rodin céramiste.* Paris.

1908 CLADEL Judith. *Rodin, l'homme et l'oeuvre.* Brussels.

GRAUTOFF Otto. *Auguste Rodin*. Leipzig.

1909 MAUCLAIR Camille. *Auguste Rodin*. Duckworth. London.

1910 DELTEIL Loys. *Rodin*. "Le peintre graveur illustré," Vol. VI. Paris.

1912 CIOLKOWSKA M. *Rodin*. London.

1913 *Auguste Rodin*. The Metropolitan Museum of Art. New York.
COQUIOT Gustave. *Le vrai Rodin*. Paris.
DUJARDIN-BEAUMETZ. *Entretiens avec Rodin*. Paris.
RILKE Rainer-Maria. *Auguste Rodin*. Leipzig.

1914 RODIN Auguste. *Les Cathédrales de France*. Colin. Paris.

1915 COQUIOT Gustave. *Rodin. 57 statues*. Paris.

1917 COQUIOT Gustave. *Rodin à l'Hôtel Biron et à Meudon*. Paris.
RILKE Rainer-Maria. *Auguste Rodin*. Insel Verlag. Leipzig.

1918 GEFFROY Gustave and SAUNIER Charles. *Rodin*. Paris.
MAUCLAIR Camille. *Auguste Rodin*. La Renaissance du Livre. Paris.

1919 BOURDELLE Antoine. *L'Art et Rodin*. Geneva.

1920 HAVELAAR J. *Auguste Rodin*. Leiden.

1922 TIREL Marcelle. *Rodin intime ou l'envers d'une gloire*. Editions du Monde Nouveau. Paris.

1924 BÉNÉDITE Léonce. *Rodin*. (60 héliogravures.) Paris.

1926 BÉNÉDITE Léonce. *Rodin*. (40 plates.) Rieder. Paris.
LUDOVICI Anthony. *Personal Reminiscences of Auguste Rodin*. London.

1927 GRAPPE Georges. *Catalogue du Musée Rodin*. Paris.
RIOTOR Léon. *Rodin*. Alcan. Paris.

1928 RILKE Rainer-Maria. *Lettres à Rodin*. Paris.

1932 SIGOGNEAU Dr. *A propos de Rodin, mécanismes psychologiques*. (Thesis.) Bordeaux.

1933 *Sculpture de Rodin*. (42 photographs by Sougez.) Paris.
SIGOGNEAU Dr. *Le tourment de Rodin*. Bordeaux.

1934 GRAPPE Georges. *Le Musée Rodin*. Paris.

1936 CLADEL Judith. *Rodin, sa vie glorieuse et inconnue*. Grasset. Paris.

1937 BOURDELLE Antoine. *La Sculpture et Rodin*. Paris.

1938 BOEHMER Günter. *Rodin*. Weise. Berlin.

1939 STORY Sommerville. *Auguste Rodin*. Oxford University Press. New York.

1946 RODIN Auguste. *L'Art*. Entretiens réunis par Paul Gsell. Mermod. Lausanne.
Rodin. Photographs by René-Jacques. (Preface by Georges Lecomte.) Les Publications Techniques et Artistiques. Paris.

1949 ROH. *Rodin*. Bern.

1951 CHARBONNEAUX Jean. *Les Sculptures de Rodin*. (Photographs by Marc Foucault.) Hazan. Paris.
STORY Sommerville. *Auguste Rodin*. Phaidon. New York.

1952 AUBERT. *Rodin Sculptures*. Tel. Paris.
MARTINIE Henri. *Rodin*. Braun. Paris.

1954 *Exhibition Auguste Rodin*. Curt Valentin Gallery. New York.

1960 ELSEN Albert E. *Rodin's Gates of Hell*. University of Minnesota Press. Minneapolis.

1962 Catalogue of *Rodin Sculpture Exhibition*. Museum of Modern Art. New York.

ROSSO Medardo.

1909 PIERARD Louis. *Un sculpteur impressionniste: Medardo Rosso*. Edition de la Société Nouvelle. Paris.

1929 SOFFICI Ardengo. *Medardo Rosso*. Florence.

1945 PAPINI G. *Medardo Rosso*. Hoepli. Milan.

1950 BARBANTINI Nino. *Medardo Rosso*. Neri Pozza. Venice.
KRAMER Hilton. "Medardo Rosso." *Arts*, Vol. 34, pp. 30–37, December. New York.

RUDE François.

1888 BERTRAND Alexis. *François Rude*. Paris.

1904 FOURCAUD Louis de. *François Rude sculpteur, ses oeuvres et son temps*. Paris.

1910 DELTEIL Loys. *Rude*. "Le Peintre graveur illustré," Vol. VI. Paris.

1946 QUARRÉ Pierre. *François Rude*. Catalogue de ses oeuvres conservées à Dijon. Musée des Beaux-Arts. Dijon.

1955 *Catalogue de l'Exposition commémorative du centenaire de François Rude*. Musée des Beaux-Arts. Dijon.

SAINT-GAUDENS Augustus.

1907 CORTISSOZ R. *Augustus Saint-Gaudens*. New York.

SINTENIS Renée.

1935 KIEL Hanna. *Renée Sintenis*. Berlin.

TAEUBER-ARP Sophie.

1943 BILL. "Sophie Taeuber-Arp." *Werk*, No. 6. Zurich.

1948 SCHMIDT. *Sophie Taeuber-Arp*. Basel.

VALLOTTON Félix.

1936 HAHNLOSER-BÜHLER Hedy. *Félix Vallotton et ses amis*. Sedrowski. Paris.

VANTONGERLOO Georges.

1924 VANTONGERLOO Georges. *L'Art et son avenir*. Antwerp.

1948 VANTONGERLOO Georges. *Paintings, Sculptures, Reflections*. New York.

VELA Vincenzo.

1920 CALDERINI M. *Vincenzo Vela scultore*. Turin.

WITTIG Edouard.

1929   RUTKOWSKI Sz. *Edouard Wittig*. Warsaw.

WOUTERS Rik.

1923   DELEN A.J.J. *Rik Wouters, zyn leven, zyn werks, zyn einde*. Antwerp.

1944   WOUTERS Nel. *La Vie de Rik Wouters à travers son oeuvre*. Brussels.

1946   *Rik Wouters*. Boymans Museum. Rotterdam.

1947   *Rik Wouters. Sculptures et dessins*. (Preface by A.J.J. Delen.) Editions de la Connaissance. Brussels.

1948   DELEN A.J.J. *Rik Wouters*. Antwerp.

1957   Catalogue of the exhibition *Rik Wouters*. Musée National d'Art Moderne. Paris.

ZADKINE Ossip.

1929   RIDDER André de. *Zadkine*. Paris.

1949   HAMMACHER Abraham Marie. *Zadkine*. Boymans Museum. Rotterdam.

1956   *Ossip Zadkine*. The National Gallery of Canada.

1957   ENGINCK. *Begegnung mit Ossip Zadkine*. Kunst und Volk. Zurich.

1958   COGNIAT Raymond. *Zadkine*. Hautefeuille. Paris.

Index

The asterisk indicates a reference in the Biographical Dictionary; the dagger indicates a reference in the Bibliography. Neither of these sections is otherwise analyzed in the Index.

Italicized numbers are plate numbers.

A

Abstract sculpture, 164, 222–23, 226, 234–35, 248–49
Academicism, 1, 12, 44–45, 77, 80–81, 84, 131, 203, 244
Adam, Henri-Georges, 9; *19*
Angers, Pierre-Jean David d' *see* David d'Angers, Pierre-Jean
Apollinaire, 168, 206
*†Archipenko, Alexander, 212, 216, 219, 222, 238; *190, 193, 194, 195, XII*
*†Arp, Jean, 9, 226, 238; *17, 208*
Arp, Sophie Taeuber—*see* Taeuber-Arp, Sophie
Art Nouveau, 77, 212–13, 244

B

*Baily, Edward Hodges, 40–41
Balla, Giacomo, 213
Balzac, Honoré de, 60
*Balzico, Alfonso, 41; *42*
Barbizon school, 31
*Barrias, Louis Ernest, 81, 100; *70*
*†Bartholdi, Frédéric-Auguste, 80
*Bartlett, Paul Wayland, 81
Bartolini, Lorenzo, 34
*†Barye, Antoine-Louis, 44, 52–53, 96, 168, 189; *51, 52, 53*
Baudelaire, Charles, quoted, 57, 117, 120
Belleuse, Albert Carrier—*see* Carrier-Belleuse, Albert
*†Bernard, Joseph, 160; *130*
Bernhardt, Sarah, 165
*†Boccioni, Umberto, 196, 213, 216; *187, 188, 189, XI*
Bogouslavskaya, Xenia, 202
Bologna, Giovanni da, 69, 72
*Bonnard, Pierre, 146; *159, 160*
*Bonnassieux, Jean Marie, 41
Bonnat, 77
Bosio, 52
*Boucher, Alfred, *66*
Bouguereau, 77
*†Bourdelle, Émile Antoine, 85, 131, 134–35, 146, 199, 245; *104, 105, 106, 107, 108, 109, 110, 111, 112, 165, VI*
  influence, 143, 146
  influence of Rodin on, 134–35
  objectives, 135, 138
  quoted, 138
  style, 138, 143
*†Brancusi, Constantin, 124, 203, 231, 234, 238; *210, 211, XIV*
Braque, Georges, 196, 235
Brzeska, Henri Gaudier—*see* Gaudier-Brzeska, Henri
Buonarroti, Michelangelo *see* Michelangelo Buonarroti

C

Cabanel, Alexandre, 153
Calder, Alexander Stirling, 9, 216; *26*
Canova, Antonio, 31, 34, 49; *37*
*†Carpeaux, Jean-Baptiste, 64–65, 68–69, 72, 73, 76, 84, 92, 96, 121, 245; *59, 60, 61, 62, 63, 64, 65, II*
Carra, Carlo, 213
*Carrier-Belleuse, Albert Ernest, 80, 96–97, 100; *43*
Carrière, Eugène, 106
Cartellier, Pierre, 45
Cézanne, Paul, 89, 146, 157, 192–93, 213
Chaplet, Ernest, 181, 184
*Chapu, Henri Michel Antoine, 80
*†Chauvin, Louis, 234–35; *212, 213*
Chocarne-Moreau, 77
*Claudel, Camille, 131
Clemenceau, Georges, 103
*Clésinger, Jean-Baptiste Auguste, 41
Consagra, Pietro, 9; *25*
Constructivism, 226, 241
Carot, J.B.C., 31
*†Courbet, Gustave, 30–31, 77, 171, *137*
  quoted, 30
Courturier, Robert, 164, 238; *11*
*Csaky, Joseph, 212, 226; *186*
Cubism, 192–93, 196, 199, 202, 212–13, 216, 219, 222–23, 226, 238
Cubo-Constructivism *see* Constructivism
Cubo-futurism, 223

D

*†Dalou, Jules, 84, 134; *71, 72, 73*
*†Dantan, Jean-Pierre, 61
Daubigny, C.F., 31
*†Daumier, Honoré, 57, 73, 76, 92, 103, 245; *54, 55, 56, 57, 58, I*
  background, 60
  political satirist, 60, 61, 64
  sculptor, 60–61, 64
Daumier, Madame Honoré, 61
*†David d'Angers, Pierre-Jean, 44, 48–49, 52, 134; *48, 49, 50*
  quoted, 34
David, J. Louis, 30, 45

David, Pierre-Jean *see* David d'Angers, Pierre-Jean

*†Degas, Edgar, 89, 121, 171, 174–75, 178, 181; *138, 139, 140*

Delacroix, Eugène, 30

Delord, Taxile, quoted, 27, 30

*Derain, André, 193, 196; *169*

*†Despiau, Charles, 131, 157, 160; *127*

Donatello, 97

Drivier, Léon Ernest, 146

*Dubois, Paul, 80

Dubuffet, Jean, 238

Duchamp, Marcel, 199, 216

*†Duchamp-Villon, Raymond, 212, 219, 222, 238; *196, 197, 198, XII*

*†Dupré, Giovanni, 37; *38*

Duret, Francisque Joseph, 65

E

Ecole des Beaux-Arts, 44, 49, 52, 65, 73, 80, 81, 96, 134, 146, 153

*†Epstein, Sir Jacob, 203; *175, 176*

*†Ernst, Max, 202; *173*

Etex, Antoine, 41

F

*Falguière, Jean-Alexandre Joseph, 80, 134, 165; *1*

Fauvism, 192, 213

*†Fenosa, Apel 'les, 164; *10*

Flannagan, John, 238

Franceschi, Jules, *3*

*Frémiet, Emmanuel, 73, 80

*†Freundlich, Otto, 212, 238; *184, 185*

Futurism, 213, 216

G

*†Gabo, Naum, 216, 238, 241; *214, 216, XV*

*†Gargallo, Pablo, 206, 209, 219; *177, 178, 179, 180*

Garnier, Charles, 69

Gaudens, Augustus Saint—*see* Saint Gaudens, Augustus

*†Gaudier-Brzeska, Henri, 212, 235; *191, 192*

*†Gauguin, Paul, 156, 174, 181, 184–85; *146, 147, 148, 149*

Gautier, Théophile, quoted, 52

*Geefs, Guillaume, 41

Geffroy, Gustave, quoted, 93

*†Gemito, Vincenzo, 88

Genre sculpture, 37

*Gérôme, Jean-Leon, 81, 153; *67*

Giacometti, Alberto, 143, 164, 199, 238; *6, 167*

Gilioli, Emile, *9*

*†Gonzalez, Julio, 209, 212; *181, 182, 183*

*Gris, Juan, 196, 206; *171*

Gros, 52

Grün, Jules, 1

Gsell, Paul, 97

Guino, Richard, 185, 188

Guys, Constantin, 69

H

Harpignies, Henri, 31

Haussmann, Baron, 68

*†Hildebrand, Adolf von, 85, 150, 160; *74*

Holten, Ragnar van, 178, 181

Hugué, Manuel Martinez *see* Manolo (Manuel Martinez Hugué)

I

Impressionism, 61, 77, 89, 92–93, 120–21, 146, 174, 181, 193, 196, 248

Ingres, J.A.D., 30

Italian naturalism, 88

J

Jacob, Max, 168, 206, 209

Jousse (Father), quoted, 21

K

Kahnweiler, Daniel-Henry, quoted, 196

Kandinsky, Vasili, 223

Kessler, Count, 157

Kitson, Henry H., 165

Klinger, Max, 150; *116*

*†Kolbe, Georg, 150; *113*

Kubin, Alfred, 150

L

*†Lachaise, Gaston, 164–65; *141*

La Fresnaye, Roger de, 193; *157, 158*

Landscape painting, 31

Larche, Raoul, *4*

Lardera, Berto, 9; *22*

*†Laurens, Henri, 223, 235, 238; *199, 202, 209, XVI*

Lefuel (architect), 69

Léger, Fernand, 196, 203

*†Lehmbruck, Wilhelm, 147, 161; *128, 131*

Lenoir, Alexandre, 57

*†Lipchitz, Jacques, 222–32, 238; *3, 201, 203*

Lipsi, Morice, 9; *15*

Lombard school, 37

*†Lübke, Wilhelm, quoted, 27

Mc

McWilliam, Frederick Edward, 199

M

Maeterlinck, 132

*Magnelli, Alberto, 199, 202; *170, 172*

*†Maillol, Aristide, 153, 156–57, 245; *122, 123, 124, 125, 126, VII*

*Maindron, Hippolyte, 77

Malevich, 202, 223

*†Malfray, Charles, 146–47; *118, 120*

Manet, Edouard, 89, 92
*†Manolo (Manuel Martinez Hugué), 168, 209; *142*
Marinetti, Filippo Tommaso, 213
*Marqueste, Laurent-Honoré, 81; *68*
*†Matisse, Henri, 189, 192, 235; *153, 154, 155, VIII*
Meissonnier, J.L.E., 37
Mellon, Paul, 175
*Mercié, Marius Jean Antonin, 80, 165
*†Meunier, Constantin, 85, 147, 161; *75, 76*
Michelangelo Buonarroti, 97, 106
*Milles, Vilhelm Carl Emil, 160; *129, 133*
*Millet, Aimé, 41; *44*
Minne, Georges, 147, 161; *117*
Mirko, 238
*†Modigliani, Amedeo, 196, 206; *168*
*†Moholy-Nagy, László, 216, 226, 238; *215*
*Molin, Johann Peter, 44
Mondrian, Piet, 223
Monet, Claude, 89, 120–21, 174
Moore, Henry, 165, 199, 219; *8*
*†Moreau, Gustave, 178, 181; *135, 136*
Morel, Louis, 188–89
*Morice, Léopold, *5*
Morisot, Berthe, 89
Müller, Robert, 9; *18*

N

*†Nadelman, Elie, 164–65; *134, 144*
Neoclassic sculpture, 31, 34, 37, 40, 41, 44, 244–45
Neo-Renaissance sculpture, 40, 41
Nevelson, Louise, 9, 238; *20*

O

*†Orloff, Chana, 164–65
*Ottin, Auguste Louis Marie, 41

P

Painter-Sculptors, 168, 171, 174–75, 178, 181, 184–85,
   188–89, 193, 196, 199, 202
Painting
   abstract, 223, 226
   and Art Nouveau, 212–13
   baroque, 213
   cubism and, 192–93, 222–23, 226
   Fauve movement in, 213
   impressionism and, 89, 92–93, 174, 181, 193, 196
   landscape, 31
   pre-cubism and, 213
   tradition and, 30
Pajou, 48
Pevsner, Antoine, 9, 238, 241; *21, 217*
Philipon (publisher), 60
*†Picasso, Pablo Ruiz y, 125, 168, 193, 196, 199, 209,
   235; *161, 162, 163, 166, IX, X*
Pissaro, Camille, 89, 174
*†Pompon, François, 1, 131, 165, 168; *145*
*†Pougny, Jean, 202, 226; *174*
*†Pradier, Jean-Jacques (James), 37; *40*

*Préault, Antoine-Augustin (Auguste), 41

R

Raphael, 30
*†Rauch, Christian Daniel, 41
Raynal, Maurice, 209
Realist school, 30–31
Redon, Odilon, 89
*†Renoir, Pierre August, 89, 146, 174, 185, 188–89;
   150, 151, 152
Reverdy, 206
Rewald, John, 175
Richier, Germaine, 143, 164, 238; *12*
*†Rietschel, Ernst, 41
*†Rodin, François August René, 52, 61, 73, 89, 92,
   121, 138, 143, 175, 193, 244–45; *78, 79, 80, 81, 82,
   83, 84, 85, 86, 87, 88, 89, 90, 91, 92, 93, 94, 95, 96,
   121, III, IV*
   background, 96–97, 100
   influence, 131, 134–35, 138, 146–47, 150, 153, 157,
      160–61, 203
   quoted, 107, 110, 124
   style, 107, 110, 113, 116–17
   techniques, 100, 103, 106–107
Rodin, Jean-Baptiste, 93, 96
Roig, 209
Roland, 48
Romantic sculpture, 244
Rosati, James, *13*
*†Rosso, Medardo, 64, 89, 193, 245; *77, 97, 98, 99,
   100, 101, 102, 103, V*
   background, 108, 117, 120–21
   objectives, 120–21
   quoted, 120
   techniques, 120, 121, 124–25
Rousseau, Theodore, 31
Roybet, 77
*†Rude, François, 44–45, 48, 52, 65, 244; *45, 46, 47*
Russolo, Luigi, 213

S

*†Saint-Gaudens, Augustus, 81; *69*
Saint-Marceaux, 165
Salelles, C.A. de, quoted, 72–73
Scheffer, Ary, 80
*†Schilling, Johannes, 41
Schlemmer, Oscar, 226
*Schnegg, Lucien, 146; *114*
*Schwitters, Kurt, 226
Sculpture
   abstract, 9, 164, 222–23, 226, 234–35, 248–49
   academic, 77, 80, 81, 84, 131, 203, 244
   advanced classicists in, 153, 156–57, 160–61, 164–
      65, 168, 245
   allegory and, 80
   anecdote in, 77, 244
   animal, 52, 165, 168
   baroque affectation in, 81

291

classicism in, 27, 30, 31, 34, 37, 40–41, 44–45, 48–49, 52–53, 244–45
constructivism, 226, 241
"counter-reliefs", 223
cubism in, 192–93, 196, 199, 213–13, 216, 219, 222–23, 226
cubo-constructivism, 226
"developable surfaces", 241
experimentation in materials, 238, 241
figurative, 248
futurism and, 213, 216, 219
genre, 37
geometric schematization in, 16, 248
impressionism and, 61, 89, 92–93, 120–21, 174, 181, 193, 196, 248
Italian naturalism, 88
"kinetic", 216
metal, 203, 206, 209, 212
mixed media in, 216
mythology and, 238, 244
naturalism in, 16, 77, 244
nature of, 12–13
neoclassic, 31, 34, 37, 40, 41, 44, 244–45
neo-Renaissance, 40, 41
new era in, 203, 206
painter-sculptors in, 168, 171, 174–75, 178, 181, 184–85, 188–89, 193, 196, 199, 202
primitive art influences on, 235, 238
realism in, 16, 21, 77, 84–85
religious, 13, 16, 21
romantic, 244
secular, 21
"sculpto-painting", 238, 241
space, 223, 241
spiritual character of, 13, 16, 21
tangibility of, 21
techniques in, 9
time in, 241
time-and-space-trap, 219
tradition and, 27, 30, 31, 34, 37, 57, 77
types of, 9
Seurat, Georges, 89
Severini, Gino, 213, 216

Signac, Paul, 89
Sisley, Alfred, 89, 174
Smith, David, 9; *23*
Stackpole, 238
Stahly, François, 9, 147, 238; *16, 119*
Stevens, Alfred George, 41

T

*†Taeuber-Arp, Sophie, 226
*Tatarkiewicz, Jacob, 44
*Tatlin, Vladimir Yevgrafovich, 216, 223, 226; *207*
*Tenerani, Pietro, 41
Thorvaldsen, Bertel, 34, 41; *36*
Tinguely, Jean, 9, 216; *24*
Toulouse-Lautrec, Henri de, 89

V

*†Vallotton, Félix, *156*
Van Gogh, Vincent, 89
Van Rasbourg, 97
Varèse, Edgar, 209
Vaudoyer, Léon, 40
Vela, Vincenzo, 37; *39*
*Vigeland, Adolf Gustav, 160–61; *132*
Villon, Raymond Duchamp—*see* Duchamp–Villon, Raymond
Viseux, Claude, *14*
Vollard, Ambroise, 185
*Volmar, Joseph, 41
Volti, *7*

W

*Ward, John Quincy Adams, 81
*Wolff, Albert, 41; *41*
*†Wouters, Rik, 146; *115*

Z

*†Zadkine, Ossip, 219, 222; *200, 204, 205, 206*
Zola, Émile, 116, 121